McClane's Secrets of Successful Fishing

McCLANE'S
Secrets
OF
Successful
Fishing

A. J. McClane

**Illustrations by
Dr. Frances Watkins
Ed Vebell
Francis Davis**

An Owl Book

Holt, Rinehart and Winston

New York

Copyright © 1965 by Holt, Rinehart and Winston, Inc.
Copyright © 1974, 1979 by A. J. McClane

First published in 1980 by Holt, Rinehart and Winston, 383 Madison Avenue, New York, New York 10017.

Published simultaneously in Canada by Holt, Rinehart and Winston of Canada, Limited.

Library of Congress Cataloging in Publication Data

McClane, Albert Jules, 1922-
  McClane's Secrets of successful fishing

  Based on McClane's New standard fishing encyclopedia.
    Includes index.
    Bibliography: p.
    1. Fishing. I. Title. II. Title: Secrets of successful fishing.
SH441.M332   799.1'2   78-24367

ISBN Paperback: 0-03-021126-3

Designer: Helene Berinsky
Printed in the United States of America
10 9 8

ISBN 0-03-021126-3

Contents

Preface

In one sense, angling is an ancient morality play, a set piece in what Izaak Walton called a "contemplative recreation." But it can also be a competitive game of the most demanding kind. That sport fishing offers something for almost everybody is evidenced by the fact that one out of every four Americans, or more than fifty-five million people, now participate. It is a game that can be pursued throughout one's lifetime, with energy demands regulated according to individual physical fitness. And the thrills of angling—whether stalking a wary bonefish on a white sand flat or casting in the bouldery shallows of a northern lake for acrobatic smallmouth bass—can be shared by the entire family. No one is ever too young or too old to enjoy this total sensory experience of the great outdoors

Learning to catch fish is not difficult, but becoming reasonably expert at it does require time and study. The primary purpose of *Secrets of Successful Fishing* is to provide an integrated course on the basic casting disciplines. It doesn't matter whether you fish in freshwater or saltwater—the essential skills are identical. This guidebook is designed to get you started without the manual errors that often prove a handicap later on. The angler who has mastered his tackle to the degree that casting of any kind has become reflexive will not necessarily have more fun but will be able to progress into specialized forms of fishing.

The source volume of this handbook, *McClane's New Standard Fishing Encyclopedia* (Holt, Rinehart and Winston, 1974), is a book of 1,156 two-column pages, covering many subjects of direct and indirect angling interest. The section on surf-fishing by Frank Woolner was excerpted directly from that volume. The selection of other material here is based on years of teaching fundamentals, not solely on my part, but in critical analysis with some of the most competent instructors in the U.S. today: Homer Circle of *Sports Afield;* Gilbert Drake, Jr., of *Field & Stream;* Chico Fernandez, who teaches casting professionally in Florida; Tom Mc-

Nally of the *Chicago Tribune;* Mark Sosin of *Sports Afield;* and Bing McClellan, past president of the American Fishing Tackle Manufacturers' Association. Collectively, they represent more than two centuries of practical fishing experience. It required a thirty-hour conference over a period of four days just to agree on what a beginner should be taught from "ground zero." Our first photocopied instructional manual was then put to the classroom test—condensed, modified, excised, and expanded according to the students' progress. It evolved into *Secrets of Successful Fishing.*

To quickly bring the reader to a practical understanding of rods, reels, lures, knot tying, and technique, we have reduced that great body of knowledge to a viable minimum. For example, there are hundreds of recognized knots, yet if you learn to tie five or six basic ones, you will be prepared to rig nearly all kinds of equipment; there are thousands of plugs on the market, but these are all variations of five *types*, and learning to recognize a lure's function is more important than collecting them in infinite colors and shapes. As the student angler becomes more sophisticated he undeniably will want to expand his knowledge (particularly in advanced techniques); but remember the old parable of learning to walk before you run. Fishing is such a geographically diverse sport that the transition can go on forever.

Fish identification, habits, and habitat are other important aspects of angling success, and, as companion volumes in our tacklebox library, *McClane's Field Guide To Freshwater Fishes of North America* and *McClane's Field Guide to Saltwater Fishes of North America* (Holt, Rinehart and Winston, 1978) will serve this purpose. Many excellent books have been published on angling, and the reader should by all means develop a reference shelf. (A suggested list of books can be found on page 267.) There are also casting clinics and schools operating periodically throughout the country, which are well worth attending.

Spinning

Spinning is the simplest casting method. It is the easiest way to learn to fish when starting from "ground zero," and is especially recommended for teaching children, as it quickly provides a sense of accomplishment. Naturally, the method has more advanced applications, but for youngsters with a short attention span, its mechanical advantages inspire the confidence necessary to eventually master all the angling disciplines.

Advantages of the Spinning Reel

The spool of a spinning reel remains stationary when casting and retrieving. The pull of the lure uncoils the line from the spool as it travels through the air. Unlike the conventional revolving-spool reel, upon which inertia must be overcome by the momentum of the lure being cast, a fixed spool offers no initial resistance; the chief cause of backlashes is thereby eliminated. Because there is no inertia to overcome at the start of a cast, the spinning reel also permits the use of extremely light lures that would not have the weight to set a revolving spool in motion. So the advantage for a beginner is that he can learn to cast in a fraction of the time required to master orthodox tackle. For the expert, spinning is a method that is ideally suited to casting lures that are too light for practical bait-casting equipment (less than ¼ ounce); this has broad application, ranging from fishing the flats for bonefish to casting on small brooks for trout. There are other advantages: ease of casting in headwinds, a greater versatility in the effective lure weights that can be used, and cost; also, a more efficient spinning reel can be manufactured at a lower cost than a comparable bait-casting reel, in which parts and tolerances must be more critical.

Reel Sizes

Spinning reels are designed for all types of freshwater and salt-water fishing. Excluding reels used for ultralight spinning, their general weight range is 10–25 ounces, with spool capacities of 200–400 yards. Although reel weight is not the sole feature to evaluate, the lighter models of 10–12 ounces are ordinarily designed for lines up to 8-pound test. Spinning reels that weigh 12–18 ounces encompass the 8- to 15-pound-test-line class, and those exceeding 18 ounces are spooled for 15- to 30-pound-test lines. This classification represents light, medium, and heavy categories, which the manufacturer may further delineate on the basis of purpose, such as *general freshwater, light saltwater, heavy-duty, surf spinning,* or by whatever descriptive method is suitable to his inventory. Trained tackle salesmen determine the correct reel for a rod on the basis of the various sizes of line to be used and the maximum capacity required. For general freshwater purposes, it is not necessary to spool more than 200 yards of 8-pound test; thus, the model selected will be light (less than 12 ounces). If the reel is to be used in surf casting for large gamefish, where a minimum of 250 yards of 15-pound test is essential, then the choice would tend to be in the medium category instead. Therefore, the significance of spinning-reel weight is a relative factor; it should be as light as possible for comfort within the limits of durability and design.

The Spool

For stability in casting, and keeping the line from slapping against the rod, a spinning reel is mounted underneath the grip. The spool is inclined slightly upward (3–5 degrees) from horizontal by the curvature of the reel leg, so that its axis centers or passes slightly below the first or "butt" guide. Due to centrifugal force, the line "spins" in a larger arc than the circumference of the spool would indicate, until it is choked through the first ring. By mounting the reel below and some distance away from the butt guide, gravity causes the uncoiling line to fall away from, rather than upon the rod. For this reason there is an optimum size to the spool diameter for any given rod.

The diameter of spinning-reel spools may vary from 1⅝ to 3⅛ inches. Generally speaking, a larger spool has the advantage of permitting longer casts and a faster rate of retrieve. When the line uncoils from the spool, its level sinks deeper and deeper. The friction of the uncoiling line against the spool flange increases as the length of the cast is extended. Obviously, a large-diameter spool, with its greater circumference, is less subject to friction (within the limits of any comparable cast) because the line level does not dwindle as rapidly. The width of the spool bears a similar relationship; that is, the uncoiling line does not sink as fast on a wide spool as a narrow one. However, there are mechanical limits to both dimensions, which must be considered in the reel's design. The greater the circumference, the more the line tends to "slap" the rod because of the larger coils formed; the greater the width, the more friction is created by adjacent coils of line (this is reduced to a large degree by cross-winding).

On all reels, it's important to keep sufficient line on the spool. At no time should the spool be filled to less than $1/16$ inch below the outside diameter of its rim.

Modern spinning reels have a skirted spool that completely covers the rotor housing. This eliminates the problem of getting line trapped behind the spool lip and tangled around the spindle.

Pickup Mechanisms

The pickup is the part of a spinning reel that engages and winds the retrieved line back onto the spool. There are three types of pickup mechanisms: *bail pickup, manual pickup,* and automatic

Spinning-Reel Nomenclature

1. Brake Screw or Drag
2. Bail or Pickup Arm
3. Line Guide or Roller
4. Handle
5. Anti-reverse Lock
6. Gear-Housing Cover Plate
7. Leg
8. Foot
9. Cup or Flyer
10. Reel Spool
11. Flange

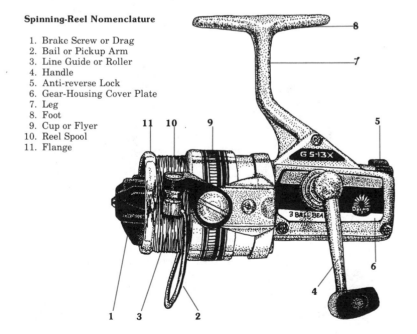

pickup arm. Each type has a roller over which the line passes. The roller may be fixed, or it may actually roll under the movement of the line. Since the rotating kind cannot be wholly efficient (the slightest dirt or corrosion will freeze it), the fixed roller is commonly employed. All rollers are subject to wear and should be checked periodically for possible replacement.

BAIL PICKUP   The bail is the most popular pickup for conventional spinning reels. The bail consists of a metal hoop that forms an arc across the face of the spool, one end being set in a socket on the revolving cup, and the other end attached to the pickup bracket. To open the bail, you merely pull it out and down with your free hand—although it can also be opened by holding the

Casting with Open-face Reel

For conventional spinning, hold rod with reel foot between second and third fingers. Your thumb should be on top. Disengage bail pickup with left hand and take line on extended index finger. Do not hook line around finger joint, and do not hold line against rod.

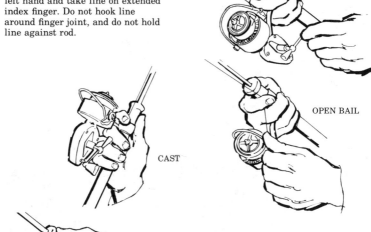

ENGAGE LINE

OPEN BAIL

CAST

RELEASE

Your forefinger serves three important roles: it holds line free of spool, preparatory to casting; it retards lure speed and prevents overshooting target by touching line as it uncoils; and it stops the cast completely at any point.

forefinger of your casting hand against the spool and rotating the crank handle. The bail closes when you operate the reel again, moving over and around the spool. As the bail starts rotating, the line automatically slips along the bail until it comes to rest against the roller.

MANUAL PICKUP   The manual pickup simply consists of a roller mounted on the revolving cup instead of on a bail or pickup arm, and the angler's forefinger flips the line over the roller before a retrieve is made. Many experienced casters feel that this is the simplest and most-foolproof design for a spinning reel, as there are no working parts to get out of order. A manual pickup becomes so easy to operate after a little experience, that your finger motions become automatic.

AUTOMATIC PICKUP ARM   The automatic pickup arm was most popular in the years 1940–50. It is still preferred by many anglers and is featured on several standard reels. The pickup device consists of a spirally curved metal arm that engages the line automatically. The whole assembly rotates through an angle of about 45 degrees from open to closed position. When casting, the line is held on the angler's forefinger, and the pickup is rotated backward and out of the way before being disengaged. After the cast is made, the crank handle is turned, and the pickup automatically closes when contacting a cam or stud. The objection to this type of pickup is that the line sometimes catches the metal arm when casting in strong winds.

The Brake or Drag

The drag in a spinning reel is an adjustable arrangement whereby a hooked fish can take the line out without breaking it while the reel handle is stationary, held either by the angler's hand or by the anti-reverse lock. Its function is identical to that of a star drag on conventional bait-casting reels. While the principle of operation is the same in all spinning reels, the mechanical details differ with the make. In general, the reel-spool seat is mounted in an exact position on the spindle. Its round flat side faces forward. The flat rear side of the line spool rests against the spool seat with a brass, asbestos, or composition friction washer in between. The spindle protrudes through the spool, and this portion of it is threaded to receive the adjustable wing-nut washer, creating increased friction or drag, which resists spool rotation. Loosening it reduces the drag. Perhaps the most important quality of a good spinning reel is an absolutely smooth drag that operates without jerkiness or "freezing."

The Anti-reverse Lock

The anti-reverse lock is a ratchet-and-dog combination that may work against the revolving cup, the main gear, or the main-gear shaft. When a large fish is hooked and begins taking out line, putting the lock in the "on" position immobilizes the crank handle, except when you want to take line back. The lock should remain on until the time you net your fish. This leaves one hand free to use the net, and if the fish decides to make a last-minute flurry, it is held in check by the friction of the dragbrake. The lock is also used in trolling. After you let your bait or lure drop back to trolling distance, snap the lock on before putting your rod in the holder. In this way, the bait is held against the dragbrake, which you've presumably set lower than the breaking strain of the line. When a fish strikes, the pull will overcome the resistance of the drag, and there will be an audible click as it takes line, but the brake tension is sufficient to set the hook. The anti-reverse lock is also used when traveling from one spot to another; reel your line up tight with the lure hooked in the keeper ring or over the butt guide, and snap the lock on. In this way the bait won't dangle or get snagged in bushes or clothing.

The Spinning Rod

Spinning rods run 4–12 feet in length and may weigh 2–30 ounces, depending on the function of the individual rod. The great majority are made of fiberglass or graphite, although some excellent bamboo models are handcrafted by a number of builders. Generally speaking, spinning rods can be divided into five classes: *ultralight, light,*

Spinning Rods

Small guides or improperly spaced guides cause line to slap against rod (*top*).

Large conelike series reduces spiral quickly and thereby minimizes friction (*bottom*).

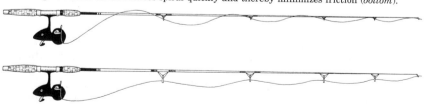

medium, heavy-duty, and *extra heavy.* These classifications are determined by the optimum lure-weight range of each rod (see table for Balanced Spinning Tackle, p. 10). For single-handed casting, we are concerned with weight up to ⅜ ounce.

Spinning rods are of one-, two-, or three-piece construction and are distinguished by a comparatively long handle and a set of graduated ring guides, which, if properly spaced, appear in a cone-like series when viewed from the rear. The guides are responsible for reducing the spiraling motion of the line, so that it passes from the reel without slapping against the rod shaft and with a minimum of friction. The size and spacing of guides is a critical factor in designing a good spinning rod.

Types of Spinning-Rod Handles

Sliding Rings

Fixed-Reel Seat

Surf Rod with Foregrip

Rod Handles

Spinning reels may be secured to the handle in one of several ways—by a pair of sliding rings, a fixed-reel seat, or a sliding-reel seat. Sliding rings are the most comfortable to grasp, but because the reel foot is squeezed directly against soft cork, the arrangement has never proven to be perfectly secure. However, with modern *tapered* sliding rings, the problem is negligible. The fixed-reel seat is the metal, screw-locking type and provides maximum security of reel foot to handle, which is advantageous on saltwater rods used for big fish. But the fixed-reel seat sacrifices some comfort and may cramp the hand after long periods of casting. The sliding-reel seat is something of a compromise, consisting of sliding rings over a metal sleeve. This is not always a satisfactory seat, as metal is uncomfortable, and it still has some tendency to slip around the corks. On rods with sliding rings, it's often practical to secure the reel in place with transparent tape and remove the rings, or tape them to both ends of the handle. Modern plastic tapes are extremely strong and pliable. The angler can custom-tailor his rod handle by binding the reel foot to the corks, thereby eliminating metal corners entirely.

How to Select a Spinning Line

The two types of line used for spinning are *braided* and *monofilament*. Which to use depends in equal parts on your casting ability and the qualities you consider most important in a line. Generally speaking, braided line is easier for the beginner to use on a spinning reel. It is less elastic than monofilament, and it spools evenly. Braided line is completely limp, a quality that tolerates many casting errors without producing a snarl. Monofilament will "lay" loose unless the retrieved lure is kept under constant tension; for this reason, it's a poor line for fishing with surface plugs. However, monofilament is more durable than braided line and has a greater resistance to abrasion. The smaller-diameter monofilament line casts easier, absorbs less water, and is less visible. Monofilament also has a smoother surface, which minimizes friction against the housing or lip of a spinning-reel spool, thereby permitting longer casts. But, because of its inherent stiffness, there is a limit to how large a diameter of monofilament you can put on any reel. No matter what the maximum practical size might be in monofilament, you can always spool a heavier (i.e., stronger) braided line on the same reel.

Whichever type of line you choose, the spinning-reel spool should be filled with line to its maximum, which is $1/16$–$3/16$ inch below the flange. If a spinning reel is overfilled, it will not lay evenly, and it will tangle after the first cast. If a spool is underfilled, friction will retard the cast. Keep in mind that, on a spinning reel, friction increases over the lip of the spool as the level of the line diminishes. It is important, therefore, to keep a spinning line at the correct level. As the line is used, the end portion wears and must be removed, foot by foot, and replaced when the level of the filled spool is appreciably below the spool lip.

For nearly all freshwater spinning you do not need a leader on monofilament line. It's durable enough even in light tests to resist normal abrasion. Also, one of the advantages of monofilament in clearwater is that it's almost invisible. With braided line, a leader is often advisable, particularly on shy fish like brown trout. The simplest rigging is 4–5 feet of monofilament, which can be joined to the casting line by means of a nail knot (see p. 194). Although leaders are used primarily to disguise or reduce the visible attachment of line to lure, they are a safety measure in saltwater fishing. The addition of 12–18 inches of piano wire, braided wire, or any of the vinyl-coated wires will save a lot of lures. Ocean-bred gamefish are rough scaled and sharp-toothed; the short leader in this case keeps your line away from abrasive danger zones.

TEST AND ELASTICITY   A light lure will not function with a heavy line, nor will a light line with a heavy lure. Light lures can't create enough velocity to pull a heavy line any distance, and the heavy lure is going to snap a light line when you whip the rod into a casting bend. A relationship exists, therefore, between the strength (or diameter) of a line and the weight of a lure. The line must be strong enough to take up the shock of casting when the rod produces backward momentum, and light enough to follow the lure off the spool with a minimum resistance to the lure's velocity.

There is also an obvious correlation between the stiffness factor of a rod and the line test. In effect, the line should not be stronger than the rod's capacity to absorb any given weight. A heavy line belongs on a stiff or heavy rod. Although a fine line can be cast with a very stiff rod, the chances of holding a fish on this mismatched combination are slight. If it requires a pull greater than the line's strength to make full use of the rod's flexibility, the line will snap. In other words, it wouldn't be practical to use a 6-pound test on a heavy-duty or extra-heavy rod. At close range, a strong gamefish could pop the line with one quick jerk. The rod must be sensitive enough to work as an elastic unit with the line at all distances.

When a running fish like the bonefish, permit, or steelhead swims for the horizon, the natural tendency of the angler is to tighten his drag. This is the precise moment when drag should be minimized. The strain on a line is multiplied by water resistance as the length taken from the spool increases. Furthermore, an additional strain is created as the dwindling amount of line on the spool increases friction. Mechanically, the strain on the line may be six times greater as the spool nears empty without the angler even touching his drag. The principal burden of the rod now is to "fight" the line rather than the fish. Paradoxically, and this is where experience counts, the more line a fish peels off (within reasonable limits), the easier you can handle him. By holding the rod tip high to decrease water resistance along the surface, and by taking advantage of the full bend of your rod, you can finger the spool and use the stretch of the line to subdue a heavyweight into submission. The most critical moments are when the fish has literally emptied the spool and when you play a "green" fish just a few yards away.

BALANCED SPINNING TACKLE

Line Diameter (inches)	Approximate Test (pounds)	Lure Weight (ounces)	Rod Class
.005–.006	1.75	$^1/_{16}$–$^3/_{16}$	Ultralight
.006–.007	2.25	$^1/_{16}$–$^1/_4$	Ultralight
.007–.008	3.00	$^1/_{16}$–$^5/_{16}$	Ultralight
.008–.009	4.00	$^1/_4$–$^3/_8$	Light
.009–.010	5.00	$^1/_4$–$^3/_8$	Light
.010–.011	6.00	$^3/_8$–$^5/_8$	Medium
.011–.012	7.00	$^3/_8$–$^5/_8$	Medium
.012–.013	8.00	$^1/_2$–1	Heavy-duty
.013–.014	9.50	$^1/_2$–1	Heavy-duty
.015–.018	14.00	1–2	Extra heavy
.018–.020	17.00	1–3	Extra heavy
.021–.024	22.00	2–4	Extra heavy

The Overhead Cast

In spinning, as in all types of casting, the overhead cast is basic and can be used at all times, unless branches or other obstructions require an underhand cast. Actual fishing may suggest modifications, but the comfortable stance for a right-handed caster is to face the target, then take a quarter turn to the left, so that your right shoulder is pointed toward the target, with your left foot a little to the rear of your right foot. When casting, your body weight should be shifted to the right foot. The procedure should be reversed by a left-handed caster.

Next, lift the line free of the pickup by holding it on the ball of your index finger and backing the pickup mechanism off a quarter turn to disengage the ball or arm. Some casters prefer to hold the line by placing the index finger against the spool rim; however, this will prove to be uncomfortable, unless you have long fingers, and impractical when using the larger saltwater reels and heavy lures. It is easier and in perfectly good form to hold the line with a relaxed forefinger. Just remember not to hook your finger around the line and not to hold it against the rod handle.

To make the overhead cast, hold the rod so that the tip is at eye level with the shaft centered on the target. Your forearm and rod should form a straight line, with the elbow at a right-angle position, and the upper arm close to but not pressing against your body. Begin the cast by raising the hand to eye level, pivoting on your elbow so that the forearm and rod come to vertical and stop.

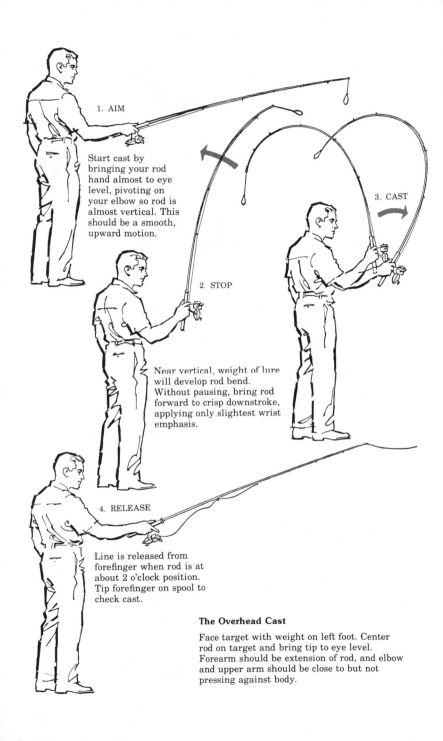

1. AIM

Start cast by bringing your rod hand almost to eye level, pivoting on your elbow so rod is almost vertical. This should be a smooth, upward motion.

3. CAST

2. STOP

Near vertical, weight of lure will develop rod bend. Without pausing, bring rod forward to crisp downstroke, applying only slightest wrist emphasis.

4. RELEASE

Line is released from forefinger when rod is at about 2 o'clock position. Tip forefinger on spool to check cast.

The Overhead Cast

Face target with weight on left foot. Center rod on target and bring tip to eye level. Forearm should be extension of rod, and elbow and upper arm should be close to but not pressing against body.

At this point the weight of the lure is flexing the rod in a rearward direction. Without pausing, bring the rod forward with a smooth, crisp, chopping motion of the forearm. Some wrist emphasis is proper, but if the arm action is correct, the extra punch will come naturally. Casting is not a "wrist flick." The rod itself is being loaded during the backward and forward strikes, and in that fraction of a second when the energy is transmitted into the tip, it's perfectly capable of tossing the plug across the pond. The cast is not executed by the actual forward motion of your arm, except insofar as it provides energy and direction to the rod. As the rod approaches its starting point, release your fingerhold on the line; the lure should be in the right trajectory for an accurate and long cast. The correct release point does take some "feel" or, at least, previous experience at casting, so that you don't release too early and send the plug straight overhead or release too late and bounce it at your feet. Through practice, however, you will quickly learn when to let go.

After the lure is in flight, you can retard its speed to prevent overshooting the target by bringing your forefinger back toward the spool to create friction against the uncoiling line. This is called *feathering*. To stop the lure completely, simply touch the spool rim with your forefinger. Even if your cast was absolutely on the target, the forefinger should come down to the spool automatically to prevent winding up slack. Slack coils of line will tangle on a spinning reel. To minimize the problem, always finish each cast by touching the spool rim. Immediately catch the line with your forefinger and lift the rod tip, taking all the slack out of the line before you begin to retrieve.

The Underhand Cast

When casting from the bank of a pond or a stream, you will often get into a position where obstructions prevent the use of an overhead cast. In such places, the underhand cast is most practical. Because the underhand cast is essentially a "toss," and because the lures used are often very light, there is an inclination to help the rod in this particular cast by emphasizing the hand motion. The trick is to rely on the rod, which has enough recoil power to do the job with very little help from you. The rod is loaded with a quick, upward lift and then is instantly reversed by a sharp, downward push, which develops the maximum resistance to bend. When practicing, assume your stance by facing the target. Then take a quarter turn to the right (which is opposite to the overhead position) so that the left shoulder is pointed toward the target and the heel of your right foot is opposite the ball of your left foot. The feet, incidentally, should be spread comfortably apart, with your weight shifted largely to your left foot. Of course, the stance is reversed by left-handed casters. Extend the rod parallel to the water at waist level so that it points directly at the target. Free the line from the pickup mechanism and hold it across the tip of your forefinger.

Start the cast from the horizontal rod position with an upward motion by bending your elbow—not the wrist—until the rod tip is at about eye level. Without hesitating, bring the rod back down to the starting position, using a positive thumb push on the handle as you do so. When the starting position has been reached, stop abruptly. The combined upward and downward movements provide the necessary casting energy to your rod tip, and when the downward thrust is stopped, the lure will flex the rod in toward your feet. As the rod tip begins to reach the horizontal position again, release the line from your finger, and the lure will sail out in a low arc. Remember, let the rod do the work. Do not attempt to help things along by adding a tossing motion with your hand.

The Side Cast

There is a great similarity between making the side cast and hitting a baseball. The rod is literally swung from the rear to the forward position across a horizontal plane, with increasing power to the point of release. The stance for the side cast differs from the overhead in that your left foot and shoulder point at the target and your feet are spread well apart. Hold the rod horizontally with the line free of the pickup mechanism and resting across your forefinger. To get a full body swing, point the rod at a right angle to your target, and slowly sweep the rod back slightly below horizontal so the tip is pointing in a line with, but directly opposite to, the target. This movement shifts your body weight from the left to the right foot, and your hips turn with your shoulders. When done smoothly the rod will bend slightly, although the idea is not to make a back cast in the overhead sense. As the rod swings back to casting position, sweep it forward with accelerating force, "hitting" your release point just before the tip comes over your target.

The Two-handed Spinning Rod

The two-handed spinning rod is a heavy-duty freshwater or saltwater model. Most rods in this class are 7–8 feet long, with a glass

The Underhand Cast

Point rod at target so hand is at waist level and the rod is absolutely horizontal.

1. AIM

2. STOP

Begin cast with an upward motion by bending the elbow but not the wrist. The tip should come to eye level. Without pause, snap the rod down to horizontal again with thumb push on handle. Stop abruptly at horizontal; the rod develops maximum bend down toward feet.

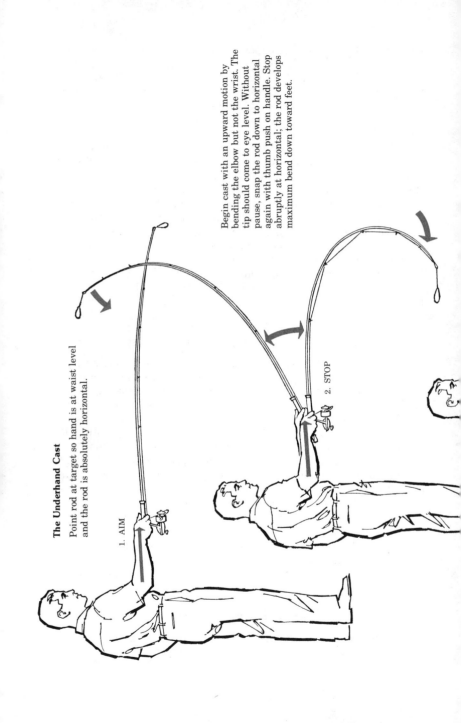

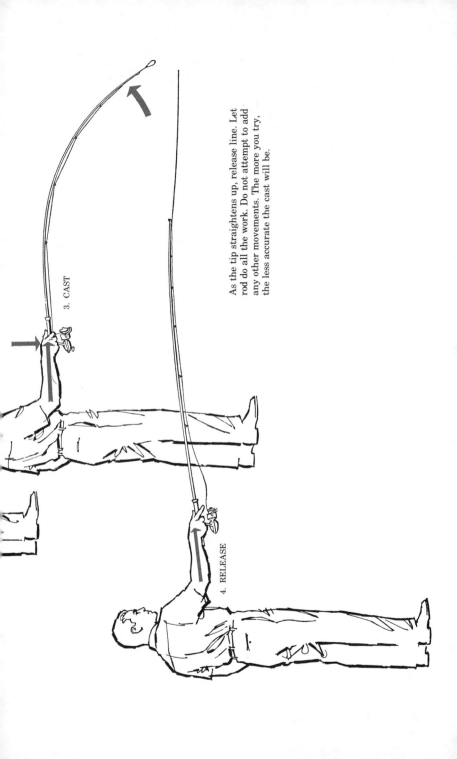

3. CAST

4. RELEASE

As the tip straightens up, release line. Let rod do all the work. Do not attempt to add any other movements. The more you try, the less accurate the cast will be.

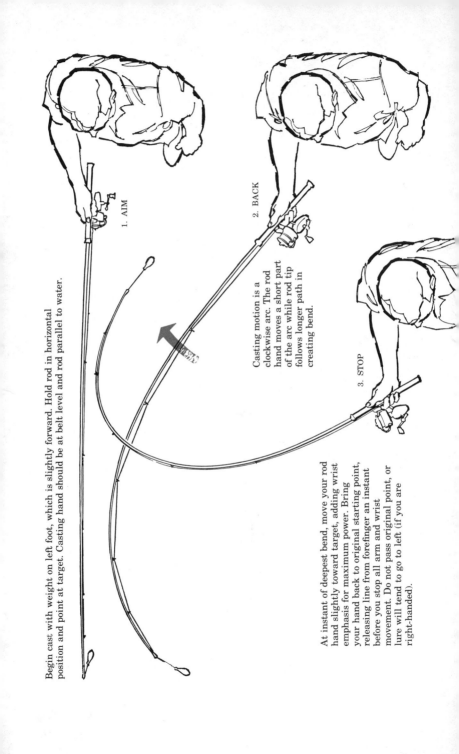

Begin cast with weight on left foot, which is slightly forward. Hold rod in horizontal position and point at target. Casting hand should be at belt level and rod parallel to water.

1. AIM

2. BACK

Casting motion is a clockwise arc. The rod hand moves a short part of the arc while rod tip follows longer path in creating bend.

3. STOP

At instant of deepest bend, move your rod hand slightly toward target, adding wrist emphasis for maximum power. Bring your hand back to original starting point, releasing line from forefinger an instant before you stop all arm and wrist movement. Do not pass original point, or lure will tend to go to left (if you are right-handed).

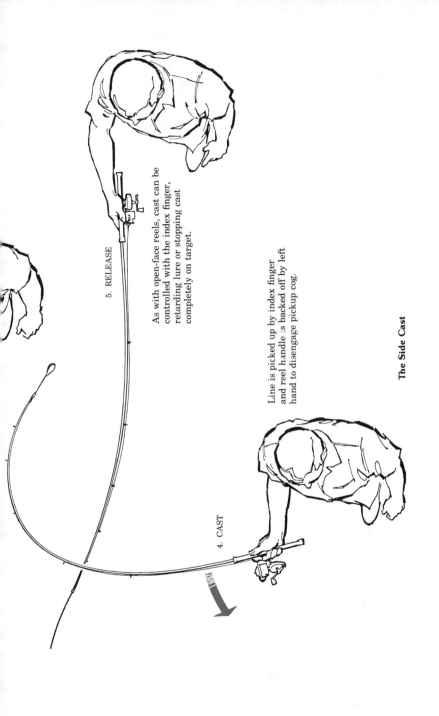

5. RELEASE

As with open-face reels, cast can be controlled with the index finger, retarding lure or stopping cast completely on target.

4. CAST

Line is picked up by index finger and reel handle is backed off by left hand to disengage pickup cog.

The Side Cast

The Overhead Snap Cast

Face target squarely. Free line from pickup
and rest across the forefinger. Swing rod back,
but in line with the target. Both hands should
not be at eye level.

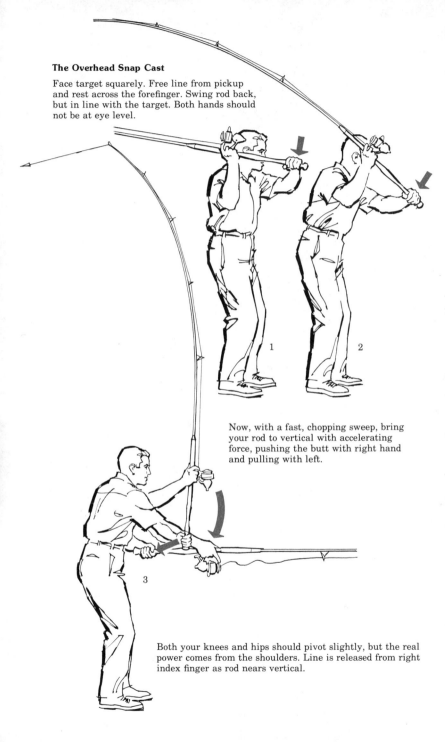

Now, with a fast, chopping sweep, bring
your rod to vertical with accelerating
force, pushing the butt with right hand
and pulling with left.

Both your knees and hips should pivot slightly, but the real
power comes from the shoulders. Line is released from right
index finger as rod nears vertical.

blank weight of 4–6 ounces. They may be termed as intermediate between standard spinning rods and surf-spinning rods. The chief targets are tarpon, snook, winter steelhead, and salmon. Both hands are used in this style of casting because the weight of the lures involved is too heavy for continuous single-handed work. Such baits weigh ⅞ ounce or more, and require active rod manipulation for popping and rapid retrieving. To some extent, the two-handed spin stick is a counterpart of the more specialized popping rod. Logically, big lures require powerful rods and heavy reels, so the shift to a two-hand style is a compromise to the tackle.

Two-handed Casting

The basic difference between the two-handed cast and other styles is that no actual back cast is required with the two-handed rod. The caster may swing his rod back to get body rhythm, as much of the casting power comes from the hips and legs, or he may start from a stationary position with the rod already extended to the rear. Essentially, however, it's the rod's taper and speed plus the right application of force behind it that make the cast. With the standard light spinning rods, which have a shorter bending length, the angler must develop recoil power by first making a back cast. In brief, the angler's body becomes a dominant factor in all forms of two-handed casting, and personal styles vary greatly as the rods get longer and heavier.

There are two fundamental casts with the two-handed rod— the overhead snap cast, which is used in normal winds, and the side cast, which can be delivered with a flatter trajectory and, therefore, is more suitable for casting against the wind.

To make the overhead snap cast, stand with your left foot slightly in front of your right foot and face your target. With the line free of the pickup mechanism and resting across your forefinger, point the rod to the rear so that the tip is below horizontal. Your weight should be on your right foot with your body leaning slightly backward and to the right from the hips. Your right arm should not be extended. The casting motion is in a complete overhead arc, during which power is applied progressively. Start slowly, and increase the tip speed by swinging the rod up and forward with your right hand and turning both shoulders in much the same way as you would if chopping with a two-handed ax. Your body weight will shift from the right foot to the left at the moment you reach the release point. The left hand merely follows through, acting as a fulcrum on the rod butt.

Surf Spinning

Surf-spinning rods are 8–11 feet long and can cast lines from 8- to 45-pound test. These specifications also encompass the range of the standard high-surf rod, but the real virtue of spinning from the beach is in the use of light tackle, i.e., with rods 8–9 feet long, handling 8- to 18-pound-test lines and lures of ¾–2 ounces. This gear is particularly suited to working in a calm-to-moderate surf when small artificial lures are in demand. Heavier surf-spinning tackle reduces the backlash problem but doesn't match the distance of the standard surf rod. Large spinning reels are made especially for surf-fishing with either a bail or manual pickup.

There are two basic casts to be made with the surf-spinning rod—the overhead cast and the side cast. As with the lighter two-handed spinning rod, no actual back cast is required. The angler may swing his rod back to get body rhythm, generating the power from legs, hips, and shoulders, or he may start from a stationary position with the rod already extended to the rear. When fishing with bait rigs, many casters simply drop the sinker on the sand behind them and cast from that position.

To make the overhead cast, stand with your left foot slightly in front of your right foot and face your target. Free the line from the pickup mechanism, and rest it across your forefinger. Now, twisting your body at the hips and bending the right knee slightly, lean as far back as possible without losing your balance. Your body weight should be almost entirely on your right foot. With the rod fully extended to the rear, make your cast by pivoting hips and shoulders as you swing the rod up and forward with increasing speed. Your body weight will shift from right to left foot.

To make the side cast, stand with your left foot placed well ahead of your right foot. Both feet should be quartering away from the direction of your target. Release the line from the pickup mechanism, and rest it across your forefinger. Grasp the butt near the end with your left hand, and swing the rod to the rear with the reel down. Both arms should be bent at the elbows. With your body weight on your right foot, twist at the hips, bending slightly on the right knee. The cast starts with a body pivot from the right heel, and your weight will shift from right to left as the cast progresses. Swing the rod up in a 45-degree plane with your right hand pushing upward while the left hand pulls backward. As the rod nears the forward position, release the line from your finger and follow with the rod pointing toward the outgoing line.

SURF-FISHING   As a casting discipline, the two-handed rod

used in surf-casting (which can employ either the open-face spinning reel or the revolving-spool reel) has mechanical similarities
with the equipment used in casting with one hand. However, the
tackle and techniques in actual fishing differ greatly and would be
out of context here; for complete details on surf-fishing, see p. 218.

How to Avoid Line Twist

It is axiomatic that when you crank a spinning reel against a dead
weight the line becomes twisted. Not that the fish is dead—but it
does become an immovable object at various times and creates the
same effect. The line, which is stretched against the fish's weight
and is at a right angle to the path of resistance, turns back on the
spool in twists as it passes over the roller mechanism. When a
heavy fish is played incorrectly with spinning tackle, the line will
become a tightly snarled mass of hoops the moment all tension is
released. Of course, a small fish that swims directly back to the
angler won't cause much trouble. The correct way to regain line
is by pumping. Actually, it is more of a stroking motion—a gentle
upward sweep of the rod, which prods the fish in your direction.
When the fish shows signs of weakening, press your forefinger
right against the spool and raise the rod slowly backward; then
lower it quickly and reel in the slack. The slack will not twist.
Never, under any circumstances, crank the reel when your quarry
is stationary and unyielding. The fish must be continually prodded
with gentle nudges of the rod.

Certain lures and even live baits will create line twist when
casting or retrieving. For example, a poorly designed lead-head jig
or a whole curved shrimp will spin in the air and, after a few casts,
snarl your line. Poorly designed spinners also twist line by blade
rotation when retrieved through the water, and while these can be
counteracted to some extent in using a swivel or snap swivel, it's
better to eliminate faulty lures.

Spinning-Reel Maintenance

The spinning reel used in freshwater fishing won't require too
much maintenance. About twice a year, the gear-housing cover
plate should be removed and the gears cleaned and greased. The
mechanism can be washed in gasoline using an old toothbrush to
scrub all the working parts. When it is dry, the gears should be
repacked with grease, and all moving parts should be lubricated
with a light machine oil. Otherwise, in most inland regions, an
occasional oiling according to the manufacturer's instructions

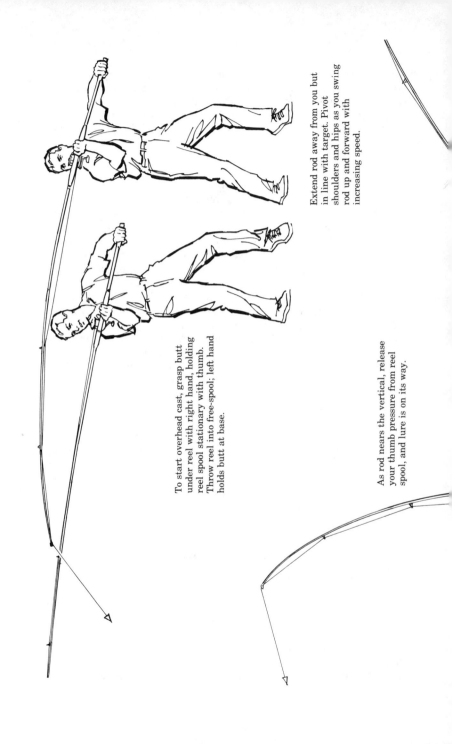

To start overhead cast, grasp butt under reel with right hand, holding reel spool stationary with thumb. Throw reel into free-spool; left hand holds butt at base.

Extend rod away from you but in line with target. Pivot shoulders and hips as you swing rod up and forward with increasing speed.

As rod nears the vertical, release your thumb pressure from reel spool, and lure is on its way.

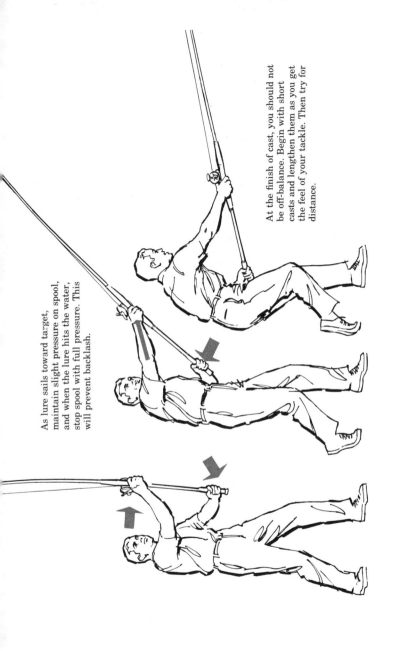

As lure sails toward target, maintain slight pressure on spool, and when the lure hits the water, stop spool with full pressure. This will prevent backlash.

At the finish of cast, you should not be off-balance. Begin with short casts and lengthen them as you get the feel of your tackle. Then try for distance.

How to Surf Cast (Revolving-Spool Reel)

is sufficient. However, if used in saltwater fishing, the reel must be washed each time it is used.

No reel, regardless of how well it is made, will remain functional if it's allowed to corrode. Once corrosion begins, it is only a matter of days before all moving parts become inoperable. To prevent corrosion, you must conscientiously clean the reel in tap water immediately after fishing. Don't wait until the next day; that's too late. The best method of cleaning is to remove the spool, then hold the reel under warm water, turning it in all positions to make certain it is washed thoroughly. To clean the spool, use a bit more water force to get as much of the salt off as possible. An unwashed line has a tendency to cake, and the residual salt will cause the spool to corrode inside the flanges. When the reel is clean, it should be dried carefully. All moving parts can then be given a coat of reel oil, making certain the areas around the pickup, the crank, and crank knob are well saturated.

How to Select Lures

The basic lures used in spinning are spinners, spoons, jigs, soft plastic lures, and plugs. A variety of other baits may be employed; however, these five types receive the widest application to fresh- and saltwater fishing. The selection of a spinning lure depends in part on the species of fish sought, the casting conditions, and the water conditions. For detailed information on the various types of lures, see Spinners (p. 105), Spoons (p. 112), Jigs (p. 118), Soft Plastic Lures (p. 121), and Plugs (p. 126).

Spin Casting

Spin casting is another form of spinning. Unlike the regular spinning or "open-faced" reel, the spin-casting reel is enclosed in a cone-shaped hood. However, it also works on the same fixed-spool principle.

The casting action is controlled by the thumb resting on a push button or lever rather than by your forefinger. Although the line spirals off the end of the spool, this motion is contained within the hood, and the line passes out through a hole in the front. The friction created by the spiraling line as it escapes from the inside of the hood is the only limitation to closed-spool reels. Friction cuts down the distance, but from a practical point of view, a well-made closed-spool reel does a quite effective job at average casting ranges. As far as most plugging situations are concerned, the loss in efficiency isn't even noticeable. The optimum lure weights are ⅜–⅝ ounce. Casting distance falls off sharply with very light lures not only because of friction but because the fine lines they require have a tendency to foul in the housing.

Spin-Casting Reels

There are two general types of closed-spool reels. One type is mounted below the rod, the same as the regular spinning reel. Some models require grasping the line to control casts. Other models have release mechanisms for line control, including a reel built as an integral part of the rod with the push button located in the rod-butt section. This is a most comfortable unit, providing for rod options in that the reel can be unscrewed and removed if you need to use a lighter or heavier tip.

The other type, the top-mounted spin-casting reel, is designed for any bait-casting rod having an offset-reel seat. Although it can be slipped on a straight-grip rod, this combination is not too comfortable. You will have to reach up with your thumb, which is both awkward and fatiguing. It's a good idea to buy both the rod and reel at the same time to make certain that one fits the other.

Many manufacturers prewind the reel spool with line, but if this is not the case, make certain to use the recommended size. The general range for closed-spool reels in monofilament is from 6-pound test to 15-pound test. Don't use braided line because it will pile up inside the housing. Occasionally, a monofilament line will be missed by the pickup pin; if so, simply pull on the line with your left hand or raise the rod tip to eliminate the slack, and it will engage.

Spin-Casting Rods

The rod for a top-mounted spin-casting reel is an adaptation of the bait-casting rod. It differs only in having larger ring guides, which reduce friction from the spiraling line, and a decurved rod grip. When buying a spin-casting rod, match it to the reel to make certain that the push button is at a comfortable height from your thumb. These rods vary from 5½ to 7 feet in length. The 6- and 6½-foot shafts in a medium-action rod are most popular for general freshwater fishing.

Spin-casting reels that mount under the handle cannot be used with regular spin-casting rods. These speciality reels are designed for conventional spinning rods or are sold as an integral part of the rod, with a push button located on top of the grip.

How to Spin-Cast

Body position is important in all casting, and, while actual fishing conditions may require some modifications, you should practice in what might be termed the "natural" stance. Face your target; then make a quarter turn to the left so your right shoulder is pointed directly toward the target and your left foot is a little to the rear of your right foot. Spread your feet slightly, get comfortable, and stay relaxed. Line up the target with your eye and the rod. Hold the rod so the tip end is slightly above your head, with the reel handle up, the button depressed, and the rod handle above your belt but extended forward, and with your forearm paralleling the angle of the rod. Don't stiffen your wrist; try to keep it relaxed. Cocking the wrist doesn't help in gaining accuracy. Both the back stroke and the forward stroke consist of a forearm movement with just the slightest wrist bend on the forward stroke for emphasis. Start your cast by lifting elbow in line with the target until your hand comes up to eye level. The rod must stop in a vertical position and should never be allowed to drift back over your shoulder. Without hesitating, begin the forward stroke in exactly the same path the rod made before. The movements should blend together with the forward stroke made in a crisp, chopping motion. When the rod reaches a position halfway between vertical and your starting point, release your thumb pressure from the button to permit the lure to start its flight. A properly designed rod virtually does all the casting; so don't try to force the rod, as too much arm movement will merely break up the rhythm of the bending and straightening shaft. Try to shoot the plug in a low arc. If you cast too high, the monofilament will drift or "float," even in a slight wind, and reduce your accuracy.

One thing the veteran bait caster misses working with the closed-face reel is the lack of "feel." Stopping the flight of a lure can be done through the push button. However, you can't actually thumb it, and consequently feathering the plug to its target is not a precise maneuver. Some reels have a feathering device (a spring-controlled pin that the line spirals against), and some anglers develop a sensitivity even for the nonfeathering buttons and can more or less "bump" the line into a corrected speed. The purpose of a closed-face reel is to keep fingers off the spool in any case. Through practice, you can establish an exact release point for various distances. The plug can be stopped at any point, of course, by depressing the button.

Retrieving with a closed-face reel is simply a matter of turning the handle. The line will be caught by a pickup pin and wound back on the spool. The spool of an orthodox spinning reel oscillates or rides in and out to cross-wind the line, so that one coil doesn't snag another coil. On closed-face reels, the spool may or may not oscillate, depending on its design. Obviously, an oscillating spool can be made wider and have a larger capacity than a nonoscillating one, but both kinds are popular. The closed-face spool lies inside a spinner head or winding cup that works on the same principle as the rotating head of an open-face reel. Instead of a bail, however, to engage the line, the closed-face reel has a pin to do the same job. Although many models have just one pin, some reels have two pins, and still others are notched completely around the winding cup. Multiple pins or notches not only help to distribute wear but allow a much faster pickup of the line. When the reel is in the casting position with the button depressed, the pickup pin is retracted flush with the winding cup. When the handle is turned, the pin extends and catches the line. To keep the line from spiraling off the spool when you push the button and retract the pin, the winding cup moves forward and presses against the nose of the hood. The line is held in place against a smooth nylon or rubber ring so that it can't be damaged.

When retrieving and working the plug, many anglers like to "palm" their reels; this is probably the most comfortable way of holding the outfit, because the reel usually fits naturally in the hand. By laying one side of the reel in your palm you can also let the line pass between your thumb and index finger when there's too much slack on the water to maintain an even tension. The reel should have a substantial handle to provide a good cranking radius so that the line comes back at a reasonable speed without tiring the other hand. And, of course, the drag must be conveniently

Hand Positions of Casting Sequence

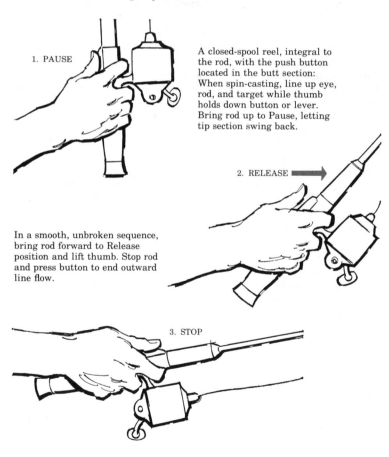

1. PAUSE

A closed-spool reel, integral to the rod, with the push button located in the butt section: When spin-casting, line up eye, rod, and target while thumb holds down button or lever. Bring rod up to Pause, letting tip section swing back.

2. RELEASE

In a smooth, unbroken sequence, bring rod forward to Release position and lift thumb. Stop rod and press button to end outward line flow.

3. STOP

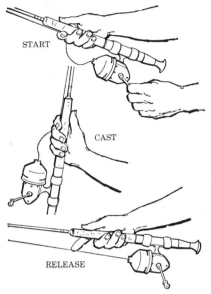

START

CAST

RELEASE

Closed-Spool Reel (Overhead Cast)

A closed-spool reel without the push-button feature, designed to be placed behind your hand: to start, hook your index finger around the line and press it to the rod grip. Turn the reel handle to release line from the pickup pin. Make your cast with the line pressed firmly against the grip.

When the line is released on the forward cast use your finger to feather, or control, the flight of the lure.

located and easy to operate. The adjustable drag mechanism of a spin-casting reel may be located on the front, top, or side of the spool. In any case, it should be smooth and display no jerkiness or buildup in operation. The drag isn't too important for most freshwater fishing, but heavy gamefish are definitely going to put it to the test.

REELS MOUNTED BELOW THE GRIP   These speciality spin-casting reels provide a different balance—more like a fly-rod outfit in feel—and are preferred by some anglers. Essentially, the casting movements are no different with respect to the rod, but your finger positions are changed.

Ultralight Spinning

Ultralight spinning is more a technique than a distinct method. It is recommended for the experienced caster rather than the beginner. As the name implies, ultralight spinning is accomplished with refined tackle: lines of less than 3-pound test and rods of less than 3 ounces (total weight) are usually employed. The value of ultralight is in the capture of small gamefish and panfish, but it also serves a definite tactical purpose. The art of *hairlining* is based on two fundamental premises: (1) certain fishing conditions, which more or less fall in a pattern, demand the use of tiny lures; and (2) tiny lures can only be cast with the lightest tackle. In general, the advantage of spooling lines in the .002- to .005-inch diameters is that they will cast a $^1/_{16}$- to $^1/_{20}$-ounce spinner 50–60 feet away with little or no splash and no disturbing shadows on the stream bottom. Of course, the lure itself is so small that a hungry gamefish is not apt to inspect it carefully. On streams that have been thumped daily with hardware, even cautious fish like the brown trout are attracted to baits no bigger than a collar button. With the higher number of strikes comes a greater number of line breaks, and the beginner, especially, will not only need patience, but considerable dexterity to get the feel of it. The almost-invisible line is hard to see and difficult to control, particularly in a wind. Hairline technique requires an absolute mastery of spinning tackle; some points that are only incidental to the use of standard gear can make the difference between success and failure.

The Ultralight Rod

The correct rod for hairline casting will be 4½–6 feet long and weigh in the neighborhood of 1½–2½ ounces. It must have a very sensitive action, soft without excessive vibration, and flexing well down into the butt. A short, stiff rod is no good even if it's very light in weight. Many ultralight lures are in the $^1/_{20}$- to $^1/_{10}$-ounce class, and in themselves, they can hardly provide one flea power toward developing a rod's resistance to bend. These diminutive spoons and spinners don't have the feeling of an orthodox casting weight. It's there, but it's delicate and takes some practice for the caster to get the right touch.

The Ultralight Reel

The reel must be first-class. A wispy line requires a sensitive drag. The dragbrake of most spinning reels is in principle an adjustable, frictional resistance against spool rotation. This works with a slipping clutch ordinarily composed of a pressure spring, a washer, a wing nut, and the spool. By tightening the wing nut, the spool is compressed between the seat and the washer, creating the friction that resists rotation of the spool. Mechanically, no friction-type brake is 100 percent efficient. On rare occasions a drag will "freeze." Trying to loosen the wing nut while a runaway fish stretches the monofilament requires considerable presence of mind. With a hairline you seldom get that chance; if the spool merely hesitates, the line breaks. However, modern reels are generally more responsive than their anglers. The trick is to set the drag on the low side. You don't need any more than a *suggestion* of drag when casting with ultralight. If you set the drag high, or close to the breaking strain of the line, everything from air temperature to the elasticity of the monofilament becomes a potentially adverse factor. Bear in mind that the force required to start the drag working is at a right angle to the spool—over the roller mechanism—and all the impact strain is confined to a few inches of line. When hand-testing a drag, you pull the monofilament off smoothly, but fish rarely hit and run with the same precision. Their response to the sting of a hook is wild head shaking and body rolling, which comes back to the reel in violent and jerky pulls. None of these forces is sustained enough to get a high drag setting started; yet they may exceed the strength of the line. For this reason, the great majority of breaks occur at the reel, and these can be minimized by using the drag sparingly.

Finger Control of Cast

Due to the fact that much of the fishing is done facing upstream in very shallow water, even a small spinner or spoon sinks very quickly and snags in the bottom if you do not control the cast manually. When using an orthodox spinning reel your forefinger does three important jobs: it holds the line free of the spool preparatory to a cast; it retards the flight of the lure by touching or feathering the line as the loops spin off; and it stops the cast on target. Some casters shoot for the bull's-eye and don't bother to check the cast manually. For a delicate presentation, however, it's necessary to aim slightly beyond the target and stop the lure in flight to knock some of the momentum out of it. The hairline angler should get in the habit of checking each cast, because when the lure is stopped by touching the forefinger against the spool, it's a simple matter to raise the rod and give the blade some initial forward motion before turning the handle to close the bail. With this technique, the lure is moving ahead—not diving for the stones—while the bail is snapping down. Precious moments are lost if you finish your cast and then retrieve in the normal manner without bringing the rod up and back. The bail must gather slack before the spinner gets started. True, your trout or smallmouth may be hiding in a deep pocket behind a boulder, but in low, summer water such stations are invariably surrounded by shingles of moist gravel. The crafty hairliner will place his lure on these bare spots and swim it back into the holes to minimize splash and shadow. By using initial finger control, he can glide the spinner through a wet dishpan.

The Importance of Line Elasticity

Although many anglers feel that the kind of gear employed is too fragile for serious work, the fact of the matter is that, with a little experience, almost anybody can use it. By holding the rod high, keeping as much line as possible out of the water, and taking advantage of the full bend of the rod, you can finger the spool and make the stretch of the monofilament wear the fish to exhaustion. The elasticity of the line acts as a shock absorber. In fact, the more yardage the fish peels off, the easier you can control the situation. Line breaks often occur because the angler snubs a green fish just a rod's length away, where sudden lunges or jumps can't be counteracted with the flexibility of the tackle. It's imperative to keep a reasonable distance between yourself and your quarry, applying finger pressure against the spool as needed and pumping with gentle upward sweeps of the rod to control the fish's direction. The anti-reverse lock should be in the "on" position until the fish has been brought to net. But don't attempt to land a lively gamefish with hairline until it's absolutely whipped.

Ultralight Lures

There is a tremendous variety of ultralight lures on the market today, encompassing spinners, spoons, jigs, and plugs. As in all methods of fishing, the smart angler will stock a selection of each. Although microscopic baits don't lose their effectiveness as readily as standard-size lures, the fact remains that a fish population can become almost immune to artificials of any kind if the stream or pond is worked intensively. The celebrated lure of yesterday can be a dud tomorrow. Consistent success in any kind of angling requires a change of pace, and one way to achieve that is by using different types of baits.

Ultralight Spinning in Streams

Generally speaking, upstream casting is more effective than fishing in a downstream direction because you can approach the fish more closely. Gamefish are easily alarmed at 40–50 feet in low water, and in view of the fact that your casting range is somewhat limited with ultralight lures, it helps to take advantage of their head-to-the-current position. In working a typical stretch of river, use the longest cast practical and select targets that are beyond the place where a fish is holding. For example, if there's a deep pocket behind a log, aim for a spot 10 or even 15 feet above it, and run the spinner back to draw the fish out. Ultralight lures have very little surface impact, but you will find that swimming the lure at the right depth and speed is very important, particularly when dealing with large brown trout. They are susceptible to ultralight baits, but the blade must be moving at the right speed. Although the size of the lure is deceptively natural, its aerial entrance invariably arouses suspicion. The same tactic applies to downstream casting. If you want to pass your spinner through an undercut or into a dark, gurgling pocket, aim your cast into the shallows well below it; the instant the lure touches the surface, bring your rod up and back to get the lure in forward motion. With the whirling blade creating tension on the line, it's a simple matter to guide the bait into the lair. You can steer a lure left or right, and even under overhanging-bank brush, by holding the tip low in the desired direction. Never aim at the fish—always try to find a natural entrance to its feeding station and swim the spinner to it. This tactic is certain to increase strikes and eliminate those follow-ups. Frequently, one type of lure will be superior to another, but their relative effectiveness depends on how artfully each is presented.

Ultralight Spinning in Saltwater

Although few ultralight casters seek large fish in saltwater, there is a great deal of sport in the variety of species that can be caught.

As a general rule, a nylon jig of $1/10$ ounce will hook flounders, croakers, snappers, lookdown, sennet, pompano, whiting, scup, and many other small inshore species that do not readily strike artificials. In addition, ladyfish, Spanish mackerel, school stripers, weakfish, and other modest-sized gamesters, which are usually caught on tackle that is too heavy for maximum enjoyment, are important to the ultralight fan. Bottom bouncing a little jig along channel edges and over shell beds is apt to produce a dozen different kinds of fish. Most of these are crustacean and mollusk feeders, and consequently the day's bag merely reflects the area being fished. The reason for the jig's attraction probably rests in the fact that many mollusks and crustaceans will "hop" when disturbed. Even a scallop can jump off the sand by jetting water through its valves, and its motion is not unlike that of the erratic behavior of shrimp and sand bugs. So the hopping movement of a correctly fished jig may resemble food forms that plugs, spinners, and flies cannot emulate. Conventional spinning tackle does not lend itself to long casts with tiny jigs, but ultralight gear greatly extends your range, and the fine line and sensitive rod of ultralight equipment is an ideal combination for bottom bouncing.

Bait Casting

The bait-casting method is more difficult to master than spinning or spin casting. The reel spool is not stationary during a cast but revolves, and therefore can overrun or backlash. However, this equipment is preferred by many anglers and is more efficient when lines of over 12-pound test are used. The tackle was originally developed in the nineteenth century solely for the purpose of casting live minnows, and thus the reference to "bait" casting. The plug is the most common lure used in bait casting, and consequently it is sometimes referred to as "plug" casting. Bait casting encompasses many kinds of fishing in both fresh and saltwater; it is especially popular for black bass, northern pike, and tarpon.

The Bait-Casting Reel

Bait-casting reels vary in weight from 7½ to 14 ounces or more. Although they are sometimes separated as freshwater or saltwater models, there is considerable overlap, with lightweight reels being used for certain small marine gamefish. Line capacity is a reliable indication of function; in addition to a star drag and minimum 4:1 gear ratio, a saltwater bait-casting reel should have a minimum 220-yard, 15-pound-test or 190-yard, 20-pound-test line capacity. This is not a critical factor in most freshwater fishing.

The heart of a bait-casting reel is the spool. It must be light in weight to start rotating quickly and to stop quickly with minimum inertia (the tendency of matter at rest to remain at rest and matter in motion to remain in motion). A heavy spool is difficult to start and stop. To minimize weight, the best spools are made of aluminum, plastic, and magnesium. In quality modern reels, the spool can be uncoupled from other parts of the reel so that the handle, main drive gear, and pinion gear are not functioning during a cast. This is called *free-spool*. These moving parts are disengaged from the spool by depressing a trip mechanism (free-spool lever or plunger) before the cast is made. Most inexpensive reels do not have this free-spool feature.

Bait-Casting Reel Nomenclature

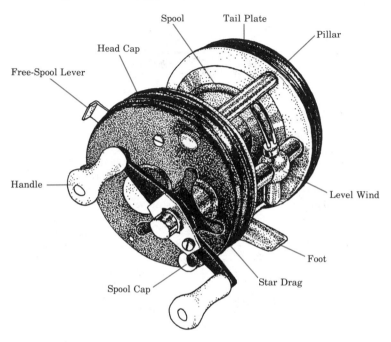

Spool   Tail Plate

Head Cap   Pillar

Free-Spool Lever

Handle

Level Wind

Foot

Spool Cap   Star Drag

Bait-Casting Reel

The device for preventing backlash in this bait-casting reel is sliding weights mounted on a bar at the end of the spool. As the spool turns faster more friction is created against the arbor.

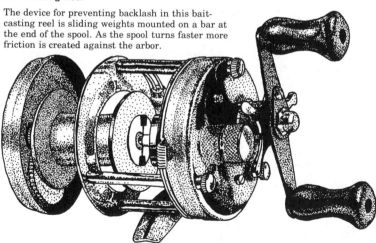

Manufacturers use different trade names for their individual antibacklash systems, but all are designed to slow the reel spool during the cast. The most popular device is weights mounted at the spool end; these create friction as spool rotation increases. The amount of friction applied can be varied by a calibrated tail-spool cap, which you adjust to match the weight of your lure. Although these controls largely eliminate backlashes, some thumb pressure is still necessary to "fine tune" each cast.

THE LEVEL-WIND MECHANISM   The level-wind mechanism on a bait-casting reel shuttles back and forth, guiding the line during a cast and a retrieve so that it leaves the spool and is respooled evenly. This cross-winding prevents the line from piling up in ridges or becoming jammed in underlying coils; a cast will stop short when the line jams and will create a backlash. As the term indicates, the coils of a cross-wound line lie on top of each other at an angle and, thus, cannot become enmeshed. On reels without a level wind, spooling line must be guided manually by your rod-hand fingers.

THE DRAG OR BRAKE   As in spinning, the drag on a bait-casting reel applies variable pressure to the spool, from very light to fully locked. The amount of pressure or drag is adjusted by turning a knurled knob or star control. A good drag has a wide range of pressure so that it works smoothly; a drag that takes up too rapidly may freeze and cause a line break. Always remember that the pressure your drag exerts against a fish increases as the amount of line on the spool decreases, on account of the friction of line passing through water. A very light drag of, say, 4 pounds with a full spool may effectively become equal to 12 pounds of pressure when a running fish has nearly emptied the spool.

The Bait-Casting Rod

Bait-casting rods vary from 4½ to 6½ feet in length. Although some are made in two sections (usually the 6- and 6½-foot shafts designed for light lures) the more common rod has a single-piece tip that inserts in the handle; this provides greater strength by eliminating the ferrule. Although this method of casting encompasses many of the same lures used in spinning, the optimum range for bait-casting tackle is from ⅜ to 1½ ounces; hence, there is greater stress on the rod. Fiberglass and graphite, or a combination of these synthetics, are superior to bamboo for the following reason: when casting, the line flows straight from the reel rather than spiraling off the spool (as in spinning), so only small ring guides are necessary. The rod handle comes in two styles: offset and straight. The offset type mounts the reel lower in relation to your hand, and for most casters, this provides better thumb control. A third type, the decurved handle used in spin casting, is also popular and, in some hands, more comfortable, especially when using the larger bait-casting reels.

How to Select a Casting Line

A quality braided line should be the choice of a beginner and even for the skilled angler in most kinds of fishing. The braided line casts easier, spools uniformly, and has a lower elasticity than monofilament. While line stretch can be an advantage with light spinning tackle, it is a handicap with the normally heavier lines and lures used in bait casting. Furthermore, braided line does not have the "memory" of monofilament, which tends to remain somewhat coiled as it leaves the spool. There are several kinds of braided line—nylon, polysynthetic, and polyester—of which the poly braids display minimal elasticity. To decrease line visibility when using a braid, a monofilament leader of suitable length can be joined to the end of the line; the leader should be of a length short of the level-wind guide so that the knot is clear when ready to cast.

There are several things to be considered in selecting a casting line, but the fundamental point is that a heavy line will not function with a light lure—nor will a light line work with a heavy lure. A delicate bait won't create enough velocity to pull the heavy line any distance, and, conversely, a spidery line will break under the load of a heavy lure when the rod is snapped into a casting bend. There is a definite relationship between the strength and/or diameter of a line and the weight to be thrown. In a sense, the line must act as a shock absorber when the rod gives the lure its backward momentum, and then the line must follow the weight through the air with a minimum resistance to the lure's velocity. These two demands are in opposition to each other. The ideal is maximum strength with minimum diameter in any casting line. So the factor to consider is what the weight range of the lures will be in a day's fishing.

This doesn't present much of a problem for the practical angler. With the standard lure-weight range of ⅜–⅝ ounce, a 12-pound-test line is usually adequate. If the fishing requires small baits of ⅛–¼ ounce, then 8-pound test would be required to get any distance. At the other extreme, with casting lures of ⅝–¾

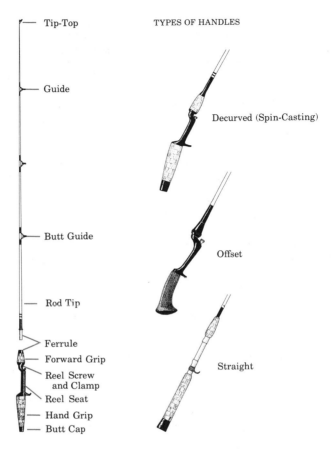

TYPES OF HANDLES

Tip-Top

Guide

Decurved (Spin-Casting)

Butt Guide

Offset

Rod Tip

Ferrule
Forward Grip
Reel Screw
  and Clamp
Reel Seat

Straight

Hand Grip
Butt Cap

Bait-Casting Rod Nomenclature

ounce, a 15-pound test is about right. This, of course, is a rule of thumb.

The Bait-Casting Outfit

LIGHT OUTFIT   The light bait-casting outfit is matched primarily for lures from 120 grains or ¼ ounce to 240 grains, or ½ ounce. This also implies clearwater conditions with a minimum of obstructions, such as gravel-bottomed lakes and rivers, where fine lines and small baits are most effective. Suitable rods vary from

5½ to 6½ feet in length, but a 6-foot rod is most popular. A slow-to-medium-action rod is preferred for accuracy.

The reel should be a narrow-frame level-wind one with free spool. There are some precision-built level winders, notably those developed for Skish accuracy work, that are sensitive enough to cast light baits even though the handle turns. The lines suitable for light bait casting are 6- to 12-pound test. For this class of tackle, monofilament rather than braided line is often used because of the visibility factor and the finer diameter per test. Be especially careful, however, that the end plates of the reel spool fit snugly against the frame. Fine monofilaments can easily get tangled inside the reel.

MEDIUM OUTFIT   This tackle class is the most popular all-around gear for freshwater casting. It's also used to some extent for saltwater work. Line tests range from 12- to 18-pound test. The lure weight range is from 300 grains, or ⅝ ounce, to 360 grains, or ¾ ounce. Rod lengths are 4–6½ feet, depending primarily on the fishing. Some anglers prefer very short rods in regions where casting is commonly done on heavily wooded creeks. They want a flat trajectory to avoid overhanging branches. Although longer rods deliver a high-arc flight, they are preferred by anglers who seek delicacy in presentation. Generally speaking, the 5-foot and 5½-foot lengths are most popular. Reels for the medium outfit can be narrow-frame, level-wind ones with or without free spool, or the standard wide-frame ones with or without free spool. Some casters are partial to heavier lines in this class, and, consequently, wide-frame reels are favored. It's not uncommon to use 25-pound-test line with medium tackle when casting for bass, pike, muskies, or any husky gamefish living in snag-filled waters.

HEAVY OUTFIT   The heavy outfit is matched chiefly for saltwater casting. But the gear is also popular regionally, among muskie, steelhead, and salmon anglers using lures from 360 grains, or ¾ ounce, to 600 grains, or 1¼ ounces. A heavy rod is required not only for casting but to set the hooks when using large baits on big fish. Rod lengths are 5–6 feet, with a 5½-foot tip in a medium- or fast-action rod most practical. Few wrists can comfortably support more than 480 grains, or a 1-ounce casting load, so the length and weight factors more or less stop at this point. With the 5-foot, heavy rod, you would need the standard wide-frame reel, with or without free spool. Lines in this class range from 18 to 25 pounds. For big game like tarpon, salmon, or muskies, select tackle on the heavy side of medium and try to keep the lure weights in the 300-

to 360-grain range. A 15-pound-test monofilament is perfectly adequate, even for tarpon in the up-to-150-pound class—provided, of course, you select a quality reel with a smooth drag.

How to Bait Cast

A fairly flexible rod in the 4½–5 foot lengths is easiest for the beginner to use in his first practice sessions. Longer rods or fast tip-action rods can feel awkward at the start. For lawn or indoor casting, use a ⅜–⅝-ounce rubber practice plug. The line should be a braided 12-pound test.

THUMB CONTROL The value of an antibacklash mechanism on a bait-casting reel is considerable; however, to get consistent results under adverse winds, you must learn the correct thumb

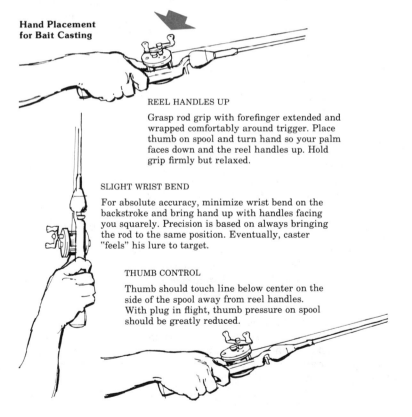

Hand Placement for Bait Casting

REEL HANDLES UP

Grasp rod grip with forefinger extended and wrapped comfortably around trigger. Place thumb on spool and turn hand so your palm faces down and the reel handles up. Hold grip firmly but relaxed.

SLIGHT WRIST BEND

For absolute accuracy, minimize wrist bend on the backstroke and bring hand up with handles facing you squarely. Precision is based on always bringing the rod to the same position. Eventually, caster "feels" his lure to target.

THUMB CONTROL

Thumb should touch line below center on the side of the spool away from reel handles. With plug in flight, thumb pressure on spool should be greatly reduced.

control. Some manual dexterity is required. Thumb pressure is applied in varying degrees, and only experience can teach you how much to use. The thumb is also used as a brake against running fish (unless the reel is equipped with a mechanical drag), and when the reel is palmed for retrieving, the thumb can apply tension to the line for tight, smooth spooling.

HOLDING THE ROD   Grasp the rod grip without squeezing it tightly. Your forefinger should be extended and wrapped comfortably around the trigger. Place your thumb on the spool, and turn your hand so that your palm faces *down* and the reel handles are *up*. The up-handle position allows complete wrist freedom. A ⅝-ounce casting weight should be ½–1 inch below the top guide; the ⅜-ounce weight should be about 3 inches below the top guide. The position of the weight (lure) is important in bait casting; as you use lures of less and less weight, they should be suspended progressively further away. For absolute accuracy, remember to minimize your wrist bend on the backstroke and to bring your rod and reel up with the handles facing you squarely. Precision is achieved by always bringing the rod to the same position. Eventually, you will "feel" the lure to the target.

THE OVERHEAD CAST   Face the target directly, then take a quarter turn to the left so that your right shoulder is now pointed toward the target and your left foot is slightly to the rear of your right foot. (A left-handed caster simply reverses the procedure by quartering to the right.) Of course, this position will be assumed naturally as you progress. Most of your body weight is now on the right foot. Hold the rod at about a 35-degree angle so that the tip-top is at eye level and the rod handle is above hip level. Your elbow should not touch your body, and your outstretched forearm should parallel the angle of the rod. The rod shaft should be "splitting" the target.

Start the backward phase of your cast by lifting the forearm and pivoting slightly on your elbow until your hand comes smoothly to eye level. The rod should stop at the vertical position, where the lure weight will develop a casting bend. Do not let the rod drift back over your shoulder. Without hesitating, begin the forward phase by moving the rod downward, following the same path it made on the upward stroke. This motion should be a crisp forearm chop using a slight elbow-and-wrist pivot for added power. At a point halfway between the vertical rod position and your original starting position release the thumb pressure from the spool to start the lure in flight. Control the spool speed with your thumb while continuing the downstroke; ordinarily, this requires a gradual *increase* of pressure until the lure hits the surface, at which point the spool is stopped completely. Through practice, you will learn the minimum pressure required to prevent a backlash.

All movements in the overhead cast should be made smoothly. Do not attempt long casts at first, but concentrate on blending the backward and forward phases without jerkiness, so that the rod tip bends and literally "kicks" the plug out.

THE SIDE CAST   The side cast is of limited value and not safe to use when fishing with a companion in a boat. Only a person thoroughly familiar with casting can use it properly. After you have mastered the overhead cast, practice the side cast alone, and with a rubber practice plug. The side cast is practical when casting from under obstacles such as tree limbs. The mistake that most beginners make is in moving their arms back at a right angle to the body.

The casting motion is a clockwise arc. Although the measurable arc of the rod hand is short, the rod tip makes a much longer arc in creating the casting bend. At the instant of deepest bend, the hand is moved slightly toward the target, adding wrist bend for maximum power. Begin with your casting hand at belt level, holding the rod parallel to the surface of the water and aimed directly at your target. Grip the rod with your palm facing left and the reel handles to the right. Your left foot should be slightly in front of your right foot, with the left side of your body angled toward the target. Distribute your body weight on both feet. With a crisp movement, bring your rod back, and stop at a right-angle position to your body. At the instant of deepest bend, move the rod forward with wrist and forearm emphasis, releasing thumb pressure from the spool at the forward impulse. It is important to get the release point that, correctly, "feels" early, or the lure will swing to the left. The tendency to angle casts away from the target is due solely to improper release and follow-through. Once mastered, the side cast is easy, accurate, and safe.

THE UNDERHAND CAST   The underhand or *flip cast* serves the same purpose as the side cast in working under obstacles, although it is safer to use and a great deal more accurate. It does have a limited range, but properly executed, it can deliver a plug to practical fishing distances. As in the overhead cast, the rod grip should be grasped palm down with the reel handles in the up position. However, unlike the overhead stance, quarter your body to the right so that your left shoulder is pointed toward the target

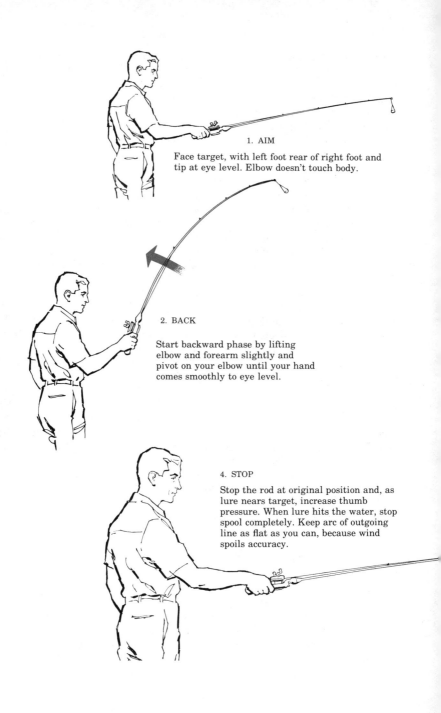

1. AIM

Face target, with left foot rear of right foot and tip at eye level. Elbow doesn't touch body.

2. BACK

Start backward phase by lifting elbow and forearm slightly and pivot on your elbow until your hand comes smoothly to eye level.

4. STOP

Stop the rod at original position and, as lure nears target, increase thumb pressure. When lure hits the water, stop spool completely. Keep arc of outgoing line as flat as you can, because wind spoils accuracy.

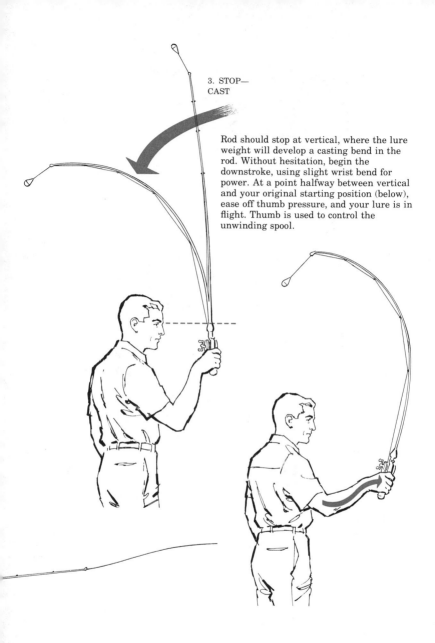

3. STOP—
CAST

Rod should stop at vertical, where the lure weight will develop a casting bend in the rod. Without hesitation, begin the downstroke, using slight wrist bend for power. At a point halfway between vertical and your original starting position (below), ease off thumb pressure, and your lure is in flight. Thumb is used to control the unwinding spool.

The Overhead Cast

The Side Cast

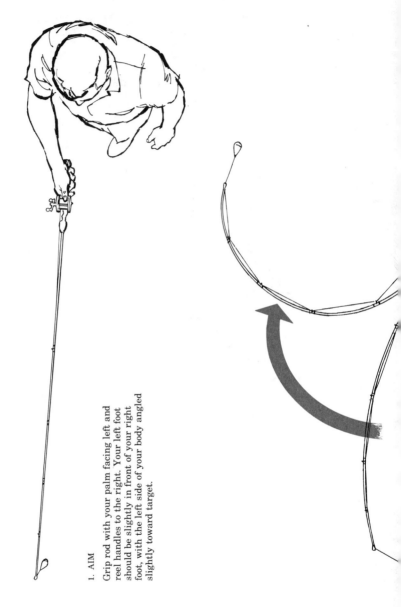

1. AIM

Grip rod with your palm facing left and reel handles to the right. Your left foot should be slightly in front of your right foot, with the left side of your body angled slightly toward target.

2. STOP

With a crisp movement, bring your rod back and stop at a right-angle position to your body. At the instant of deepest bend, move the rod forward with wrist and forearm emphasis, releasing thumb pressure from the spool at the forward impulse. It is important to get the correct release point—not too late—or the lure will swing to the left.

3. STOP

Stop again at your original starting point. Do not pass it, or the lure will mush left if you are right-handed and right if you are southpaw. The tendency to angle casts away from the target is due solely to improper release and follow-through. Once mastered, the side cast is easy, accurate, and safe.

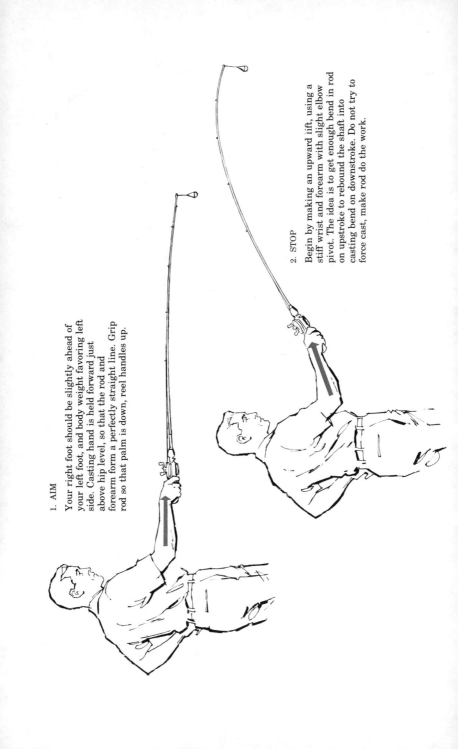

1. AIM

Your right foot should be slightly ahead of your left foot, and body weight favoring left side. Casting hand is held forward just above hip level, so that the rod and forearm form a perfectly straight line. Grip rod so that palm is down, reel handles up.

2. STOP

Begin by making an upward lift, using a stiff wrist and forearm with slight elbow pivot. The idea is to get enough bend in rod on upstroke to rebound the shaft into casting bend on downstroke. Do not try to force cast, make rod do the work.

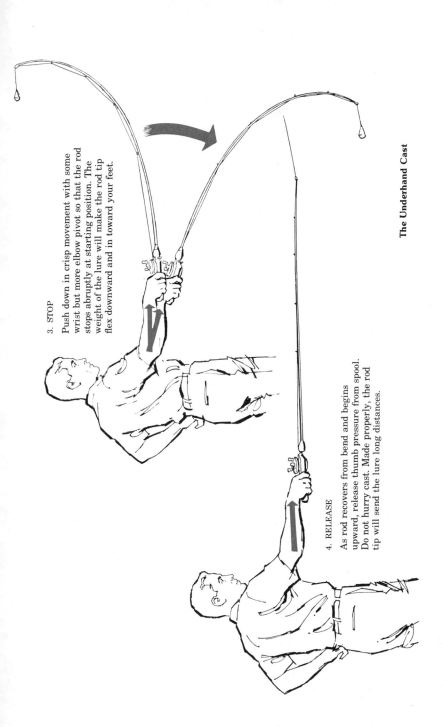

3. STOP

Push down in crisp movement with some wrist but more elbow pivot so that the rod stops abruptly at starting position. The weight of the lure will make the rod tip flex downward and in toward your feet.

4. RELEASE

As rod recovers from bend and begins upward, release thumb pressure from spool. Do not hurry cast. Made properly, the rod tip will send the lure long distances.

The Underhand Cast

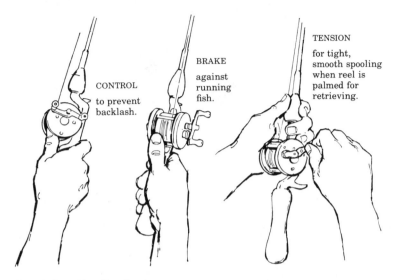

CONTROL
to prevent
backlash.

BRAKE
against
running
fish.

TENSION

for tight,
smooth spooling
when reel is
palmed for
retrieving.

Thumb Control in Bait Casting

and your weight is shifted to the *left* foot. There is a natural and perhaps effective tendency to lean toward the target when casting in this position. Your casting hand should be held forward above hip level, so that the rod is parallel with the surface of the water and both rod and forearm form a straight line.

Begin the underhand cast by making an upward lift with the rod, keeping a stiff wrist and forearm and pivoting on the elbow. When the tip reaches shoulder level, reverse the direction immediately with a crisp, downward push so that the rod returns to its starting position and stops abruptly. The weight of the lure will cause the rod tip to flex down and in toward your feet. As the rod recovers from its bend and begins upward, release thumb pressure from the spool. The lure will snap outward in a low arc. Do not attempt to push the rod forward. When the underhand cast is executed properly by the angler, the casting bend of the rod itself will provide sufficient velocity to the lure.

Fly Casting

Fly casting is more difficult to learn than other methods. It takes more patience and practice as compared to spinning, for example, but it is the most graceful and satisfying method in the anglers' art. It differs from other forms of casting in that the *weight of the line* is propelled through the air rather than the weight of the lure.

Although a serious fly-fisherman will acquire a number of different rods, reels, and lines over a period of time, the beginner only needs one outfit while learning the fundamentals. These need not be expensive.

The Fly Rod

Fly rods may be made in one to three sections or more, although two- and three-section rods are most common. When the sections are joined, the total rod length may vary from 6 to 14 feet; those of more than 10 feet long are all doublehanded salmon rods, which are popular among European anglers. The lightest fly rods weigh slightly more than 1 ounce, and the heaviest doublehanded rods, up to 20 ounces. Fiberglass and graphite are the most widely accepted rod materials; however, many fine fly rods are made of the traditional split bamboo. Bamboo rods, which are entirely handmade, are generally more expensive, but the "cane" craftsmen have a loyal audience among expert casters.

Naturally, the more you spend, the greater the quality of the rod, within limitations. You can find serviceable glass fly rods at very low cost and exquisite models of the craftsmen's art in bamboo at over $200. However, you can have just as much fun with one as the other. Except for specialized equipment, there's a point beyond which you are just paying for the window dressing, so to speak, which is a gratifying, though not essential, indulgence. Bamboo rods are more costly because both the material and the number of technicians who still custom-build are becoming scarce. Regardless of your budget, it is important to select a rod that will be easy to cast with and suitable for the type of fishing you plan to do. There is no absolute rule to follow, but most casting instructors find an 8- to 8½-foot rod to be most practical. A short fly rod of 7–7½ feet requires perfect line control to handle smoothly, while rods of 9

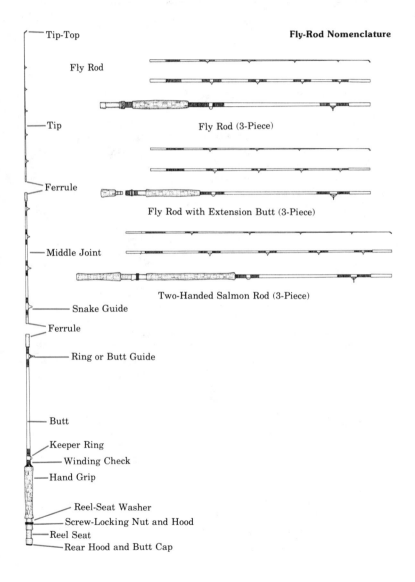

Fly-Rod Nomenclature

Tip-Top

Fly Rod

Fly Rod (3-Piece)

Tip

Ferrule

Fly Rod with Extension Butt (3-Piece)

Middle Joint

Two-Handed Salmon Rod (3-Piece)

Snake Guide

Ferrule

Ring or Butt Guide

Butt

Keeper Ring

Winding Check

Hand Grip

Reel-Seat Washer

Screw-Locking Nut and Hood

Reel Seat

Rear Hood and Butt Cap

feet or more put a premium on line weight, making it easy to cast, but only in specialized angling such as the popular 9½-foot tarpon rod designed for No. 11–No. 12 lines. The 8- to 8½-foot lengths taking a No. 7- or No. 8-weight lines are ideal for a beginner and generally suitable for most kinds of fishing. Your tackle dealer or the rod manufacturer can make a specific recommendation.

ROD ACTION   To a large extent, *action* is a built-in quality dependent on a rod's taper. But this is closely linked with the stiffness factor of the material or its ability to resist bending. Compared to an oak tree, bamboo grows to a height out of proportion to its girth, yet it survives because of its unique structure. This tropical grass must bend under the severest winds of hurricane force without breaking, then return to an upright position. So it grows in the form of a tube enclosed in vertical fibers that are stronger than steel; these are cushioned from one another by a corklike pith, and when the bamboo is bent, the fibers compress it; when the stress is relieved or the winds cease, it has the resilience to snap back. This ability to resist bending is the very same quality needed in a fishing rod. The difference is that the rod builder attempts to control the recoil power of his material, so that it bends more or less or at a faster or slower rate under varying stresses. Whether a rod is made of natural cane or any other material, the principle is the same.

The action of a rod is best described as the curvature it assumes when stressed. If all the curvature takes place in the upper quarter of the rod, it has an extra-fast action. If the curvature is confined to the upper third of the blank, it is described as having a fast action. If the curvature is in the upper half of the rod blank, the action is described as medium. A slow-action rod assumes a progressive curvature all the way from the butt of the blank to its tip. It is possible to design any type of rod—whether for fly-fishing, spinning, or bait casting—to have any of the actions outlined above. However, in actual practice, it is accepted that certain types of actions are more or less suited for certain types of rods.

Fly-rod design is influenced primarily by casting conditions. Only in certain types of saltwater angling does the strength of the fish become a more important consideration than the requirements for casting. Quality fly rods are manufactured either with slow or moderate actions. The choice really depends on the preference of the angler. His individual casting stroke may be more suited to the moderate action than the slow rod, or vice versa. On the other hand, fly rods with a fast action are very difficult to cast and very tiring to the caster. If only the tip of the rod is working, it becomes difficult to roll the fly line through the air. But if the rod flexes throughout, it is possible to apply smooth, consistent power to the line.

The amount of glass fiber at a given point in the rod blank determines the power and action of the rod. The amount of fiber is determined by varying the pattern that is cut from a roll of glass cloth at the beginning of the manufacturing process.

The pattern itself is tapered. The butt portion is of greater width than the tip. Different rod actions are achieved by increasing or decreasing the width of the taper over any portion of its length.

Increasing the number of glass fibers at any point will stiffen the action of the blank at that point. Conversely, fewer fibers result in greater flexibility. A multitude of different actions may thus be achieved by making small alterations to the pattern at any point along the length of the blank.

A hollow blank is made by rolling the tapered cloth pattern onto a tapered mandrel. The type of mandrel used is very important. If a small-diameter mandrel is used, a thick-walled blank is the result. But if the manufacturer has the necessary sophisticated machinery and know-how, he may apply the same pattern to a large-diameter mandrel and produce a thin-walled blank. Because identical patterns were used, both blanks would weigh the same, but the thin-walled blank would have far greater power because of its larger diameter.

FLY-ROD HANDLES   When selecting a fly rod you should carefully examine the construction of the handle and the quality of the materials used. Nearly all fishing-rod grips are made of cork, though other materials are used occasionally. Cork is used primarily because it is light in weight, easily shaped, and has a

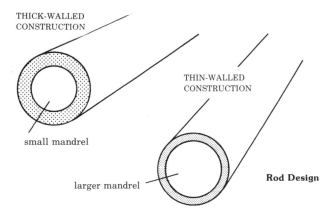

THICK-WALLED CONSTRUCTION

THIN-WALLED CONSTRUCTION

small mandrel

larger mandrel

Rod Design

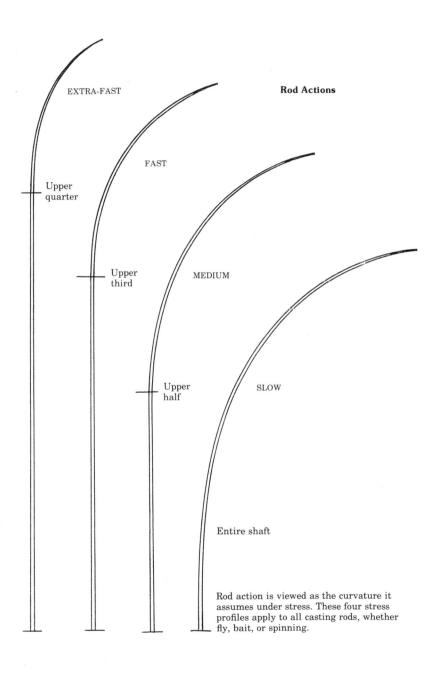

Rod Actions

EXTRA-FAST

FAST

MEDIUM

SLOW

Upper
quarter

Upper
third

Upper
half

Entire shaft

Rod action is viewed as the curvature it
assumes under stress. These four stress
profiles apply to all casting rods, whether
fly, bait, or spinning.

composition that keeps it from becoming slippery when wet or covered with fish slime.

Two types of cork are used in rod construction: specie cork and mustard cork. Specie-cork rings are cut from cork-tree bark on an axis perpendicular to the core of the tree. This gives the rings an appearance of consisting of multiple layers, but in fact these layers are merely the growth rings of the bark. Mustard cork is cut in rings on an axis parallel to the core of the tree, and the layers are not seen in the finished product. Mustard cork is less durable than specie cork.

Different types of rods require grips of varying design and placement. In fly-rod construction, the reel seat is placed at the extreme butt of the rod so that the reel may be kept out of the way while the angler handles the rod and line to make a cast. The grip is placed just forward of the reel seat and may be shaped in any one of a number of traditional patterns.

REEL SEATS   Reel seats are made from a variety of materials, including aluminum, cork, and walnut. Aluminum tubing probably is used most commonly. It is strong, light in weight, and inexpensive. Its disadvantage is that when it is exposed to seawater or other corrosive solutions it has a tendency to deteriorate rapidly, even if it has been anodized. For this reason, a reel seat of chrome-plated brass is used extensively on saltwater rods, particularly where weight is not a factor.

Reel seats of reinforced plastic also have been developed, and while these have been maligned as being "cheap," they are superior to either aluminum or chrome-plated brass on lightweight saltwater spinning and fly rods.

There has been quite a diversity of opinion over the best design for a reel seat. The straight reel seat with fixed and movable hoods has been adopted by most manufacturers. In this type of reel seat one end of the reel's foot is inserted into the fixed hood, and the movable hood then is screwed into position over the other end of the foot by means of screw threads in the reel-seat shaft. Some manufacturers place the movable hood and screw threads at the butt end of the reel seat; others place them at the tip end; and there are various arguments in support of both designs.

FERRULES   Nearly all fishing rods are built in two or more sections. This is done so that the rods may be disassembled for ease in transportation. In the long history of rod development, a number of methods have been devised to join and separate the different sections of a rod.

Fly-Rod Handles

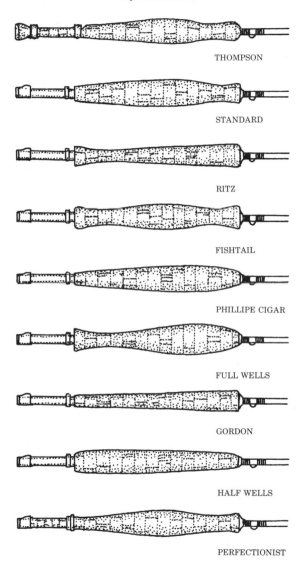

THOMPSON

STANDARD

RITZ

FISHTAIL

PHILLIPE CIGAR

FULL WELLS

GORDON

HALF WELLS

PERFECTIONIST

The fly-rod handle in nine of the traditional grip patterns. Cork reel seats in the Thompson and Perfectionist handle are designed to reduce weight on very light rods.

The most common method now used is the metal ferrule, which consists of two parts. On a two-piece rod, a female section is mounted on the butt section of the rod, and a male section is mounted on the tip. The rod may then be joined easily by fitting the tip section into the butt, and separated by pulling the two sections apart.

Chrome-plated brass is used in the manufacture of some metal ferrules. The advantage of this material is that it is easily shaped; the disadvantage is that it is heavy and has a tendency to wear easily.

Nickel silver also is commonly used. It lends itself to deep drawing and the types of forming necessary to produce a ferrule of high quality, but its high cost precludes widespread use.

Another common metal used for ferrules is aluminum. It is

Ferrules

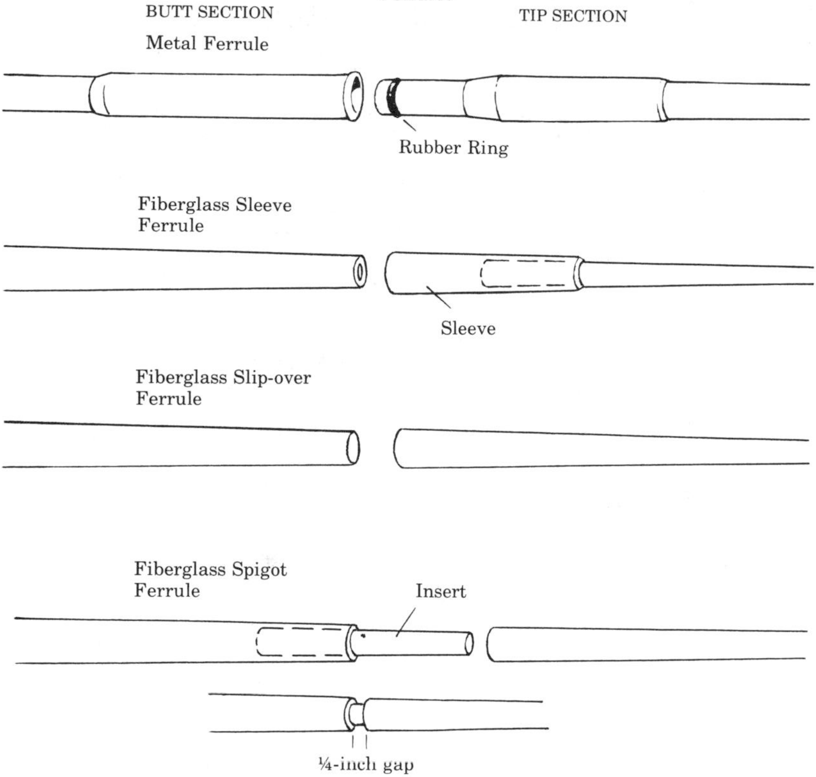

BUTT SECTION   TIP SECTION

Metal Ferrule

Rubber Ring

Fiberglass Sleeve
Ferrule

Sleeve

Fiberglass Slip-over
Ferrule

Fiberglass Spigot
Ferrule   Insert

¼-inch gap

light, strong enough to do the job, and well suited to drawing and shaping by machine.

For the most part, metal ferrules rely on the friction generated between the inside of the female ferrule section and the exterior of the male section to hold the rod together. The fitting of these ferrules is critical, and it is of utmost importance to keep to the proper clearance in the manufacturing process. A small amount of wear may cause this type of ferrule to loosen; the angler soon will experience problems if this occurs.

A development of major importance in recent years was the perfection of a fiberglass ferrule. Nearly all the manufacturers of fiberglass rods and graphite rods now use some form of this prototype.

The slip-over ferrule (in which the tip section of the rod slides down over the butt section) was pioneered by the Fenwick Rod Company with its Feralite Ferrule in 1962. This ferrule is protected by patent, but there is a variety of alternatives available. Slipping the tip section into the hollow butt has proven practical and is utilized by some manufacturers. Others use a sleeve type of ferrule. Probably the most common fiberglass ferrule is the spigot type, and while this adds stiffness at the ferruling point, it still provides a measure of flexibility and has proven satisfactory in most instances.

Fiberglass ferrules and graphite ferrules rely upon a taper fit. Because of this, wear is not a problem as it is with metal ferrules. Nonmetal ferrules also do not have a tendency to stick, as friction-type ferrules do, because once the taper fit of the fiberglass ferrule is broken, the lock is released over its entire length, and the two sections may be separated easily.

The Fly Line

In all forms of casting, except with the fly, it is the weight of the lure that is cast. The most efficient casting weight is a compact lead sinker. Artificial flies in themselves have no weight, but the line does, and by propelling it back and forth, we achieve enough velocity to shoot it through the air. However, the usable weight of fly lines is distributed over 30–40 feet of surface area; thus, air friction rapidly absorbs the energy that goes into fly casting. To utilize that energy to its maximum, the weight of a fly line must be arranged in a shape or profile that will maintain velocity for the longest possible time. There are three common profiles among fly lines: a weight-forward (WF), a double-taper (DT), and a level (L) distribution (see page 61). For the beginning flycaster, a double taper is the easiest to handle. The weights of various lines differ, and you must buy one that is proportionate to the stiffness of your rod, or more precisely, to its resistance to bend. Until 1961, line sizes were designated by alphabetical symbols, such as HDH or GAF. This never was a very good system because it only related to line diameters and not their weights. Another method that is somewhat better was devised (see Fly-Line Standards, p. 66). This indicates the profile of the line alphabetically, the weight with a numerical symbol, and the specific gravity by another alphabetical symbol. Thus a DT-5-F is interpreted as a double-taper line of approximately 140 grains in the first 30 feet, floating. Or a WF-7-S means a weight-forward line of 185 grains, sinking.

HOW TO SELECT A FLY LINE   A properly designed fly line will not sag in the air but will extend and turn over smoothly, keeping its weight portion off the water until the cast is completed. The distribution of that weight is the basic consideration in selecting a fly line.

The most effective casting weights are lead sinkers; therefore, any elongation of the projectile, such as a fly line, becomes less and less effective as its length is increased. A 1-ounce sinker is a compact mass, but an equivalent weight of fly line must be arranged over 30–40 feet of surface area; thus air friction rapidly absorbs the energy that goes into fly casting. To utilize that energy properly, the weight of a fly line must be distributed in a shape that will maintain velocity for the longest possible time. Once your cast is released, all parts of the line in the air, from your leader to your rod tip, have an identical velocity, but this speed rapidly decreases as the line rolls over and becomes extended.

As we have already noted there are three profiles or shapes in fly lines: a level, a double-taper, and a weight-forward distribution. At the extremes, we have the level profile, which is a constant diameter throughout, and the weight-forward or torpedo-taper profile, which is of varying diameter and with its weight portion occurring at one end of the line. Both theoretically and practically, the weight-forward profile provides longer and easier casts. In a level line, air friction absorbs the casting energy rapidly, because a diameter of *equal* weight is coming out of the rod guides and therefore adding more burden on the declining momentum of the already extended cast. On the other hand, a weight-forward taper, with its effective weight in the air, is more nearly comparable to the sinker because it can pull a great length of line through the guides before losing momentum from the inertia and weight of the fine-diameter shooting line. Obviously, the slack you hold in your

LEVEL

DOUBLE TAPER

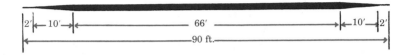

WEIGHT FORWARD

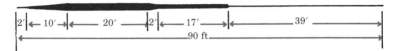

Fly-Line Measurements

hand has no velocity to contribute to the cast when you make your shoot. It merely waits to be pulled forward. This is made easier by the lightweight shooting line of a weight forward, but the success of such a line depends on the front taper. It is responsible for completing the turnover of line and leader at the exact instant the line stops shooting, regardless of the speed of the cast. In theory, it is impossible to slap the water with a weight-forward line if the front taper is correctly made.

Although the belly section provides casting weight, the front taper must remain in the unrolling line loop until the last instant and then deliver the final kick to your leader and fly. If the front taper is too long, you'll have great difficulty in unrolling the loop. Your leader will simply fall back next to the line at the finish of a cast. The fly will fall to the right or left or back over the line. With a long front taper you can never turn the leader and fly over against a wind and seldom with a wind, because your back cast will not straighten. Thus, the distance you intend to cast determines the size and length of the belly in a weight-forward line, while the length of the front taper is responsible for pulling and stabilizing that weight until the shoot is completed. The back taper is unimportant except to provide a reduction in line diameter. So, actually, you can use several sizes of weight forwards on one rod, depending on how far you have to cast. Remember, most trout are caught within a 35–40 foot radius, and the heavier your line, the less chance you have of doing a proper job at short distances. It is fallacious to believe that the more weight you concentrate in a line the better you will cast. There's a law of diminishing returns in this case, because as the belly section is made longer or heavier, the forward taper must be made longer, and there's a limit to how much speed you can apply to turn the taper over. But the longer you can delay complete unrolling of the forward loop, the longer the cast will be, provided the belly of the line maintains its velocity. Although the front taper must be just long enough to hold the weight portion up off the water until the cast is completed, you can, by aiming the rod high on a long cast, delay the turnover and give a more gradual and prolonged flight to the line. The lower you aim your cast, the more rapidly gravity will overtake the belly section, thereby causing you to lose the extra-long footage that is provided by momentum.

A properly designed weight-forward line promotes the caster from water slapping to perfection. A smooth elbow pivot will suffice for the pickup, then another for the false cast, and away the line goes across the river, turning over in the air, not unrolling on the water. Inasmuch as the function of lines built with all their weight forward is to make that weight immediately available to the cast, you can readily understand that short, stiff rods will throw the same size line as some of the longer and heavier rods. But if the rod is overburdened, the line will touch the water in front and rear when you're making your false cast. The same effect is created with a double-taper or even a level line, in that there is a point beyond which the rod can no longer lift and speed up the weight of the line already extended. You can recognize the difference when a proper casting weight of level or double taper is extended; the weight of the line that this casting length will have to pull is out of proportion to the created momentum. Instead of pulling a finer, lighter-shooting line, such as the weight-forward taper does, the double taper and level are forced to pull a heavy section of line, which quickly retards the speed of the pulling load. Do not underestimate the role of the double taper, however; any double taper is better than a poorly balanced line, and it is superior for roll casting, which is important to small-stream anglers.

To sum up, if the length of the front taper is too long, the fly goes out of control, falling anywhere, right or left or even on top of the leader and line. If the length of the front taper is too short, the fly and leader will turn under and slap the water.

SPECIFIC GRAVITY   In both wet- and dry-fly fishing, as a general rule, the line should float. The leader, of course, should sink, and if you want the fly to go down deep, the leader should be long enough to permit you to do so. The reason for the floating line is that it is very difficult to pick up a line that is beneath the surface. The strain on a light fly rod would be too great. Moreover, the floating fly line gives the fisherman more direct contact with the fish when it strikes. A sunken line that is bellied out beneath the water requires some skill to handle correctly. But these are only generalizations that we should examine more closely.

A sinking fly line offers a great advantage to the average fisherman. Simply stated, it brings the fly down to fish level. An ordinary floating line is perfectly all right for wet and nymph patterns on small streams, where you work in knee-deep water, and certainly on lakes, when the fish are foraging close to the surface. Under both conditions, the fly seldom has to sink more than a foot or two to reach pay dirt. In fact, a floating line terminated with a 12–15 foot leader is superior to the sinking type in fast, shallow rivers, particularly when using weighted nymphs. You can watch the line point like a bobber, and the slightest nip is signaled by a pull that would otherwise be hard to see. But when fish are feeding 10–20 feet below the surface, a floating line is useless.

The original sinking fly line was a metal-cored silk made in England around 1938. The body of the line was simply braided over fine bronze wire, and as long as the silk didn't separate from its core, the line sank to reasonable depths. There was, however, the uncomfortable feeling of casting a piece of wire, and the manufacturers didn't find an eager audience for their product.

In 1958 the first real step toward a strictly sinking fly line was made with the introduction of Dacron, which differs chiefly from nylon in its specific gravity. A Dacron line sinks readily. Today, sinking lines are made in four different densities: Type 1, or slow sinking; Type 2, or fast sinking; Type 3, or extra-fast sinking; and Type 4, or high-speed Hi-D. In addition, lead-core shooting heads are also available; these sink with maximum speed but must be used on a heavy and powerful rod.

SHOOTING TAPER LINES   Shooting taper lines or shooting heads consist of 28–32 feet of regular fly line connected to a thin, usually about 20-pound-test monofilament running line. Because the monofilament offers little resistance to the pull of a shooting head, the longest casts are possible. The head portion may be made from a level, double-taper, weight-forward, or a lead-core line; this is usually joined to the monofilament by means of a loop. Another advantage of the shooting-taper system is that heads of different sizes and densities may be quickly changed by looping on the appropriate one without switching reel spools.

Shooting tapers require some casting skill. The monofilament, which must be held in loose coils, does tend to tangle, especially in a wind. Some anglers hold the slack between their lips, and others coil it in a stripping basket belted at their waists.

Although many experienced casters use the shooting-taper system for all kinds of fishing, its real value is in special situations, such as casting for chinook salmon, winter steelhead, and shad, when distance and a deep-drifting fly are prerequisite to success. The lead-core head also has applications to deep fishing in salt-water.

There are two things worth mentioning if you use a shooting head rather than a weight-forward line. First, on the pickup, you must watch the "overhang," the distance between the terminal loop of the head and the rod tip. If there is too much monofilament extended, it won't support the weight of the line when you lift it and throw it. If you bring the loop too close to the tip, you won't get a smooth haul, because it will hit the top guide. Secondly, there is a slight difference in trajectory when using a shooting head. The head—generally a short 28- to 32-foot-long single, tapered section of line weighing 275–340 grains attached to 100 feet of .020–.025 monofilament—must be aimed *higher* or released earlier than the regular weight-forward fly line, because there is less friction in the guides to retard its flight, and it will turn over too fast if aimed low. Shooting heads are not essential except in specialized angling, as anyone can learn to cast the full length of a modern fly line without one. The head has a definite role in steelhead fishing for bottom bouncing with a wet fly. But the average man can do almost anything, even with a double-taper fly line in all other kinds of fishing, provided he has learned line control.

BACKING FOR THE FLY LINE   The backing line has a dual purpose, and, on all except the smallest fly reels, which lack the capacity, it should be added in order to fill the reel (to within ⅛–¼ inch of the spool rim). By building up the arbor with this additional line, the fly line will be spooled in larger coils. The larger the coil, the less tendency there is for a line to kink, particularly after it has been stored away during the off-season. To the angler who is completely familiar with his reel, it's possible to guess how much backing is required to bring the fly line to the right level. However, to always get the desired result, it's advisable to reel the fly line on the spool first, add the correct amount of backing, and then reverse the line. This requires either an identical reel to which the backing can be immediately secured or a spacious lawn, where the entire length including the fly line can be pulled gently from the reel and then reversed. Reversing does take a bit more time, but it's worth the effort; just fractions of an inch make a difference in maintaining a supply fly line.

Braided nylon or Dacron line in 15- to 18-pound test makes a good all-purpose backing. From the standpoint of catching fish, a 25-yard length is ample insurance for the inland-trout and -bass angler on the average stream and lake. For steelhead and salmon in large rivers, 100 yards is usually adequate. Although bonefish seldom require more than 100 yards, if the same reel is to be used for permit, barracuda, and tarpon, 200 yards is more realistic. There are rare situations in which a fish will run a mile or even two miles, so, obviously, the angler must decide on a practical maximum. At the extremes (a 100-pound tarpon on the flats or large salmon in swift rivers), the angler can resort to his boat or to the bank in following a running fish. Thus the amount of backing should only serve for *average* conditions. Oversize fly reels have been made to accommodate 350–400 yards of backing; however, these are of dubious value: such reels are heavy, and line breaks from water resistance and snags are inevitable. But regardless of the quarry, some backing should always be added to a fly reel.

FLY-LINE MAINTENANCE   Fly-line maintenance consists of keeping it clean and properly stored. Both algae and salt can make a line "gummy" and cause a floating line to sink. Although it is not usually necessary to clean a fly line after each trip, it should be wiped with a damp sponge or cloth whenever it feels slightly dirty. Naturally, if you are fishing in weedy ponds or in saltwater, the line will need more frequent cleaning. Do not expose a fly line to long hours in a hot sun by leaving the reel uncovered in an open boat. And beware of solvents that damage plastic or silk, such as insect repellents, suntan lotions, or the inevitable splash of gasoline from the fuel can in an outboard. Standing on loose coils of slack in the boat or on the bank will chip and crack the plastic finish. All silk fly lines must be thoroughly dried after each trip and rubbed down with a dressing designed for silk, such as Mucilin.

FLY-LINE STANDARDS   The American Fishing Tackle Manufacturers Association established in 1961 the fly-line standards now in use. The numerical system, which replaces the letter system, became necessary because of the various materials that have, to a large extent, replaced silk. When almost all fly lines were made of silk, they were identified by one or more letters of the alphabet, running from A to I. These letters represented line diameters, ranging from .060 inch (A) to .20 inch (I) and were indicative of line weights. This system served its purpose; for example, the fly-rod fisherman could match his rod with almost any manufacturer's version of an HCH floating line.

When fly lines made of nylon and Dacron were introduced, the manufacturers continued to use the silk-diameter system of letters. However, it soon became apparent that whereas one manufacturer's HCH floating line would work with a particular rod, another similarly labeled line would be too light or too heavy with that rod.

The reason is basically simple. Nylon is lighter than silk; Dacron is heavier than silk. Thus, each of these lines made to the same diameter specifications performs differently on the same rod.

So line diameter became meaningless as a standard of identification, not only because of the different specific gravities of the basic materials, but also as a result of different types of braids and finishes developed by various manufacturers.

	AFTMA Fly-Line Standards	
No.	Wt.*	Range**
1	60	54– 66
2	80	74– 86
3	100	94–106
4	120	114–126
5	140	134–146
6	160	152–168
7	185	177–193
8	210	202–218
9	240	230–250
10	280	270–290
11	330	318–342
12	380	368–392

* In grains (437.5 gr.=1 oz.), based on first 30 feet of line
** Manufacturing tolerances

AFTMA Fly-Line Symbols

L = Level
DT = Double taper
WF = Weight forward
ST = Single taper

AFTMA Fly-Line Types

F = Floating
S = Sinking
I = Intermediate
    (Floating or Sinking)

The unit of weight selected for the new standards is the *grain,* the smallest unit in the system of weights used in the United States and Great Britain. (One pound avoirdupois equals 7000 grains.) The numbers *1* through *12* in the preceding table are assigned to the standard grain weights, ranging from the lightest to the heaviest, regardless of the line's diameter, material, braid, or finish.

The segment of a fly line that is weighed to determine its number is the first thirty feet of the "working" portion of the line, exclusive of any level tip, as measured from the very beginning of the taper. The weights of fly lines range from 60 grains (No. 1) to 380 grains (No. 12), plus or minus acceptable manufacturing tolerances.

The Fly Reel

Before the innovation of fly reels, the playing of a fish consisted chiefly of keeping the fish directly under the rod. In Izaak Walton's day, and for many years afterward, fly rods were extremely long and supple for this reason. When a trout was hooked, the angler would hold the point of his rod over the fish to prevent it from running too far from the resilient tip. The elasticity of a modern fly rod still means a great deal in handling large fish on fine leaders, but if the pull exceeds its capacity to bend, we simply allow the fish to run more line from the reel. In most kinds of fly-fishing, however, the reel isn't as important as the rod and line.

There are three types of fly reels: single action, multiplying action, and automatic. The single action and, to a lesser extent, the automatic are most popular. Fly reels generally weigh from 2 to 12 ounces. The size does not reflect quality; small reels are designed for light or small-diameter lines and can be very expensive, while some larger reels designed for heavy lines may be cheap by comparison. Reel weight is a fatigue factor in continuous casting, and the lightest freshwater models are made of magnesium alloy or graphite. In saltwater fishing, which is principally "sight" casting and not continuous, the top grade reels are made of solid-bar, stock aluminum.

SINGLE-ACTION FLY REELS Gear ratio combined with spool diameter determines the speed of retrieve. A single-action reel has the minimum ratio of 1:1, which means only one turn of line is recovered with each turn of the crank. To minimize weight and cost most fly reels are single action. To compensate they have narrow, large-diameter spools that permit a more rapid recovery, in comparison to other smaller-spool reels.

Fly-Reel Nomenclature

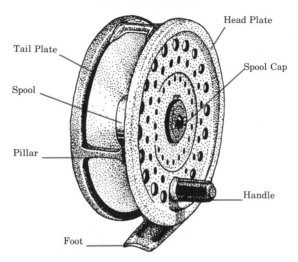

Head Plate

Tail Plate

Spool Cap

Spool

Pillar

Handle

Foot

SINGLE-ACTION FLY REEL

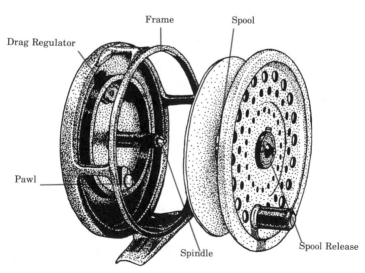

Frame

Spool

Drag Regulator

Pawl

Spindle

Spool Release

MULTIPLYING FLY REEL

You can buy a lightweight single-action fly reel at very little cost. A standard freshwater model weighs from 3½ to 5½ ounces and has a 3- to 3½-inch spool diameter. It should have a simple drag, which may be in the form of a pressure-adjustment screw or lever. Without minimal tension against the spool, it can overrun when stripping line from the reel to cast or from the sudden pull of a strong fish. Some reels have a rim on the head plate that extends over the frame; this provides extra braking by hand or finger pressure against the rotating spool, which compensates for a rudimentary mechanical drag. However, it is not recommended for any of the strong running species such as bonefish, tarpon, or steelhead.

The single-action reel should have interchangeable spools. This makes it possible to switch from a floating line to a sinking line or to change sizes or tapers as the need arises. A release lever or button on the spool cap allows instant removal.

Quality saltwater fly reels are expensive. Depending on the width of the reel, spool diameters vary from 3¼ to 4 inches, and standard reels weigh from 11 to 14 ounces. Aside from being corrosion resistant, the most important features are a strong drag system and an anti-reverse spool lock, which permits the crank handle to remain stationary while the line is paying out. Without an anti-reverse, the handle becomes a knuckle buster when whirling to the run of a heavy fish. The drag must be smooth and easily adjusted from zero to full stop.

MULTIPLYING FLY REELS   Comparatively few satisfactory multiplying fly reels have been designed. Precision gearing without a great weight increase is the problem. For most kinds of fishing a multiple ratio is not necessary but rather a convenience where reel weight is unimportant. There are quality reels built with a 2:1 gear ratio.

AUTOMATIC FLY REELS   The automatic fly reel recovers line mechanically by means of a spring-loaded brake lever or trigger. There are two basic types: one mounts vertically on the rod and the other horizontally. There is no technical advantage of one style over the other—it's simply a matter of personal preference. The ability to take up line automatically is of some importance to anglers fishing from a boat, for example, bug fishing for bass, where handling long lengths of slack can be awkward and time consuming. However, automatics are heavy in comparison to single-action reels and have a limited line capacity on a size-for-size basis. Automatics are generally limited to line sizes no bigger

Automatic Fly-Reel Nomenclature

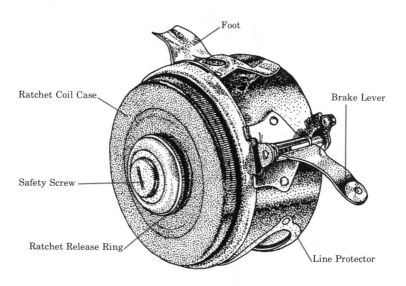

than No. 6 and weigh 8–9 ounces. These reels are of specialized interest and not recommended for the beginner.

HANDLE POSITION   When fly-fishing, the reel is mounted below the rod grip where it won't interfere with the cast. Its only manual function is to play the fish. So you should decide whether it will be more comfortable to seat the reel with the handle to the left or to the right. Most anglers prefer to have the handle on the left, the idea being that one doesn't have to change hands when a fish is hooked.

Although the average trout or bass won't pull out much line, you should always work them with the reel. Beginners especially benefit by cranking the reel instead of stripping line by hand, because the technique of getting yardage back on the spool evenly requires some practice. This will be very important later on when you deal with large fish that must be played directly from the reel.

The Fly Leader

A long, light leader is necessary, not only because it forms a nearly invisible connection between the line and the fly, but, equally important, because it allows the fly to drift and turn like a natural insect. The leader may look fragile, but the fine end will ordinarily test about three pounds, which is strong enough to hold most trout you will catch. Even if you should hook a fish weighing more than three pounds, the odds on landing him are still in your favor provided you do not attempt to "horse" the trout out of the stream. By all means get *tapered* leaders, as the level kind have very poor casting qualities. There are two facts that you should know about leaders that influence fishing with them: (1) You must select the correct length—or approximate length—to suit the water conditions. A 7½-foot leader is standard for small streams where you will be making short casts of 20–30 feet; a 9-foot leader is better for average-size streams that require 30- to 40-foot casts; and a 12½-foot leader is used during the summer months when the average stream is low and diamond clear. (2) You should also specify the correct tippet size. (The *tippet* is the fine end of the leader where the fly is tied.) A leader must have enough rigidity to transmit the energy imparted by the line during the cast. If the fly is too large or too heavy for the tippet, you cannot present the fly properly, and the leader will quickly weaken. As a general guide, the following tippet sizes are recommended for various hook sizes:

Tippet	Fly
0X	No. 2– No. 1/0
1X	No. 4– No. 8
2X	No. 6– No. 10
3X	No. 10–No. 14
4X	No. 12–No. 16
5X	No. 14–No. 18
6X	No. 16–No. 22

So there's really no mystery in leader specifications. When you ask for a 9-foot, 3X, tapered leader, you will get one suitable for the average stream, where 30- to 40-foot casts are the rule, and with a tippet fine enough to handle the average fly sizes of No. 10 to No. 14. If the water is high and roily, you might use a shorter, 7½-foot leader and somewhat larger flies that require a 2X tippet. A 12-foot, 6X leader would be ideal for extremely clear water when only the tiniest flies are to be used. Don't let long leaders scare you away. When properly made, they are just as easy to cast as short ones if you are working at the distances (40 feet or more) demanded on hot, droughty days when the river flows thin. Occasionally, you will hear of someone using a 15-foot, or even 18-foot leader, but anything over 12 feet is awkward, and it is doubtful if it serves a practical purpose. By the same token, a very short leader of 3–6 feet is much more likely to frighten fish and cause casting problems.

The Fly

Broadly speaking, there are two kinds of flies that you will need at the outset: the wet fly and the dry fly. The wet fly is fished below the surface of the water, and the dry fly is designed to float on top. The purpose of both is to imitate or suggest by shape, color, or action the natural insects upon which fish feed. No phase of angling has had so much esoteric scholarship lavished on it as the tying and selection of trout flies. Yet for all the minute perfection in thousands of patterns, the basic standards remain with us year after year. On any ordinary day, during any reasonable weather, there will be a morning rise and an evening rise of trout to the naturals. Occasionally, you may also see a midday rise. These are the periods when dry flies are most effective. Between hatches, or in floodwater or roughwater, the wet fly might be more acceptable. The best way to determine the fish's preference is, of course, to try both. Select a pattern of the size and general coloration of any insects that you see on the river—or, if none is in evidence, use a fly pattern that appeals to you. There are many standard patterns that catch trout most of the time. The following dry and wet flies are used successfully throughout the United States and in many foreign countries:

Dry Flies	*Hook*
Light Cahill	No. 10–No. 16
Hendrickson	No. 10–No. 16
Adams	No. 10–No. 16
Royal Coachman	No. 10–No. 14
Quill Gordon	No. 12–No. 16
Badger Bivisible	No. 10–No. 14
Muddler	No. 6–No. 10
Gray Wulff	No. 8–No. 12
March Brown	No. 10–No. 14
Blue Dun Spider	No. 12–No. 16
Irresistible	No. 8–No. 12
Multicolor Variant	No. 12–No. 16

Wet Flies	Hook
McGinty	No. 10–No. 12
Black Gnat	No. 10–No. 16
Leadwing Coachman	No. 10–No. 16
Wickham's Fancy	No. 10–No. 12
Silver Doctor	No. 10–No. 12
Grizzly King	No. 10–No. 12
Black Woolly Worm	No. 8–No. 10
Blue Dun	No. 10–No. 14
Quill Gordon	No. 10–No. 16
Dark Cahill	No. 10–No. 16
Gray Hackle Peacock	No. 10–No. 14

How to Fly Cast

As in any other sport, you must practice, and the more hours you work, the easier fly casting becomes. There are only two different casts to learn: the overhead cast and the roll cast. All other casts are movements. To learn fly casting quickly, it is recommended that you use an 8½-foot rod of about 5 ounces. Shorter rods require more experience, and longer rods are too heavy for the average hand in practice. The rod should be matched with a No. 7 or No. 8 line. When practicing, use a 7½-foot leader tapered to 1X or 2X. Clip the barb from the fly to prevent accidents. Except for the roll cast, all fundamental rod work can be learned on dry land. Whether you are right- or left-handed, these instructions should be clear, as the terms *rod hand* and *line hand* are used where necessary.

THE ROD HAND   When you take the rod in your hand you must be relaxed. For average fishing casts up to 40 feet the rod is going to perform most of the work. You will simply provide the motion necessary to move the rod back and forth. Hold the cork handle lightly, with your thumb on top of the grip and in direct line with the rod. Most of the squeeze in your grip should be in the lower three fingers as you raise the rod in a backward motion. At vertical, your thumb comes into play to stop the rod. Your forefinger should be so relaxed that it can be moved away from the grip. As you begin the forward cast, thumb pressure should be applied, and the squeeze will be in all fingers momentarily. When you complete the forward cast the rod should stop, again squeezed by the lower three fingers and resting across your forefinger. Your thumb simply follows through after the push.

The Rod Hand

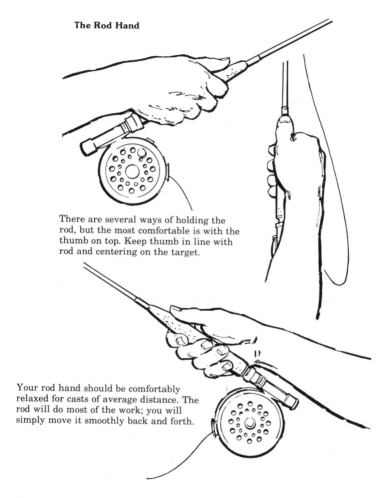

There are several ways of holding the rod, but the most comfortable is with the thumb on top. Keep thumb in line with rod and centering on the target.

Your rod hand should be comfortably relaxed for casts of average distance. The rod will do most of the work; you will simply move it smoothly back and forth.

THE OVERHEAD CAST Every fly cast consists of several movements blended together in what appears to be one motion. The basic overhead cast is a combination of backward and forward strokes, which can be made at different angles and varying speeds under actual fishing conditions. Of the two parts—back cast and forward cast—the former is most important to the beginner. A proper back cast will automatically create a smooth forward cast. When you begin practice, keep in mind that you cannot make a poor back cast if you block your wrist movement almost completely and pivot on your elbow. A straight, upward forearm movement will throw the line high in the air. If your line hits the ground behind you, you are not lifting with enough emphasis, or you are bending your wrist.

The Back Cast If you have never held a fly rod before, the first few flexes will feel awkward until you have about 12–15 feet of line out. You are literally casting the weight of the line, and the only usable part is that length extended beyond your rod tip. Strip off about twenty feet of line from the reel, and take a comfortable stance. If you are a right-hand caster, your body weight should favor the right foot, and vice versa. You are not going to use your line hand at first; so place the line under your rod-hand forefinger and keep it there; this will prevent throwing slack into your casts. Hold the rod in front of you so that the tip is at eye level, with your forearm in a straight line with the rod. Your hand should be relaxed, but your wrist, somewhat stiff; you should have the feeling that your forearm is an extension of the rod—right down to your elbow. Your elbow should be 1–2 inches from your body. Begin the cast by raising the rod smartly, lifting your hand toward your ear and slightly raising your elbow. The elbow is actually the pivot point. As your rod hand nears eye level, stiffen your wrist even more, and then block all arm movement. The rod should be in a vertical position, with the line unrolling in the rear. There is a definite *pause* at this point, which allows the line to extend and straighten. It is absolutely essential to complete the back cast. Only when the line is actually tugging at the rod and developing its bend can you begin the forward cast.

The Forward Cast With a high, smooth back cast, the forward cast is merely a follow-through phase to the overhead cast. With the rod bending on your back cast, move your forearm down through the same path, applying speed progressively. As the rod begins to turn over, give the grip more thumb squeeze and emphasize that forward stroke. You should have the feeling that you are throwing the rod tip into the cast. Finish your cast at a point 2–3 feet above the target. Do not cast directly on the water, but above it. The line should extend completely in the air and fall to the surface. Pick up the line again and repeat the back cast, allowing each forward cast to be completed. When you have mastered these two phases of the overhead cast, you are ready to blend them in continuous back-and-forth movements—known as *false casting*. You will use the false cast in fishing to dry the fly and to extend the line.

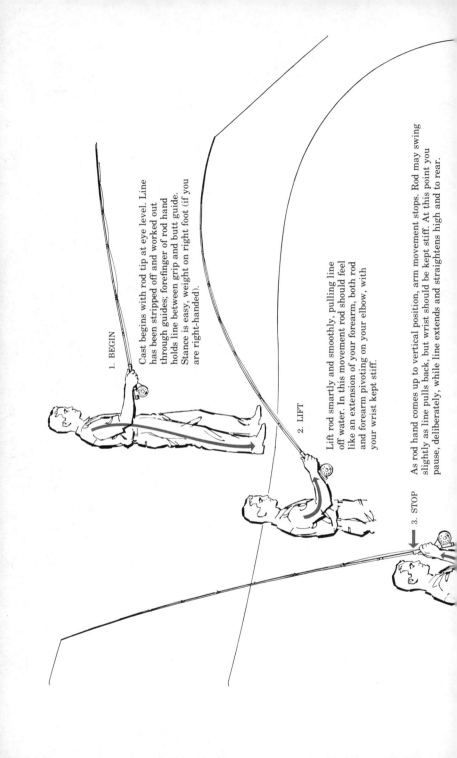

1. BEGIN

Cast begins with rod tip at eye level. Line has been stripped off and worked out through guides; forefinger of rod hand holds line between grip and butt guide. Stance is easy, weight on right foot (if you are right-handed).

2. LIFT

Lift rod smartly and smoothly, pulling line off water. In this movement rod should feel like an extension of your forearm, both rod and forearm pivoting on your elbow, with your wrist kept stiff.

3. STOP

As rod hand comes up to vertical position, arm movement stops. Rod may swing slightly as line pulls back, but wrist should be kept stiff. At this point you pause, deliberately, while line extends and straightens high and to rear.

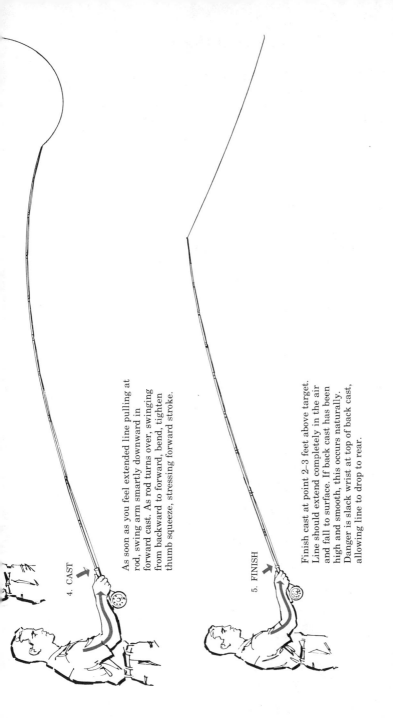

4. CAST

As soon as you feel extended line pulling at rod, swing arm smartly downward in forward cast. As rod turns over, swinging from backward to forward, bend, tighten thumb squeeze, stressing forward stroke.

5. FINISH

Finish cast at point 2–3 feet above target. Line should extend completely in the air and fall to surface. If back cast has been high and smooth, this occurs naturally. Danger is slack wrist at top of back cast, allowing line to drop to rear.

The Overhead Cast

THE LINE HAND   The work of the line hand becomes increasingly important as you cast longer distances. Its fundamental role, however, is to keep slack out of the line, maintaining constant tension on the line while casting. When fishing, the forefinger of your rod hand acts almost as an additional guide. By running the line over your forefinger, the slack between butt guide and rod grip is eliminated. This facilitates the retrieve and striking the fish. Your line hand takes up incoming line and prepares it for shooting the next cast. The easiest system for handling slack is to form loops in your line hand. Simply take the first length of line retrieved (which is the amount you can pull down in a distance from the grip to a straight-arm position), and form a half loop across your hand. Again, reach up to your rod-hand forefinger, and pull the next length of line down. Now drop both, and grasp the line again to form one big loop. Continue your retrieve, looping alternate lengths of line. A large loop is easy to handle in casting, and you can hold more line in your hand without tangling. The last pull should leave your line hand free, so that you are ready to cast again. All loops should rest over your hand with each separated from the other, the first loop formed closest to your thumb and the last loop nearest your fingertips.

For the average cast, your line hand maintains constant tension at a position near hip level. After one or two false casts, you should have enough line speed to shoot the slack as your rod is approaching a 45-degree angle. Simply open your hand, and the speed of the line traveling through the air is sufficient to pull the slack out.

CASTING IN HEAD WINDS   The ability to cast against strong winds is a decided advantage, especially in the open country of western rivers. The chief difference between an ordinary cast and the wind cast is that you exaggerate the forward phase when bucking a head wind. Make the back cast with your elbow well separated from your body, keeping your forearm stiff. The trick of casting into the wind is to keep your back cast high and your forward cast low. A high back cast is always essential to effortless form, but to buck the wind you have to exaggerate the movement by bringing your hand from near horizontal, as the line is lifted from the water, to a point above eye level as though you were trying to throw the line straight over your head. Actually, the wind will buffet the line down to a lower level. It also helps to give the line a strong pull on the lift to add speed in straightening, because the longer the line is in the air, the more the wind will push it down. The forward cast must be progressive in power. Do not attempt to

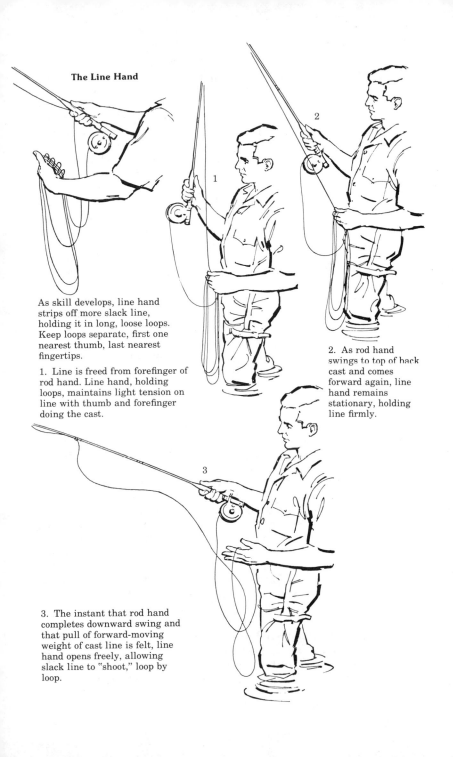

The Line Hand

As skill develops, line hand strips off more slack line, holding it in long, loose loops. Keep loops separate, first one nearest thumb, last nearest fingertips.

1. Line is freed from forefinger of rod hand. Line hand, holding loops, maintains light tension on line with thumb and forefinger doing the cast.

2. As rod hand swings to top of back cast and comes forward again, line hand remains stationary, holding line firmly.

3. The instant that rod hand completes downward swing and that pull of forward-moving weight of cast line is felt, line hand opens freely, allowing slack line to "shoot," loop by loop.

slam your line against the wind. With your hand held high at the finish of the back cast (which is at about the one-o'clock position), begin coming forward with your shoulder, elbow, and forearm just an instant before adding the real power. Keep your forearm and wrist stiff as you pivot at the elbow, and when your rod hand starts down, pull line with the left hand. Put all emphasis in a forceful wrist-and-thumb delivery. The rod should almost reach a horizontal position before you release line. In other words, you must delay shooting line until the outgoing taper is pulling at maximum. None of the movements is difficult if you remember the cardinal points: exaggerate the height of the back cast; then shoot low over the water, using a sharp line-hand pull. Once you have the knack, you'll be able to throw a 2/0 bass bug into the teeth of a gale.

CASTING IN TAIL WINDS   The fundamental rule of casting with a strong tail wind is naturally just the opposite of casting against it. Your back cast must be lower than usual and the forward cast, higher. Now if you work strictly in a vertical plane, as you do for an ordinary overhead cast, the only way you can get the line low in the rear is to let it drop or to swing the rod horizontally to the rear. Neither method is practical, because you lose line speed, and at that precise instant, the wind will bang your taper on the water. Or, on the forward stroke, you'll get the whole length of the line wrapped around your neck. Remember, also, that a tail wind is going to retard your back cast; so you must maintain maximum velocity. The easiest way is to make a low, fast back cast by moving the rod to the rear at an angle below 45 degrees and to bring it forward in a vertical plane. If the cast is executed correctly, you can reach long distances without losing line control. This method has the virtues of utilizing two well-separated casting planes and of throwing a wide loop. Begin by giving the line a brisk left-hand pull, simultaneously making a side cast; then pivot with elbow and shoulder to sweep the rod up into a vertical plane, applying power progressively. The path of your hand should be circular in traveling back and forward. When the line is tugging hard against the rod, finish your forward cast with another left-hand pull as your casting hand comes down with a forceful stroke. The tip should stop at the horizontal position. The line will literally rocket away from the rod.

CASTING IN CROSS WINDS   Under normal wind conditions, if you are a right-hand caster and the wind comes from your left there's no problem; just keep the rod tip leaning slightly to the right and cast. But if the wind comes from the right side, your line is going to drift toward your body. To some degree this can be neutralized with a forceful side cast on the right side. Experts who can cast with either hand have no trouble even in violent cross winds. An ambidextrous angler will follow the fundamental cross-wind rule of always keeping the rod on his lee side. Minus this versatility, the average caster will find use for the backhand cast in a strong cross wind.

The backhand cast is made by a right-hander with his arm held across the front of his body and the rod pointing to the left. A southpaw makes the cast in the opposite plane, with his arm held across the front of his body and the rod pointing to the right. The cast is very simple to execute. With palm facing down and thumb on top of the grip, your rod should be at a 45-degree angle quartering away from and a few inches in front of your body. Pick up the line for a back cast using the full forearm, pivoting at the elbow, and moving your shoulders slightly in the direction of the cast. The rod should stop at a 45-degree angle, quartering away from and to the rear of your body. Start the forward cast by coming closer to the vertical plane on the left side of your body, but do not cast just with your wrist. Lower your forearm slightly, and use the elbow pivot with wrist emphasis. In both the back and forward stroke, a slight left-hand pull will add speed to the line and help the turnover. Practice your backhand every chance you get. It's also a good one to use when fishing with a tree-bordered bank on your rod side.

THE DOUBLE LINE HAUL Before you are able to cast smoothly to distances of over 60 feet you must understand the brand-new role of your line hand. For a long cast, your rod movements are somewhat exaggerated in that there is more line weight to handle. This means your line hand cannot remain stationary during the actual cast. As you have already seen, your line hand is responsible for keeping the line under control at all times. Now, in distance casting, you will actually lift your rod arm in a higher plane, so your line hand must be coordinated with your rod hand. If your line hand remains stationary, the distance between right and left will constantly vary, jerking the line on your back cast and throwing it slack on the forward cast. There must be tension both backward and forward, because with this control you can add speed to the flight of the line whenever needed. When both hands work together, you can correct casts that are affected by the wind, correct your own errors in timing, and get greater distance, because the slightest pull on the line will shoot it much further. Although the double haul is applicable to all types of lines, the weight-forward line is designed for distance work and is therefore easier to cast.

The reason for the first haul is to make a perfectly straight back cast. It is also axiomatic that a high, straight back cast will result in a perfect forward cast. It's almost impossible to make a bad forward cast if the line has altitude and speed when coming from the rear. By pulling the line toward you as you lift the rod, you overcome the resistance of the water (which is variable against the differing diameters of a tapered fly line) and actually slide the line off the surface. Secondly, the haul gives greater initial speed to the line; so much so that it's perfectly easy to pick up 35–40 feet and shoot it to 60 feet with one back cast. Under actual fishing conditions you may use a modified line haul, even when casting on small streams with light tackle. Just the slightest left-hand pull will break the surface tension, and the fly can be picked off the water cleanly without making a disturbance. This doesn't require raising the rod hand any higher than the normal casting position, while the actual movement of the line hand is no more than a tug of 5–6 inches. If the casting range is short, it probably won't be necessary to make the second haul. In either case, you will find that very gentle movements do the trick at normal distances.

The reason for the second haul is, again, to increase the line speed. Whatever speed you gained with the first haul in laying out a back cast will be dissipated in sending the line high and straight. So when your left hand starts for your hip pocket, you are giving the taper a downhill ride at its maximum velocity. (Remember, the line is a projectile in this case, and momentum only takes over after the line has straightened and lost its forward speed.) This movement, which can resemble a man scratching his chin or a man swinging a two-handed ax, depending on his own style and the immediate casting conditions, must be timed perfectly so that the rhythmic flow of the line is not broken up. This takes practice.

Grip for Double Haul   Although your rod hand should remain in the same position as described for the overhead cast, it cannot be as relaxed, because you will be handling greater (i.e., heavier) lengths of line. Distribute your squeeze evenly through all fingers. Some experts with very strong hands and forearms prefer to turn their thumbs off-center and pinch the grip from opposing sides. This, however, is a matter of individual physique and doesn't necessarily assist all casters.

The Lift for Double Haul   Ordinarily, you can lift 15–20 feet of line from the surface by a direct pull from water to back cast without too much disturbance and without losing line speed. However, if 40–50 feet of taper is extended on the water, a direct lift would splash, and because of surface tension against the line, it would travel at about half the speed required for an easy back cast. Therefore, the double haul is always started with a smooth, short pull of your line hand simultaneous with raising the rod. This simple movement will slide the line off the water and take the extra burden of weight off your rod.

Presuming that you want to cast 60–70 feet, lay out about 40 feet with an ordinary overhead cast. On nearly all weight-forward lines, this length has the belly extended and the rod tip holding the last foot or so of back taper. Strip off of the reel whatever additional yardage you want to shoot. You can let the slack fall on the water or keep it in hand loops. Begin with your left foot (if right-handed) forward, and lean slightly forward at the waist. Then reach out to the butt guide and grasp the line between thumb and forefinger. Start moving the line toward you an instant before your rod hand begins the upward stroke. Pull the line smoothly to your hip and stop as your rod hand comes to a point opposite your ear. This will throw the line in a high back cast. Your body weight, which was primarily on your left foot, should shift onto your right foot as you lean back into the cast.

Role of Line Hand   Your hands are now widely separated, but with the back cast unrolling in the rear, move your line hand toward the reel. If executed correctly, the momentum of the back cast will pull the line upward. The instant your back cast is perfectly straight and tugging against the rod, your line hand must start to move down toward your hip again in a smooth, fast pull. Now start the pull a fraction of a second before you begin the forward cast, and follow through with greater emphasis on the rod turnover than ordinarily applied. Your body weight should now come back from the right foot to the left foot. Remember, as you pull and add speed to your line, do it progressively.

At this point you can shoot the line as you would for a regular overhead cast (see illustration, "The Double Line Haul, Forward Cast," pp. 86–87)—or continue false casting if you have not achieved sufficient line speed. Usually one or two false casts accompanied by the pull are sufficient to get maximum velocity.

In order to understand fully the double haul, it's a good idea to look over your shoulder while practicing and watch how the line unrolls and how it responds to your left hand. Your back cast should lay out straight without fishtailing, and as the forward motion is applied and you make the second pull, there should be

The Double Line Haul, Back Cast

(1) With line laid out, reach to butt guide, grasp line with thumb and fore-finger of line hand and pull (2), sliding line off water as rod hand starts upward. Continue pull with line hand as rod hand swings up (3). As rod hand reaches point about opposite your ear (4), line hand should be about same level as hip. Body weight shifts to rear (right) foot.

As the back cast unrolls, allow line hand to be drawn upward (5), keeping tension on line so that line hand comes opposite reel as back cast straightens. The instant back cast is straight and you feel its weight tugging (6), begin pull with line hand. As line hand moves down, rod hand swings forward and weight shifts (7).

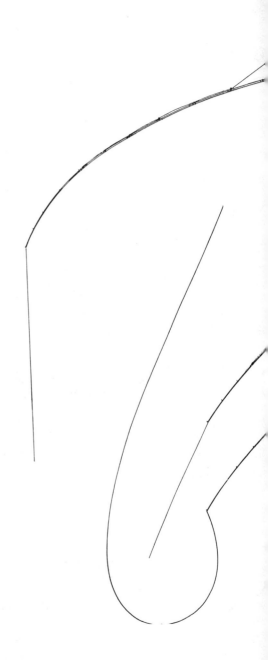

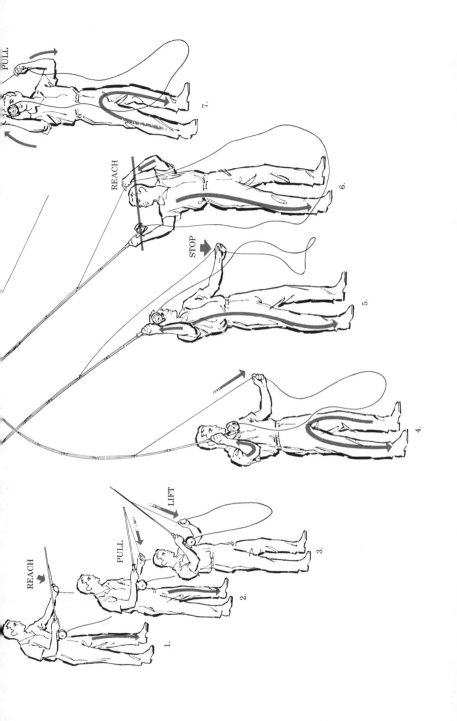

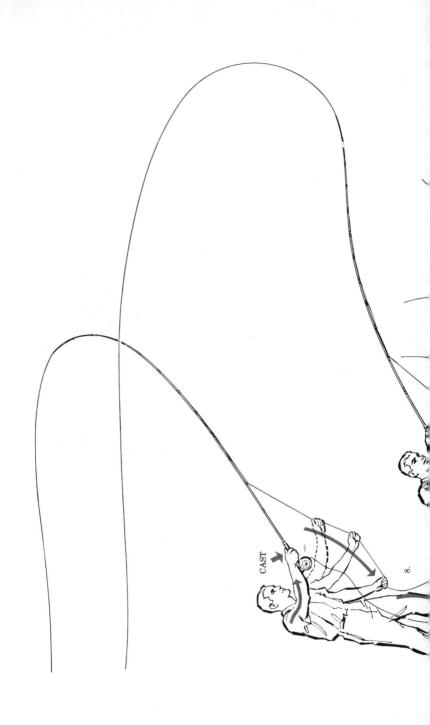

CAST

8.

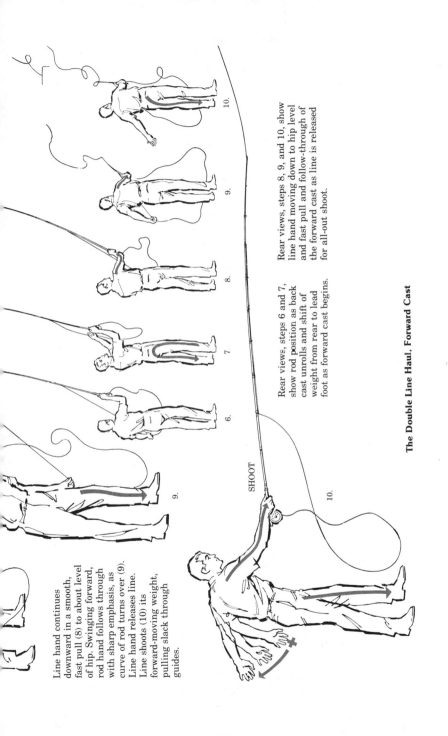

Line hand continues downward in a smooth, fast pull (8) to about level of hip. Swinging forward, rod hand follows through with sharp emphasis, as curve of rod turns over (9). Line hand releases line. Line shoots (10) its forward-moving weight, pulling slack through guides.

Rear views, steps 6 and 7, show rod position as back cast unrolls and shift of weight from rear to lead foot as forward cast begins.

Rear views, steps 8, 9, and 10, show line hand moving down to hip level and fast pull and follow-through of the forward cast as line is released for all-out shoot.

SHOOT

The Double Line Haul, Forward Cast

a noticeable increase in its speed. Above all, work to achieve a fluid action throughout the cast. Remember, the least bit of jerkiness in your hand and rod movements will destroy the flow of the line.

Handling the slack or shooting line may be a little difficult at first, but you'll soon get the knack of it. During practice sessions you can drop the line at your feet in large, loose coils. When actually fishing, you can use the same system if working from a boat, or drape the coils around your hand when wading. Some casters use a specially designed *shooting basket,* which may be strapped at the waist or suspended from the shoulders. The line is stripped into and shot from the basket. Other anglers drape the coils over clothespins secured to their wader tops, and the more adept casters prefer to hold a monofilament shooting line between their lips and open their mouths on the forward cast.

Although the double haul can look extremely gymnastic, particularly on a casting platform when a person is going for extreme distance, it really doesn't require powerful yanks to get the line going. The haul may consist of nothing more than a gentle tug at the line in either direction, barely perceptible pulls that send the taper over 100 feet with energy to spare. The trick, of course, is in perfect timing and the *smoothness* with which the haul is applied. One thing you'll discover very quickly is that if you jerk at the line and cause it to "snake" or deviate while unrolling toward the perpendicular back path, you'll lose line speed instantly. The best casts are made when the line travels absolutely straight, high, and to the rear, and when the increase in speed is applied with gradual emphasis. If you pull just a shade too hard, or at the wrong moment, your hand will create little air-resisting curves that break up the rhythm of the cast, cause the line to sag and lose momentum. Unless you can cast a high, straight line, it's almost impossible to get the maximum yardage out of a double haul. Of course, under practical fishing conditions, it's often difficult to make a perfect back cast because of gusting winds or your own body position in a balance-rocking current or boat. You can false cast until you feel the line is under perfect control.

The standard procedure is to make two or sometimes three false casts when starting cold with no line extended. When standing in the bow of a boat, for example, drop the shooting line on the deck and leave about 10–15 feet dangling out of the rod tip. The object, of course, is to get the maximum range with a minimum of movement. The first cast—or really a flip skyward—does nothing more than put the line in the air. The second false cast is to extend the line to about 40 feet with a double haul to get the belly section completely out of the guides. Very often at this point, the range is already adequate to present the fly. On the third false cast increase the line speed, still using the double haul, and let it go. With a balanced WF-8, one can easily hit 80 feet, or roughly twice the length of line extended.

If on the second false cast the line is not completely straight, try to correct it with a harder (but smooth) pull. Even though the strokes may be perfect, there's no accounting for the yawing of a 3/0 bucktail, for example, as it fights the air. Generally it sails overhead die straight, but the slightest puff of wind can grab a hairy wing and cause a chain reaction that finds the line moving faster than the fly, that in turn slows down the leader, and that holds back the line point; then each unit is moving at different speeds. If this occurs, the angler who can apply a sharp haul (in either direction) to regain line speed, altitude, and a straight path backward and forward will pull out of trouble with ease.

THE ROLL CAST   One of the chief difficulties in fly casting on small streams, or rivers that are overgrown with trees, is that an overhead cast must extend in the air behind the angler before it can go forward. The roll cast solves this problem. When executed correctly, the line will not travel more than 10–12 inches behind your elbow. Bear in mind that you are not to lift the back cast into the air. Do not practice on dry land, as the roll requires some degree of water-surface tension to complete.

First, work out about 15 feet of line by using a horizontal cast in any free direction, or even by stripping line from the reel and shaking it out through your tip. Then pull more line off the reel, which you can drop on the water for shooting. The rod should be pointed forward as for the overhead cast. Raise the rod slowly until your hand is at a point behind your eye and the rod is angled back slightly over your shoulder. When the rod has reached this position, with the belly of the line slightly behind your right elbow, there is a definite pause as in the regular overhead cast. The forward phase of the roll is made by driving the rod sharply downward with stiff wrist and forearm. The impulse given the line causes it to travel forward before the leader and fly have left the water, with the result that they are pulled after the rolling line. To get more distance, shoot your slack as you would in the overhead cast, and repeat the rod movements. Remember, as more line is added, you must put additional emphasis in the forward stroke.

One trick worth learning is to keep the line in slight motion toward you when the forward cast is started. With a long line already on the water, you should gauge the instant between pause and downstroke before the line comes to rest. A practiced roll caster can handle 50–60 feet of line without much difficulty.

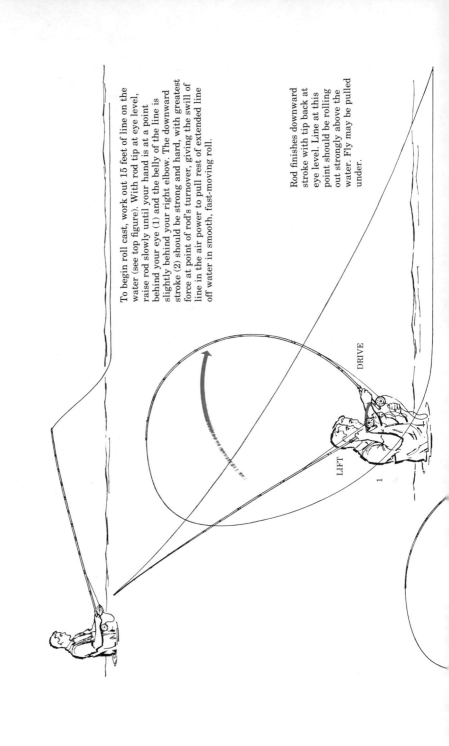

To begin roll cast, work out 15 feet of line on the water (see top figure). With rod tip at eye level, raise rod slowly until your hand is at a point behind your eye (1) and the belly of the line is slightly behind your right elbow. The downward stroke (2) should be strong and hard, with greatest force at point of rod's turnover, giving the swirl of line in the air power to pull rest of extended line off water in smooth, fast-moving roll.

Rod finishes downward stroke with tip back at eye level. Line at this point should be rolling out strongly above the water. Fly may be pulled under.

DRIVE

LIFT

1

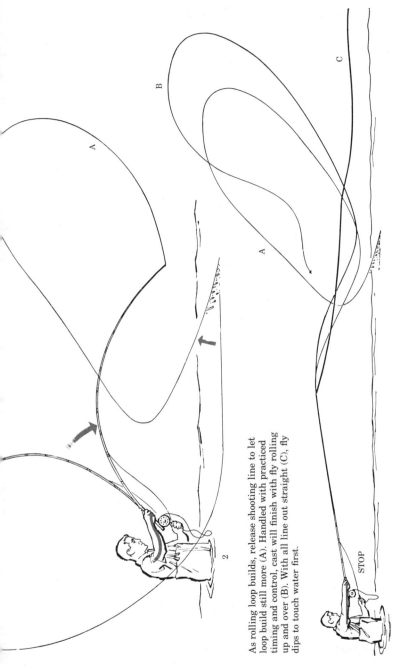

As rolling loop builds, release shooting line to let loop build still more (A). Handled with practiced timing and control, cast will finish with fly rolling up and over (B). With all line out straight (C), fly dips to touch water first.

The Roll Cast

In making the roll cast, the angler again must guard against the tendency to drive the rod forward with all his strength. The movement must be controlled and precise, with the caster starting slowly and then speeding up.

The Pickup

The correct handling of a fly line after a cast is fished out is important. It is sometimes difficult for a beginner to lift the line smoothly from the water and get it into the air for a new cast. If too much line is picked up, the ensuing splash is enough to frighten any fish. If too little is lifted from the water, the fly will simply hover over the angler's head until the rod is given more line (weight) for proper flexing. As a general rule, you should have a minimum of 1½ rod lengths of line extended from the tip for an effortless pickup. There are four ways of getting line off the water: with a smooth, left-hand pull, slide the line directly into a back cast, or you can roll it from the surface, snake it off with a few shakes of the rod, or make a snap pickup by throwing slack down the line.

THE ROLL PICKUP   When dry-fly fishing, many anglers use the roll pickup. This is nothing more than an unfinished roll cast in which you snap the tip downward to lift the line, then pick the fly out of the air and go into an ordinary back cast. When fishing with a sunken fly line, using nymphs and wet patterns, some anglers make a short, left-hand pull to raise and move the line before making the back cast. Others prefer the pull followed by a straight lift when casting a very long line or in places where there seems to be no likelihood of taking fish close to the rod.

These two methods are the most commonly used. There are two other pickups that are useful to know, however, particularly when fishing fastwater streams, where you get varying degrees of slack. They also excel in shallow streams where most of your casting is done in knee-deep water. Frequently you will be working pockets 30–40 feet away while most of your line is drifting around stones, branches, and other obstacles. Making an ordinary pickup or even a roll is difficult, because the line continually snags when drawn *across* the surface. Obviously, any pickup that lifts line upward from the water will escape getting hung.

THE SNAP PICKUP   The snap pickup is easy to execute. It literally jumps the line out of any debris or from behind rocks. The snap pickup has the further advantage of permitting you to work the fly right up to your boots. It doesn't make any difference about the slack between the tip and the fly, even if a fish hits, because one quick wrist movement will set the hook. Essentially, the snap pickup consists of nothing more than moving your rod from a ten- to an eleven-o'clock position, then snapping the tip back to ten o'clock. The snap motion forms a moving curve that instantly runs down to the leader, lifting line off the water, and—*flip*—it becomes airborne. Make your normal back cast just at the point when the leader clears the surface. You might be a bit splashy on the first few attempts, because there's a tendency to use too much power or use it at the wrong angle. But when done correctly, there is no splash, and the fly is flicked off the water as if by magic.

THE SNAKE PICKUP   This pickup consists of waving the rod from side to side and forcing a series of S curves into the line. It has the virtue of lifting a heavy front taper or bass bug off the water, and just as the leader comes free, you can flip the bug into a neat back cast without splashing. Naturally, it also can be done with trout flies. Hold your rod at the ten-o'clock position, and start shaking the line in a side-to-side motion, gradually elevating the rod to eleven o'clock. Don't rush it, because neat execution depends on getting the S curves running down to the leader to free the line from surface tension. When made correctly, the leader snakes out of the water without so much as a ripple.

The Importance of a Fly Leader

From an angling standpoint, a perfectly presented fly at 40 feet is far more effective than an awkward, splashing cast at 40 yards. Complete mastery of the rod at normal distances from all positions and under varying wind conditions is the ideal most of us seek. However, a large measure of success that one experiences in fly casting is due to paying careful attention to details like stretching the leader before fishing. This can be done with a small piece of soft rubber. Cut off a 2-inch square from an old inner tube and keep it in your leader pouch. This will earn more fish than a dozen new patterns. Before you begin fishing, rub the leader until it's perfectly straight and pliable. This will get some of the stretch out of it and prevent kinking. It takes only a few seconds to do this, and it will make a big difference in your casting.

It is also frequently necessary to lengthen the butt section or correct the tippet diameter. A leader is not only the connecting link between line and fly, but it also causes the feathers to be delivered softly to the surface. Even when a cast is checked high in the air, the weight of a falling line is sufficient to send out alarming ripples in calm water. To make a perfect presentation, the leader must be designed correctly. The length and weight of a leader are a compromise to the fishing conditions, and the taper, which is a vital component, is responsible for the transmission of energy from the line to the fly.

THE LEVEL LEADER   The level leader is one that has a uniform diameter throughout its length. It can be made simply by cutting off the desired footage of monofilament and tying a loop at one end. It is used chiefly for bait and spinner fishing rather than fly-fishing. The level kind is a poor substitute for a tapered leader, and, considering the low cost of modern synthetics, it is no longer justified even for reasons of economy. Tapered leaders work better no matter what they are made of, and, like a well-designed fly line, each portion will progressively transmit the energy of the cast right down to the fly. Level leaders were in common use before 1940 owing to the relatively high cost of Spanish silkworm gut; these level leaders were made of Japanese gut, which was the only synthetic material available at that time.

HOW TO DESIGN A TAPERED LEADER   The two main parts of a tapered leader are the *tippet,* which is the end section or strand of material to which the fly is tied (its diameter is determined by water or fishing conditions and the size of fly used), and, at the opposite end, the *butt,* or first strand, to which the line is connected. The butt is the heaviest portion, and, generally speaking, it should approximate two-thirds the diameter of the line point. Most American double-tapered fly lines are .030 at the end, so a .020 butt is generally correct. If you use any of the modern weight-forward lines made with a plastic coating, their points will measure .033–.037, and for these, a .022 leader butt is necessary. Unless you are certain that the line and leader materials with which you will be working are accurately identified, it is advisable to obtain a micrometer. This is a valuable instrument to have for leader making. It's difficult to build leaders by pound-test ratings; these can vary so widely in diameter that you might easily tie fine sections behind heavy ones. With the great variety of spooled synthetics available, from both foreign and domestic sources, the materials are not always accurately identified according to size.

The most common error in leader design is making too light and too short a butt. Some of the tapers in current fashion start at .014, which was customary in the days when gut leaders were the only kind available. The reason for the light butt was twofold. Finer silk line points were the rule, and only a limited number of gut strands could be used in making leaders commercially. To arrive at a 3X or 4X tippet, the butt had to be light. Natural gut strands longer than 15 inches are almost impossible to find. So the taper consisted of regular gradations, just like so many steps of stairs. To maintain its knot strength, gut can only be varied by .001 between strands, which means the leader had to drop from .014 to .013 to .012, and so on for eight or nine sections. This made for a very knotty taper. Mechanically, the old-time leader maker was a conformist because of his material. When making a synthetic leader today, we can jump .002–.004 between sizes without sacrificing strength—and go to 62-inch lengths or longer, if the design requires it.

Generally speaking, you will have to do a considerable amount of fishing until you find the leaders with which you can cast best under different conditions. They will vary from line to line, depending on their forward tapers and the length and diameter of their points.

Try to duplicate the proper leader in subsequent purchases. Of course, if you tie your own, the chances of learning exactly the right formula are much better. A general design that can be recommended in making leaders is 60 percent butt, 20 percent graduation, and 20 percent tippet. The long, heavy butt turns over perfectly under most wind conditions. Begin by using a bit more than one half of the total length in heavy diameters, say .020–.018. Following the heavy material, tie in short, graduating strands. These step-down pieces serve the purpose of reducing the diameter rapidly from .018 to the finer tippet sections you would normally use. The tippet section itself should be 20–30 inches long, the exact length depending on how well it turns over. As a rule of thumb, a fly that is proportionately large in relation to the diameter of the tippet will require a shorter length. A 30-inch, .006 (5X) tippet, for instance, will roll over perfectly with No. 16 and No. 18 flies; if you tie on a bushier hackled No. 10, the fly will tend to fall back over the leader. It will also twist in the air and weaken the tippet. This can be improved somewhat by cutting the .006 down to about 8–10 inches, but it's better to replace the tippet with a heavier diameter. For a No. 10 fly, the tippet size should run .008 (3X).

LENGTH AND WEIGHT   It should be apparent that the length and weight of the leader to be used is dependent on the water conditions and the size of the fish. For instance, when the water is discolored and you're using a large hook like a bucktail, you can safely work with a leader on the heavy side. It doesn't have to be too long, either. If you're casting small flies in clearwater, the leader should be light and long; it's impossible to present a tiny fly properly on a short, heavy leader. We usually consider a 7½-foot leader as short, and anything over 9 feet as long. Experts commonly use lengths of 10–12 feet and go up to 15 feet on occasion. For most trout fishing, don't be concerned about the pound-test ratings. On the average stream, we seldom hook many fish over 1½ pounds, and while we may break off on the infrequent heavier trout with 5X or 6X, these tippets will hold up to three pounds or more if handled gently. The fine diameters are a problem if the fish come big, but sometimes it's the only way to move them, and the higher ratio of strikes provides some success. In rivers where 4-pound trout are common (and there are few such waters), try to stay at 3X, but don't hesitate to go down to 5X if the conditions require it. Of course salmon, steelhead, and black bass are going to demand heavy diameters, not merely because of their weight but because of the need for much larger flies and lures.

IMPORTANCE OF A LEADER BALANCE   The impact a fly makes on the surface often has a great deal to do with its effectiveness. There are days when stoneflies and grasshoppers literally slam the water, and an artificial spanked down in the same fashion will bring furious strikes. This is not the ordinary situation, however, and, by and large, the man who drops his floater quietly is going to raise fish. If you're a beginner, it's a good idea to spend some time on a very quiet pool just studying your line and leader. Make average casts of 30–40 feet, using a 9-foot leader with fly attached. Remember to massage the nylon first with a piece of rubber so that it falls perfectly straight. Watch both the back and forward casts. If the back stroke isn't rolling out straight to begin with, then you have a casting problem. But if the line unrolls without humps, and if the leader flops around as though unrelated to the cast and falls in a heap on the water, then it's time to start building a new taper. One that is practically foolproof for line points of .025 or a shade heavier starts with a butt of 42 inches of .018, then adds a second, heavy section of 29 inches of .016. This is about 60 percent of a 9-foot leader. Now add three 6-inch graduating strands of .014, .012, and .010. For the tippet, tie on 20 inches of .008. This all runs a fraction over 9 feet, but after stretching the leader with a piece of rubber you'll be able to cast it with your bare hand. Any fly from No. 10 to No. 14 should sail out, turn over, and sit down as daintily as a mayfly.

BALANCED LEADER TAPERS   The following profiles are suitable for all wind conditions. Under normal winds and in clear water, the 20-inch tippet sections may be lengthened to 30 inches, when using small flies.

9 Feet—1X		9 Feet—2X		9 Feet—3X	
Diameter	Length	Diameter	Length	Diameter	Length
.018	41″	.018	41″	.018	41″
.016	35″	.016	29″	.016	29″
.014	6″	.014	6″	.014	6″
.012	6″	.012	6″	.012	6″
.010	20″	.010	6″	.010	6″
		.019	20″	.008	20″

9 Feet—4X		9 Feet—5X		9 Feet—6X*	
Diameter	Length	Diameter	Length	Diameter	Length
.018	34″	.018	54″	.018	48″
.016	30″	.016	12″	.016	12″
.014	6″	.014	6″	.014	6″
.012	6″	.012	6″	.012	6″
.010	6″	.010	6″	.010	6″
.008	6″	.008	6″	.008	6″
.007	20″	.006	20″	.006	6″
				.005	20″

*This taper can be reduced to 7X by substituting a tippet of .004 in place of .005.

SALTWATER FLY LEADERS   For heavy saltwater work when casting to fish that require 60- to 100-pound-test shock tippets in addition to the regulation 12-pound-test or 15-pound-test qualifying tippets, the following profile (by test) in best-grade, hard-finish monofilament for a 9½-foot leader is widely applicable for snook, dolphin, striped bass, sharks, barracuda, tarpon, and sailfish:

	Test (pounds)	Length (inches)
Butt	40	72
Tippet	12	30
Shock Tippet	60	13*

*Shock tippet reduces to 12 inches when the knot is tied.

The butt section of the leader can be joined to the fly line with a nail knot. Due to the heavy diameter of 40-pound test, any kind of knot will be somewhat bulky; to smooth its passing through rod guides, apply two coats of Pliobond cement to the knot. The butt can be joined to the tippet with a nail knot, and the tippet to the shock tippet with a surgeon's knot, if 60-pound test is used; with the heavier 80- and 100-pound-test tippets, join the tippet to the shock tippet with an offset nail knot. The fly is tied to the shock tippet with a Homer Rhode loop knot or a nail-knot loop (For detailed information on various knots, see Knots, p. 191).

Accuracy Casting

Thus far we have concentrated on the mechanics of spinning, spin casting, bait casting, and fly casting. To a beginner, the ability to cast long distances might appear to be the ultimate goal, but, in everyday angling, the skill that really pays off is achieving accuracy. When you can drop a plug within an inch of the bank at 50 feet or float a fly over a rising trout at the same distance, successful fishing is guaranteed. The most important factor in all accuracy casting is total *concentration on the target*. You must forget the mechanics of casting. If your eyes focus on the tree limbs instead of that fishy pocket next to the bank below them, all you will catch are tree limbs.

The Release Point

Accuracy with the fly rod differs from other forms of casting in that we are extending a variable weight (the line) as opposed to a known weight (the lure) when using a spinning or bait-casting rod. Nevertheless, all three methods require that you establish the correct release point of a cast. In other words, before the line or lure is set free, the rod must always come to the same point in space in the flattest possible trajectory. If you cast too high, the line will drift, even in a slight breeze, and reduce your accuracy. Only the rod's speed will vary, according to the distance required to reach the target. If you release the cast a microsecond too soon or too late, the lure will over- or undershoot the target. With constant practice, you will "feel" the correct point subconsciously; it will become a reflexive motion to sight and split the target. However, when casting a known weight, such as a plug or a spoon, it is extremely important to learn the correct distance between your rod tip and a lure of any given weight, and then always hold that weight in exactly the same position. It may be 4 inches for a ⅜-ounce lure, 3 inches for a ½-ounce lure, and 2 inches for a ⅝-ounce lure, but the relationship is absolute. If you are casting a ⅜-ounce lure at a target 50 feet away, and it's suspended 2 inches below the tip-top on one cast and 4 inches away on the next—you will get two different results. There is no hard-and-fast rule for rods or people in general. It requires personal experiment to find the perfect "hang," because the length and stiffness factor of individual rods varies greatly. This may seem inconsequential, but it's the first thing every successful tournament caster works out for himself.

Bait Casting and Spin Casting

Whether you use a bait-casting or a push-button type reel, the casting style is identical. If you consistently overshoot the target, shorten the hang; if you undershoot, lengthen it inch by inch. To start accurately, grasp the rod handle just firmly enough to keep the outfit in your hand. Do not squeeze the grip. Extend your forefinger so that it wraps comfortably around the trigger-shaped spur on the handle, and place your thumb in a comfortable position on the spool. Then rotate your hand so that the palm faces downward with the reel handles facing up. This position allows complete wrist freedom. Although casting is frequently described as "a mere flick of the wrist," this is not the case at all. Excessive wrist bending only defeats accuracy. What you are going to do is lift your forearm with the wrist remaining unbent.

Despite the fact that casters sometimes find themselves sitting on an ice chest in a crowded boat or hanging apelike from the limb of a tree on a brushy bank, your stance is important to accuracy. Practical fishing conditions may modify the ground rules, but learn them correctly, and your body weight and rod motions will conform to any handicap. Face the target, then take a quarter turn to the left so that your right shoulder is pointed toward the target. Your left foot should be just to the rear of your right foot with the right heel pointed toward the ball of your left foot. Get comfortable and relax. As the cast begins, your weight should be shifted to your right foot. Hold the rod with the tip-top slightly above head level and the rod slightly above belt level. Your outstretched forearm will more or less parallel the angle of the rod. Make sure the crank handles face up and that your wrist is relaxed to prevent cocking it during the back cast.

Aiming a cast requires complete concentration on one object. You have to keep your eyes on the target. The extended rod is just a blur—it is pointed in the right direction splitting the target, and you are aware of it, but your eyes should be focused on the spot you want to hit. You may cast for hours dropping a plug within an inch of the shoreline, and, for no accountable reason, suddenly focus on some waterside hazard and blow a perfect score. If you are catching more trees than fish, the problem is simply lack of concentration. You cannot accurately aim a rod at one object while focused on another; if you do, you will hit the wrong one. Your eye and hand must be coordinated. So before you cast, forget about any hazard as long as there is enough free space to lay the plug on target.

Start the back cast by lifting your forearm, pivoting slightly on your elbow, until your hand comes to eye level. At this point the rod should be in a vertical position and should not be allowed to drop back over the shoulder. Now, without any hesitation, immediately begin the downward cast following the same path the rod took on its upward swing. The forward cast is actually a smooth, crisp, chopping motion of the arm. When a position halfway between the vertical and your original starting position is reached, release the thumb pressure on the reel spool, permitting the lure to start on its flight. The downward position is continued until the starting position is reached, and then the rod motion is halted. As the lure approaches its target, the thumb pressure is increased. When the lure hits the target, the thumb halts all forward motion of the spool preventing overrun and backlash at one and the same time. Try to make both the upward and downward motions as smooth as possible. Any attempt to shove the lure forward by body or arm motions merely dampens the rod action. Let the rod do the work.

A side cast is more difficult than an overhead cast. It's not safe to use when fishing with another person in a boat unless you can lean out over the bow or stern to where nobody can get hit. A moving rod tip has a lot more whip than most beginners realize. The area a bending rod will cover comes as a shock to novices— not to mention their tutors. Nevertheless, a side cast is literally the only cast that can be used on some southern waters where Spanish moss and tree limbs almost touch the surface of the water. It takes plenty of practice to develop accuracy in a side movement, because the release point and follow-through are critical. The reel must be held differently, with your palm facing to the left and the crank handle to the right, rather than facing up. Also, your stance should be reversed, with your left shoulder pointing toward the target and the heel of your right foot opposite the ball of your left foot. Keep your body weight on both feet in this cast. With a crisp movement, bring your rod back, and stop at a right-angle position to your body. At the instant of deepest bend, move the rod forward with wrist and forearm emphasis, releasing thumb pressure from the spool at the forward impulse. It is important to get the correct release point that "feels" early, or the lure will swing to the left. The tendency to angle casts away from targets is due solely to improper release and follow-through. If the rod tip is allowed to pass beyond its starting point, you will miss the target. It is also well to remember that the path your lure must travel from extended rod tip to the target is *not* your actual line of sight, as in the case of the overhead casts, and any attempt to cast along your line of sight will result in a cast going far to the left. Keep in mind that the motion you desire is not given to the lure by a simple sweeping action from right to left, but by "loading" the rod tip.

Spinning

The spinning rod with its fixed-spool reel is much easier to use than a standard bait-casting outfit. For this very reason fewer anglers work at fundamentals or achieve pinpoint accuracy. Bear in mind that the usual range of lure weights for spinning are considerably lighter than those used in bait casting or with push-button reels. Depending on the recoil speed of the rod, it may be necessary to drop a $1/16$- or $1/18$-ounce bait 12–14 inches below the tip-top. The casting style to develop with the spinning rod is a smooth, chopping motion of the forearm. True, you can toss the lure out with a mere wrist snap, but using the forearm has the same advantage it does in bait casting. For one thing, you can get more elevation with the forearm; by starting with the hand low and using a short arc you can make very short, accurate casts. As the arc is lengthened and the hand raised higher, you can apply more power and reach greater distances. A pure wrist motion, on the other hand, has a definite limit; it is not a consistent movement among inexperienced casters, and it is tiring, particularly when using lures in the over-¼-ounce class. By using the forearm as well as *some* wrist action, you can achieve absolute precision and the maximum distance. This is the style used by the best tournament casters.

Accuracy begins with gripping the rod properly. You should grasp the corks of a spinning rod with your fingers split around the reel leg—with two fingers in front and two in back. Some men with exceptionally large hands might find this uncomfortable and prefer one finger in front and three in back of the reel leg, but this is rarely necessary. Your thumb should be on top of the handle, positioned over your forefinger, which is directly over the reel spool. It is important to keep your hand as relaxed as possible. Starting with a relaxed hold, you shouldn't squeeze down on the rod grip until the very instant power is applied to the back cast. To begin the cast, wind the reel so that the bail, pickup finger, or roller (depending on the type of reel) is on top and the lure is hanging about 6 inches from the rod tip, and then pick up the line so that it rests over the first joint of your forefinger. Your finger should bend just enough to lift the line free from the roller. Next, reverse the crank handle approximately one quarter turn. At this point, the pickup mechanism should be at the bottom of the reel, the line held in check by your forefinger. Do not squeeze the line against the rod grip, but hold it on the ball of your forefinger; the weight of the lure will create enough tension to keep the line tight. Now, with your left hand, snap the pickup open.

In your first practice session, hold the rod so that the very tip is slightly above eye level, with the shaft splitting the center of the target. Your arm should be relaxed. Try to estimate how much speed the rod will need to shoot the lure the proper distance. Bending at the elbow, with an upward and backward forearm motion, start the rod toward vertical, accelerating its speed until the rod is twelve-o'clock high, and stop the movement by squeezing the rod grip. The momentum of the lure will pull the rod tip back into a casting bend. As the lure pulls hard against the rod, start the forward chop with some wrist emphasis, and release the line from your forefinger as you pass the eleven-o'clock position (viewing the clock face with the angler facing left). When the line has been released, move your finger away, and to the right of the spool. If you are trying for a very long shot over open water, don't allow the line to come in contact with your finger at all. In accuracy work, however, you will want to slow the cast down by feathering the line with your forefinger, as the common tendency is to overshoot a target.

Fly Casting

There are two ways of achieving accuracy with the fly rod: one is the old tournament style of *painting* the fly on target by repetitive false casting until the feathers are almost brushing the spot you want to hit, before releasing the line. This works fine at short ranges of, say, up to 35 feet, and if you can do it with a minimum of strokes, there's little likelihood of spooking the fish. Using a slow-action rod, light line, and a balanced leader, it's a deadly way of catching trout out of miniature pockets in turbulent streams. Screened by the current, the flash of line and rod is hidden. In quiet water, and especially on sunlit days, the same technique may quickly put the fish down. The tournament technique is also a painful way of trying to reach a steelhead at 60 or 70 feet and is absolutely hopeless over often fast-moving targets such as bonefish or tarpon. The only way to deal with a variable is, as we have seen in bait casting and spinning, to eliminate it. As in casting known weights with the spinning or bait-casting rod, where a "hang" of 2, 3, 4, or however many inches is essential for consistent results, the fly line should be extended until a reference point is reached. At least one line manufacturer molds a sharp diameter reduction into its forward taper lines 10 feet behind the shooting head; when this is felt by your fingers, you have the correct length of line in the air for a perfect shoot. By the same reasoning, you can find points of reference in any size fly line simply by feel. Lack of accuracy in fly casting is to a large extent caused by under- and, more often, overextending the length of line in the air when false casting. The correct weight must always come back to the same release point, and again, only the speed varies according to distance of the target.

Practice makes perfect in all sports, and casting demands the same attention to detail as you find in golf, tennis, baseball, or any of the other sports people play.

Spinners

Spinners are used for a great variety of fresh- and saltwater gamefish. This is the basic lure used with the spinning method of casting. A spinner is a metal blade, usually oval in shape, designed to rotate when drawn through the water. The blade generally revolves around a shaft; however, there are some variations in construction. Although spinners are often mounted in tandem with other lures, the blade in itself is sufficient to attract game- and panfish. A spinner creates the illusion of a minnow, or at least something edible, in three ways: it has vibration, flash, and motion. Water is a more positive conductor of sound waves than air. External noises, such as a man shouting, bounce off the surface, and fish pay no attention to them. But let the same person step too hard on a hollow bank, and the vibrations pass through the earth into the water and into the lateral line of his quarry. Although the "ears" of a fish do not function in the same fashion as the angler's, the fact remains that fish can hear underwater sounds and can, themselves, emit vibrations that are audible to other fish. Considering the fact that spinners are often effective in muddy water and after dark, this vibration factor is of great significance. Both the size and the speed at which the blade rotates probably has more to do with earning strikes than its actual appearance in the water. Spinners used for casting are ordinarily from 1 to 3 inches long, but those made for trolling are often 5 inches long, and as many as eight blades may be mounted on the same shaft. A popular lake-trout trolling rig is composed of three Willowleaf and five Bear Valley spinners mounted on a 48-inch length of wire. This armament either gives the illusion of a whole school of baitfish, or else it has the same effect as a "silent" whistle on a dog. When a lure such as a fly or pork rind or worm won't attract fish, it often happens that the addition of a small spinner, with its glittering movement, is successful.

The Construction of Spinners

A spinner consists of a shaft and U-shaped clevis upon which the blade is mounted. The shaft is generally made of tinned piano wire, brass, or nickel silver. At one end of the shaft is a lure-locking device of either the cross-snap or coil-spring type. The cross snap is sturdy and reliable on large spinners, but it may have a tendency to pop open on small sizes because of the fine-diameter shaft. The coil spring is, conversely, the better one for small spinners, but the old-fashioned kind tends to creep up the shaft in the large sizes. The clevis is the revolving arm or ring that holds the blade to the shaft. It is important to remember that the clevis can be bent in the mouth of a heavy fish or damaged against rocks; then the spinner won't rotate properly. The clevis is usually separated from the eye and the lock by two or three metal or plastic beads. These beads keep the clevis from jamming against either end of the shaft. They also provide some decoration; for example, in the case of the Bear Valley, which usually has bright-red beads. The Bear Valley is a Colorado blade with a bit of decorative flash. Other spinners, such as the Junebug, do not have a clevis, but are attached blade to shaft, being braced at an angle by an underextension of the blade, which can be cocked or bent to vary the amount of spin. The only other basic component is the hook, which may be single, double, or treble; it can be feathered, covered with bucktail, or mounted with a weed guard. Many anglers dislike treble hooks and avoid using them on any lure that doesn't require one. Certainly, all fly-rod spinners and many weighted blades used with orthodox spinning tackle can be mounted ice-tong style with two single hooks face to face. These are less apt to snag bottom and won't cause any injury to small fish.

BLADE FINISHES   Spinner blades are finished in brass, nickel silver, copper, and gold. They are also enameled in various colors, such as black, white, and yellow. By far the most popular in both fresh- and saltwater, however, is a highly polished nickel-silver blade. Yet, under clearwater conditions, gamefish often shy away from bright blades, and the duller brass, copper, and even black spinners can be more effective. Nevertheless, the size and shape of a blade are equally important from the standpoint of providing constant movement and the right amount of vibration. There seems to be a time for small, slow spinners as well as a time for the large, fast ones.

BLADE DESIGN   Unlike a spoon, which is a curved blade that breaks rotation because of its shape and, thus, wobbles, a spinner embodies the principle of a blade mounted on a shaft so that it revolves completely when drawn through the water. Therefore the basic distinction made among spinners is the shape of their blades. The shape is important because it determines how fast or how slow the blade turns and the angle at which it rotates with relation to its axis. A near-round blade, such as the Colorado, swings wide and rather slowly, while the narrow Willowleaf design spins fast and close to the shaft. This suggests two things: (1) The Colorado has more resistance in the water and is best adapted to slow currents and ponds; and (2) the Willowleaf has a minimum resistance, and can be used in fastwater without twisting the leader. Between the Colorado and the Willowleaf are a number of designs that are oval in shape, such as the Indiana, Idaho, and Bear Valley patterns, which rotate at an angle close to 45 degrees from their shafts. But both the thickness and the size of the blade have a cumulative effect.

BODY DESIGN   Most spinner blades are too light to be cast without some added weight. A molded metal body or metal beads are added to the shaft for this reason. The lures used for spinning and spin casting generally range from $1/16$ to 1 ounce in size. A good lure has an aerodynamically balanced body in its weight distribution so that the spinner doesn't "tumble" in the air, which shortens the cast or wraps the hook back over the line.

Spinner-Blade Sizes and Types

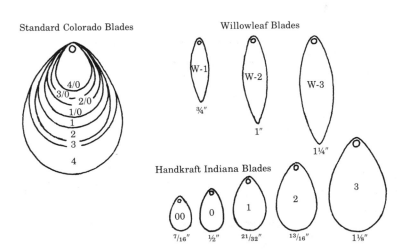

Standard Colorado Blades

Willowleaf Blades

Handkraft Indiana Blades

Spinners

Spinners are made in a variety of sizes and finishes with different blade and body shapes. The blade, which is mounted on the shaft by means of a U-shaped clevis, rotates in the water. A narrow blade spins closer to the body and can be retrieved faster and deeper than a broad blade, which revolves effectively at very slow speeds.

How to Fish with Spinners

In lakes, spinners are used mainly for black bass, pike, muskellunge, and panfish. Except for the smaller panfish, which usually require lures in the ¹/₁₆- to ¼-ounce range (⅛ ounce is a practical starter), a ½-ounce spinner is usually more effective for the larger gamefish.

The areas to fish vary greatly with the season; shoreline casting is generally productive in the spring, and the deeper parts of a lake in summer and fall. In addition to known underwater structures, you should watch for points of land, gravel bars, inlet streams, shores with a sharp drop-off, and visible surface cover, such as stumps and weed beds. Always use the lightest monofilament line that is practical for the water being fished; with spinning or spin-casting tackle, 4- to 10-pound test is recommended, and with bait-casting gear, 10- to 15-pound test. Monofilament sinks better than braided line, and the lighter it is, the more strikes you will feel. Spinners are often taken on the "fall" as they drop toward bottom after a cast is made. Because of the inevitable slack, the strike of a big fish may be no more apparent than a twitch of the line. In lakes, spinners can be fished at all depths and speeds, they can even be buzzed on the surface. Any of the narrow blades similar to a Willowleaf will run deeper and faster than other designs.

In brooks or small streams, spinners are used principally for trout and panfish. For shallow water the oval blades, such as the Colorado, are ideal, because they can be fished slowly without snagging bottom.

The trick in using a spinner here is to estimate where the fish are hiding and then bring the lure near the lie. In shallow brooks where most of the casting is done in pockets 1–3 feet in depth, working downstream will probably be more effective until you have mastered the ultralight-spinning method. You will have absolute control over the lure, and it can be fished at any speed, or even held stationary against the pull of the current. If the water is a bit deeper, with riffles running 3–5 feet deep, you might try working directly upstream. At these depths, you can swim a spinner without snagging, and you're less apt to alarm the fish. In other words, make it a rule to cast against the current wherever the conditions are suitable. The ideal lure weights under these conditions are $1/16$–$1/8$ ounce. This requires light spinning tackle with a 3- to 4-pound-test line.

In a big river, your problem is to get maximum water coverage, and this is easy to accomplish by casting across and slightly upstream, swimming the lure in long swings or drops. Here you might run into difficulty by fishing too "high" in the stream; so the lure weight can comfortably run from $1/8$ to $1/4$-ounce. The $1/4$-ounce size will probably be your best bet. To cover a pool thoroughly, quarter your first cast about 40 feet upriver; the current will carry the spinner down with a semicircular sweep until it swings around below your position, where it will hang spinning in the current near bottom. Don't hurry the lure back. The second cast shouldn't be as far *up* the river but quartered more toward the opposite bank, to a distance of about 50 feet this time. Let it swim downstream again to the lowest point of its arc. By casting in a pattern of widening half circles you can cover every inch of a pool or deep riffle, then move on to the next spot. This sounds like a mechanical procedure, but it takes some skill to keep in contact with the spinner and adjust its speed according to the current to keep it working deep.

Spinner Baits

A spinner bait is a compound lure that incorporates one or more
spinner blades with a jig (see Jigs, p. 118); these are joined at
opposite ends of a wire arm so that the lures work independently.
The jig hook is masked with a rubber or plastic skirt or a soft
plastic body. Spinner baits range from ⅛ to ⅝ ounces in size. They
are primarily designed for black bass, pike, muskies, and panfish.
Spinner baits can be fished at all depths and are often deadly when
"buzzed" across the surface.

Spinner Baits

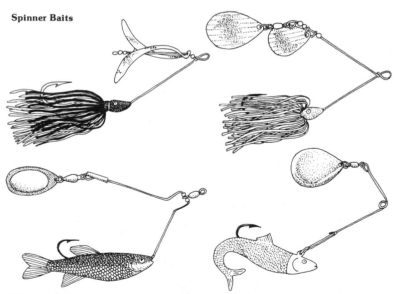

Spinner baits are a combination of two lures, the spinner and the jig. The jig
usually consists of a soft plastic body or skirt with a lead head for added weight.
The spinner blade is attached to a wire arm, either by means of a clevis or a
swivel. Oval or broad blades are most popular for maximum action, but curved
blades are also effective, particularly when "buzzed" along the surface.

Spoons

Spoons are used with bait-casting, spinning, and spin-casting tackle. These metal lures are made in a variety of sizes, from little, 1-inch-long, $1/16$-ounce blades suitable for panfish and trout to 10-inch-long, 7-ounce trolling spoons designed for wahoos and giant barracuda. They can be fished at all depths, from surface to bottom. Despite the fact that the first patent for a metal spoon was issued in 1834 to Julio Buel (his lure was actually a large trolling spinner) of Whitehall, New York, primitive people used pieces of polished shell and bone for the same purpose as early as 3000 B.C. Presumably the spoon simulates a fish swimming through the water because of its erratic motion and flash, which attracts any larger predatory species. Yet, like any other fishing lure, it has limitations as well as virtues.

The basic wobbling spoon resembles an oval-shaped metal blade, not unlike the familiar teaspoon. The blade may vary somewhat in being broader to reduce its swimming speed or more elongated to increase its speed, but all spoons are meant to "wobble" rather than spin. Regardless of the actual blade shape, the distinction is that it does not perform like a spinner. A correctly designed spoon has a calculated balance instability that causes it to break rotation from one side to the other. The chief difference between spoon patterns is the relationship of weight to mass in hundreds of possible curvatures. The theoretical ideal is to design a spoon that swims with a maximum motion through any speed range. The perfect spoon, like the perfect shape for a fish, has never been created; each variation suits a particular environment and circumstance.

The spoon's castability and sinking coefficient are interrelated; a blade heavy and streamlined enough to sail across the pond will also drop to the bottom rather quickly. A wide, shoehorn-shaped spoon may achieve only half the distance yet be more "fishable" in sinking and swimming slowly. Obviously, the larger the surface area of a lure for a given weight, the greater its wind and water resistance. At times the most effective lures are the most difficult to cast and vice versa. As a rule of thumb, lure weights and blade lengths can be categorized according to the tackle employed as follows:

	Ultralight	Spinning	Bait Casting
Line test (pounds)	1½–3	4–8	10–12
Lure weight (ounces)	$\frac{1}{16}$–¼	¼–⅝	⅜–⅞
Blade length (inches)	1–1¾	2–3	3–4

Trolling spoons are not cast, and while the angler may troll a small wobbler on occasion with spinning and bait-casting gear, in a strict sense, the line tests used by specialists ordinarily range from 12 to 50 pounds, with spoon weights varying from ⅝ to 7 ounces and blade lengths, from 3 to 10 inches. The selection of a lure for this equipment is dependent on how deep the spoon runs and how fast it works. Some trolling spoons are made paper-thin and have very little weight; these are designed to use behind a sinker so that the light blade achieves a maximum fluttering action. Such lures are particularly effective for landlocked salmon and lake trout. On the other hand, the angler who casts a spoon can be defeated by fractions of an ounce or the slightest variation in blade shape, because wind conditions do not always complement fishing conditions.

Spoons come in a great variety of colors and finishes; gold, nickel, silver, or red-and-white are standards for most kinds of fishing. They are also made with weed guards over a single or treble hook, and these are particularly useful for black bass, pike, or muskie fishing. The single-hook spoon is usually dressed with a mask of bucktail, a strip of pork rind, or a plastic skirt.

How to Select Spoons

Selecting the right spoon is not difficult. The only thing to keep in mind is that between two spoons of equal weight but of different size, the one with the smallest blade area will sink faster, work deeper, and cast easier against strong winds. The spoon with the greater surface area (which may be better for your purposes when casting in lakes) will sink slowly and swim higher in the water.

For example, a good choice in river fishing is a compact wobbler 1½–2 inches in length, weighing ¼ ounce. Such a blade will

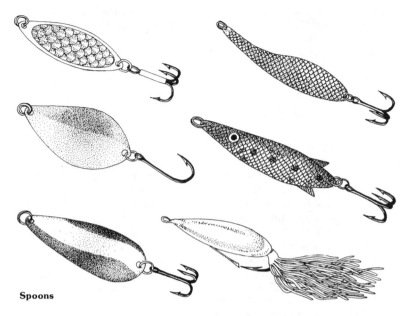

Spoons

Spoons differ from spinners in breaking rotation when drawn through the water. The blade wobbles as opposed to revolving. Spoons are made in a wide variety of shapes, sizes, and finishes. Blade thickness determines castability, with the thicker, more compact spoons delivering maximum distance and the thinner blades providing more lifelike action, so most designs are compromises to specific kinds of fishing.

sink deep in fastwater. Aim the lure quartering upstream, and work it back at the same pace as the current, as close to the bottom as possible. The best spots for presenting a wobbler are in pools and at the feet of heavy riffles. You'll have to judge the depth of the water as you move along and correct the angle of your casts so that the spoon is wobbling at fish level. In the average big stream, the effective swim of a lure is 6–8 feet down, and, generally, the speed of the current is such that you have to cast well above the fish's lie. If you cast directly at or even a short distance above its position, the wobbler will be at the very end of its swing before it starts dropping to the gravel. The trick is to angle the blade well upstream and let it sink before retrieving; make a few slow turns of the reel, twitch the rod, and then let the wobbler flutter in the current until it is over the hot spot.

As we have already noted, spinners and spoons will take, in

varying degrees, a tremendous variety of gamefish. However, these two types of lures are fundamental to fishing for muskellunge and northern pike. Why the muskie prefers a rotating blade and the pike prefers one that wobbles is not exactly clear in view of the fact that they are closely related species occurring in similar habitats and with similar feeding habits; but the fact remains that a big bucktail spinner is the basic artificial for the muskie and a wobbling spoon for the pike.

Fishing for Muskellunge

Muskellunge are generally taken with spinning, bait-casting, or trolling tackle. To a lesser extent, they are also caught with the fly rod by skilled casters. The key to catching muskellunge is in the retrieve. There is no hard-and-fast rule, but, unlike bass fishing, which counts heavily on slow reeling with long pauses, the veteran muskie man frequently employs a fast retrieve. One would expect that any predator that lies waiting to ambush its food is going to snap at slow-moving baits or even stationary ones; yet it doesn't always work out that way. Nothing excites the muskie more than a lively lure, and for this purpose a large casting spinner with a bucktail trailer is preferred by most anglers; these lures weigh from ½ to 1 ounce and have a single or double blade. The bucktail mask may be black, yellow, red, brown, or even purple with a gold, silver, or black blade. This type of lure is easy to retrieve even at top speeds. It is a fairly weedless lure because of the heavy bucktail mask and is effective to a depth of about 15 feet. In deepwater it not only sinks slowly but planes upward too quickly; when it's necessary to work below that level, a deep-diving plug is more productive (jointed diving plugs are especially favored).

Muskellunge usually remain out of sight in very dense weed beds at depths of 6–15 feet during hot weather. Deep trolling is popular among muskie specialists in the summer period. Bear in mind, however, that motor trolling or the use of metal lines is illegal in some states. When in rivers, muskellunge are partial to quiet backwaters and the sheltered places where there is some pad cover or thick grass. They also frequent drop-offs and channels at depths of 6–30 feet or more, depending on the season.

Most muskie fishermen will agree on the following: by far the greatest majority of muskies caught over 15 pounds are females; the most productive time of day for fishing is afternoon; three of the best months are September, October, and November; muskies are solitary fish and will stay in one spot unless driven out by a larger fish or caught; more than one cast in the same place frequently produces a strike or a follow; muskie fishing is hard work; the medium-to-short cast is better than the long cast; the fisherman who works his baits properly, makes the most casts, and stays alert will, in the long run, enjoy the greatest success; and, finally, all muskies are unpredictable.

A muskie may strike the lure at any point along the line of retrieve and has, on occasion, been known to bash its snout on the side of the boat in its belated efforts to grab the lure. Or it may follow the lure to the boat without striking and repeat this procedure several times. The muskie does have a big, toothy mouth, and, in most instances, it will lunge at the bait in such a way as to have it end up across its jaws. Since it exerts tremendous power downward, it is almost impossible to move the bait in its mouth. It is only when it realizes that the bait is not what it wants and relaxes the tension of its jaws that the hooks may be driven into its mouth, so it is very important to set the hook several times in rapid succession.

The muskie does not always agree with the fisherman in regard to what constitutes a perfect day for fishing. Weather conditions seem to play a large part in determining whether or not the fish will cooperate. An overcast sky with a light chop on the water is generally agreed as being a condition more productive than others. Since few fisherman can pick and choose those days that seem most conducive for action, their results do little to stabilize the statistics. One of the best times to try is during or after a storm on a rising barometer.

Fishing for Pike

There's no question that pike will take large spinners, but a wobbling spoon has long been the standard attractor for this species. Probably the all-time North American favorite is a red-and-white wobbler, somewhat pear-shaped, in the ½ ounce size. This is cast over and around submerged weed beds and retrieved at variable speeds. Although one can expect that a fast-swimming lure will attract muskies with some certainty, there doesn't seem to be any comparable formula for pike; sometimes a slow or moderately paced retrieve is most effective. It pays to vary the speed in any one cast, starting slow, then cranking fast at the halfway point as the spoon returns.

The northern pike is one of our most reliable gamefish, but there are times when it is more readily caught than others. In the southern part of its range, in Nebraska and Iowa and east to Ohio and Pennsylvania, the best fishing occurs in cold weather until May and June. For a very brief period after the spawning run, fishing is excellent. Almost all fish returning from spawning runs have empty stomachs, and this has proven to be one of the best times for large catches. Fish taken early in the morning invariably have empty stomachs from the previous night's digestion. This is why morning is considered one of the better fishing periods. Pike are more active during different times of the day. One study found that they were most active between 8:00 and 11:00 A.M. and between 2:00 and 4:00 P.M. There seemed to be a definite rest period between 11:30 A.M. and 1:00 P.M. After 1:00 P.M., activity reached its peak at 3:00 P.M. and then gradually declined toward evening. These periods of activity probably vary with the seasons and latitude. In the north, where days are longer, the peak of activity may be between 5:00 and 6:00 P.M.

After the water reaches 65° F., angling success lessens and the summer catches diminish. In the north, such as in Great Slave Lake in Saskatchewan, water temperatures rarely exceed 50° F. in the openwater and 60° F. in shallow water. Consequently, the average catch in June is only slightly higher than in July and August. The most consistent catches of northern pike are made in shallow water by fishing the holes in weed beds and patches of lily pads. In the spring, pike concentrate in large numbers in moderate-to-strong currents on the downstream side of barriers or falls. Fish usually strike readily in these areas, and large catches often result.

Jigs

A jig is an artificial lure consisting of a metal head to which a skirt of bucktail, feathers, or nylon is attached. The head of a casting jig is molded to the hook, while the traditional trolling jig or *feather* is threaded on a wire leader to which the hook is fastened. Jigs are made in many sizes from $1/16$ ounce to 6 ounces or more. They are designed for nearly all species of fresh- and salt-water fish. Jig heads are made slanted, ball shaped, oval shaped, bullet shaped, coin shaped, and keeled. It is the shape and weight of the head that functionally distinguish one jig from another. Being a compact mass of lead with very little air resistance, a jig casts easily and sinks readily. It rides hook up in the water and rests nose down, which provides some degree of immunity to snags. Presumably, jigs can suggest baitfish when moved rapidly through the water, not in the imitative sense of a plug, but because of motion and color. Primitive people all over the world have used crudely fashioned jigs made of bone or shell for centuries.

The Importance of Hook Sharpness

The first, and perhaps most vital, feature of a jig is the hook. On a lure of this type, a dull point just won't penetrate. Because of its hopping and diving action, a jig is often struck by the fish when the hook is at a tangent to the direction of the rod. When jigging in deepwater below a boat for instance, the hook bend instead of the point is facing the rod as the lure makes a free fall toward bottom. A great percentage of the time there is no reeling motion to start penetration, such a you have when retrieving a plug through the water. Furthermore, the jig is often grabbed by the fish when it's sitting perfectly still. Consequently, the point must be needle sharp. Until 1940, all jigs were made on heavy spear-point hooks, as they were used solely for saltwater clam busters like the striped bass. This didn't make much difference, as the heavy casting tackle of that era could drive a blunt nail home. But

Jigs

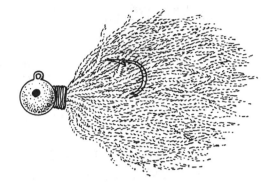

Ball

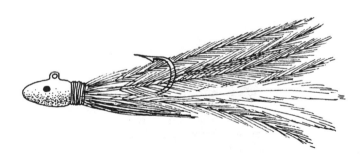

Coin

Bullet

Flat

with the advent of spinning tackle and the adaptation of jigs to freshwater fishing, hook sharpness became a real factor in success. Unfortunately, many lure makers, and anglers for that matter, felt that the flat, thick spearpoint was an integral part of the jig. More so than any other type of lure, the jig requires finely honed hollow points on properly tempered wire. The transition to quality hooks made a tremendous difference in both angling results and dealers' sales. A perfectly sharpened hook will "bite" no matter which way the fish hits.

Fishing with Jigs

In addition to jigs with hooks already masked in bucktail, nylon, marabou, and other materials, you should stock a variety of heads with bare hooks. There are numerous soft plastic lures such as worms, grub tails, splittails, and minnows, as well as attractors, such as the pork-rind eel, which can be attached to the hook. They are often more effective than the fixed skirts. These jig bodies are interchangeable, and you can switch colors or sizes quickly. Soft plastics and pork rind provide more action to the lure. In fresh- and saltwater fishing, jig heads in the ⅛- to ½-ounce range are ideal for spinning or spin-casting tackle, and sizes over ¼ ounce are for bait-casting gear. Special panfish jigs are made as small as ¹/₃₂ ounce.

Many different retrieves can be used with jigs. Whether you fish shallow or deep, letting the lure sink to the bottom then retrieving it in short hops is usually productive. When casting the wiggling plastic lures, such as worms or splittails, or a pork rind eel, a slow, steady retrieve may develop the best action. In thin-water you will need coin-shaped or flat heads for slow sinking, while in deepwater the oval or bullet heads will go down faster; ball-shaped heads provide an enticing action in deepwater when jigged up and down.

Soft Plastic Lures

These lures are made of flexible vinyl plastic. Plastic lures first become popular in the United States in 1957 and are marketed today in a variety of forms and sizes suitable for the fly rod, spinning rod, bait-casting rod, and for trolling in saltwater. Although the first soft lure was patented in the 1860s (a rubber worm), it wasn't until 1935, when the B. F. Goodrich Company produced a vinyl under the trade name Koroseal, that any significant progress occurred. This plastic material is ideal for molding, and it doesn't become brittle with age or variations in temperature. Lures designed to imitate worms, grasshoppers, crickets, hellgrammites, minnows, eels, maggots, shrimp, bloodworms, sandworms, mackerel, mullet, and a variety of other fish foods are now widely used.

Plastic Worms

The plastic worm in sizes from 1 inch to 15 inches in length, in all colors, and even flavors (various scents can be introduced to liquid plastic during the molding process) is the most popular lure of this genre. It is synonymous with black-bass fishing. Plastic worms can be purchased with hooks already rigged, but most anglers prefer to buy them in bulk, as the rigging is simple.

THE TEXAS RIG The basic method of rigging is the weedless sliding-sinker style or Texas rig. Usually a Sproat or Eagle's Claw hook pattern is used. The size selected depends on the length of the worm; 2/0 for 6-inch worms, 4/0 for 8-inch worms, and 6/0 for 10-inch worms or longer. This requires a bullet-shaped or cone sinker with a hole through the center; the sinker is threaded on the line in front of the hook. The hook point is pressed into the nose and back out the side of the worm, turned 180 degrees; the eye of the hook is then imbedded in the nose, and the hook point is pushed back into the worm so that it forms its own weed guard.

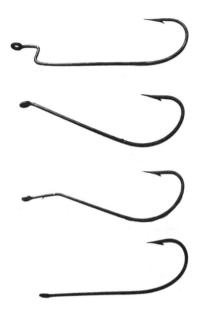

Hooks

Specialized hooks, varying
from 2/0–6/0, are made for
plastic-worm fishing. Bends or
shank barbs help hold the
worm in place.

THE SOUTH CAROLINA RIG   This rig will not work through
the heavy cover that a Texas rig is designed for but is used when
bass are suspended over vegetation or around open structures, such
as gravel bars or along clay banks. On the Carolina rig the worm
swims independent of the sinker, floating higher in the water and
2–3 feet behind it. This is accomplished with an egg-type sinker
that is secured 2–3 feet up the line behind a barrel swivel to prevent it from sliding down to the lure. A high-flotation plastic worm
is used so that it rises in the water during the pauses and stops in
a retrieve. If the sinker is left stationary on the bottom for a brief
period, you can feed out slack line and the worm will rise even
higher.

THE FLOATER RIG   The floater rig is simply a Texas rig without the sliding sinker. It is sometimes rigged with the hook point
exposed when fishing in water free of vegetation. A long worm of
8 inches or more is preferable to provide some casting weight. A
small split-shot sinker can be fixed at the worm nose, which adds
to the lure's action in a slow, headfirst dive during pauses on a
retrieve. The floating worm is most effective in shallow, weedy

The Texas Rig

Thread the monofilament through the bullet type of sliding sinker and tie on the hook.

To thread the worm, start the hook in the center of the worm's head at about a 30-degree angle, allowing some slack in the worm body so that it will be straight when it is imbedded. Then force the point outside the worm.

Turn the hook 180 degrees in the worm, covering the knot.

Impale the hook in the worm. The rig is now completed.

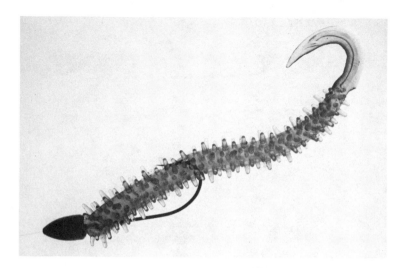

The Hook Worm®

water, and especially in the spring season. Because of its light weight, the floater rig is best fished with spinning tackle.

THE HOOK WORM®   The Hook Worm® is a design rather than a rig, first marketed in 1977. This plastic lure has spines all around the worm body acting as weed guards, which allow the hook point to be exposed. This self-hooking feature permits the use of lighter lines when cover conditions permit. It can be fished with lines as light as 4-pound test, although a somewhat heavier test is recommended under most conditions.

How to Fish with Plastic Worms

Plastic-worm fishing is a specialized technique. The most popular tackle is spinning and spin-casting gear with lines of 10- to 12-pound test and bait-casting gear with lines from 14- to 20-pound test in dense cover. A typical worming rod has a stiff action with a sensitive tip; distance casting is not important—the fishing is from the surface down to 50 feet or more.

The most popular worms are 4–8 inches in length, with blue, red, black, and purple the standard colors. Slip-sinker weights vary according to the depth fished, but the usual range is about ⅛–½ ounce. The lightest weight provides the best worm action, and this is dictated to some extent by line diameter; a heavy line will not cast or sink very readily with a light weight.

The basic worm retrieve is slow, moving the lure only 1 or 2 feet at a time. The reel is used only to take up slack line, while the rod moves the worm in short hops over the bottom. The sequence is to cast, let the lure sink with the line taut (strikes are often obtained as the worm drops toward bottom), then retrieve with the rod moving from near horizontal to vertical before lowering the tip to reel in the slack. The fisherman has to "feel" his way along the bottom. Bass seldom strike a worm hard. A typical strike is felt as if a small child were tugging at your sleeve, just a light *tap-tap*. With the buried hook point experienced bass fishermen *always* strike (or set the hook) as if they were going to break the rod. A forceful strike is necessary for two reasons. The large hook has to be driven through the worm and into the fish's jaw; secondly, the bass is usually in, or close to, heavy cover on the bottom, where any hesitation can mean a lost fish.

Lifelike Plastic Lures

There is a wide variety of imitative plastic on the market, which represents virtually all natural fish foods in lifelike detail. These can be used on fly-, spinning, or bait-casting outfits. Although none of the lifelikes have achieved the popularity of plastic worms, some of these are very effective for bass and panfish. The spider and cricket imitations are deadly for bluegills and smallmouth bass in the spring season; the plastic frog is a great largemouth and pike fooler when these fish are in shallow water.

Plugs

A plug is a lure usually designed in the shape of a small fish. These are often fanciful in both form and color. Plugs are also made to suggest frogs, mice, ducklings, and other forms of life utilized by gamefish as food. There are literally thousands of different plugs on the market, but these can be separated or selected on the basis of their individual function. There are five basic designs: popping, surface disturbers, floating-and-diving, sinking, and deep divers.

Size Standards

The first consideration in selecting a plug is its size. Back at the turn of the century, the standard bass lure weighed just a shade under 1 ounce. The weight had nothing to do with performance in the water—it was the amount necessary to put a casting bend in the stiff rods of 1900. Today's equipment is greatly refined. With ultralight spinning tackle the angler can cast $1/16$-ounce plugs, which are no bigger than a natural minnow. But for the man who uses regular spinning, spin-casting, or bait-casting tackle, the standards are ¼-ounce, ⅜-ounce, ½-ounce, and ⅝-ounce plugs. Broadly speaking, the ¼- to ⅜-ounce sizes are for refined fishing in clearwater with light tackle, while the ½- to ⅝-ounce plugs are the norm for nearly all other freshwater work. For beginners using regular bait-casting gear, an assortment of lures in the ⅜-ounce and ⅝-ounce weights are most practical. At the extremes, these are the easiest sizes to cast with a revolving-spool reel. It takes some thumbing skill to handle the lighter ¼-ounce plugs. But if you are using any kind of fixed-spool reel, don't hesitate to try these midgets on civilized ponds.

Plug Colors

The color of a plug is sometimes a determining factor in getting strikes. There is no one universal rule, not even for one species of fish. Local preferences can be learned at any tackle shop or boat livery. Just as a general guide for the beginner who is far from his fishing grounds, the following are basic: red-and-white, frog, black-scale, silver-flash, and yellow-polka-dot finishes. These five color patterns are old reliables throughout the country. If you are going to plug-cast in saltwater, then the silver-flash, blue-mullet, gold-flash, yellow-polka-dot, and green-scale finishes are good colors to start with. As a rule of thumb, small, dark, natural-looking plugs work best in transparent lakes, the kind of water where you'd fish for smallmouth bass; the bright colors and larger plugs are more suited to turbid water or periods when the light is dim. Needless to say, there are plenty of exceptions, but you can't go too far wrong by using imitative patterns, such as the perch, bluegill, shad, frog, or mullet. These are available in natural finishes. The important thing is to select plugs that function at the correct level or otherwise act in a way that will attract the fish.

Basic Plug Actions

The effectiveness of the five basic plug designs depends on your skill in retrieving. Assuming that you have learned to cast accurately to reasonable fishing distances, now it's important to develop a technique. By angling definition, *retrieving* simply means "recovery of the lure through reeling." But in actual practice, it's the final touch of success—your sword point in the delicate art of catching fish off their guard. Although technical advances have spawned a variety of nearly automatic baits, there are qualities of action that cannot be built into a plug or spoon.

Anybody who has fished very often is aware of that classic angling paradox: two men cast from the same boat, using the same lure, and one angler hooks fish to the point of monotony, while his companion feels like a charity case. A casual observer might say it's "luck," but it doesn't take a genius to realize that there is unending variation and novelty within a task, which, to a duller eye, might seem mechanical. The successful angler knows how to work his bait. Retrieving is the practice of innocent deceptions to make fish believe that metal and plastic are edible—a kind of artful storytelling in which the plug plays the role of a tired frog, leaping mullet, or whatever seems appropriate at the moment. The mere reeling of a lure is not enough. There are many retrieves that might be classified one from another on the basis of distinctive movements, but most anglers use four, which vary in speed and emphasis.

THE CORRECT SPEED   Different reels have different rates of line recovery. How many inches will be spooled with one turn of the handle depends on (1) how much line is on the reel, (2) the gear ratio, (3) the cranking radius of the handle, and (4) the spool diameter. A very small reel, with, say, a 2:1 gear ratio, is going to recover much less line than a large reel with a 4:1 ratio. It's possible, therefore, for a man to crank rapidly with the smaller reel and believe that he is making a fast retrieve, but his actual lure speed may be less than half of what it would be with the larger reel. Thus, we have a considerable degree of variation in what constitutes fast and slow, mechanically speaking. The most workable definition of a slow retrieve is the minimum speed at which the inherent action of a bait will function. If it's designed to wobble, it should wobble; if it's built to flap a pair of aluminum arms, it should flap. By the same token, a fast retrieve must imply the maximum speed at which these devices operate. If the plug is "straight," or completely without mechanical action of any kind, then we might define a slow retrieve as the maximum speed at which you can reel. In the latter case, this usually means the plug will skip over the water.

To determine the correct reeling speed on any particular day, it's a good idea to vary the retrieve every fifteen minutes, until you catch a fish or at least see one. On a fast retrieve, for instance, if a fish follows the lure for a long distance without striking, you can stop reeling and let the plug sit motionless on the water. There is a reasonable chance that he will strike when the plug is at rest or when it starts to move again. On subsequent casts, if more fish continue to follow without striking until the plug stops, it would indicate the reeling at a slower speed with pauses is going to be more effective. Conversely, you may get the same response to a slow retrieve; if the fish swims along behind the bait without hitting, then a sudden increase in reeling speed might trigger a strike. Of course, you don't have much chance of seeing fish when casting deep-running lures, but in this connection it's worth remembering that we all tend to work at a neutral speed, and it's usually the very slow or very fast retrieves that pay off.

THE CORRECT ROD POSITION   The correct rod position for any type of retrieve depends on the lure itself (its design and weight) and the length of line extended on the water. For example, a surface bait built to skip over the water is going to require your holding the rod very high. A darter, on the other hand, will require your pointing the tip downward to keep it weaving under the surface. And while you can begin all retrieves with a high rod on a long cast, the tip will have to be gradually lowered to work many baits; it becomes increasingly difficult, for instance, to pop a surface plug when the extended line length is shortened, because the lure is eventually pulled over, rather than under the water. An experienced angler gauges the correct rod position with each cast. He tries to keep the tip at an angle 45–60 degrees in relation to the line, whether he's working with tip up, down, or to the side. As much rod as possible should absorb the shock of a strike; yet it must never be so close to 90 degrees that he is unable to set the hook.

Popping Plugs

Poppers float on the surface, and when jerked with the rod tip they bury their hollow faces under the surface to create sounds and bubbles. Popping plugs come in all sizes, from the ¼-ounce spinning model to 4½-inch-long muskie baits. Some saltwater popping plugs weigh as much as 2½ ounces. They are also made in jointed models and skirted models, which add a bit of wiggle in addition to the noise, and when the face is elongated, they make a chugging sound instead of the usual *blup*. Poppers get their biggest play in shallow-water casting. It's customary to let them lie still until the splash made from falling on the surface has subsided. Then they are retrieved in a series of well-spaced jerks. Those plugs that have a pronounced action (some pop more loudly than others) will bring fish from greater depths than those that make a mere bubble. When bass are bottom feeding or even hiding among weeds in 10 feet of water, they will sometimes come up for a noisy bait. However, and this is significant, popping plugs do not always get strikes. Although a noisy surface plug might be blasted to splinters on occasion, there are times when that which attracts merely repels. Under these conditions, a surface-disturbing lure such as an injured-minnow plug or a nodding plug should provide just the right amount of action to bring the strike.

Popping Plug

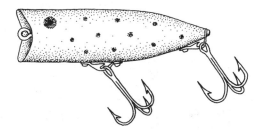

There are two fishing situations in which the popping plug is ideal. The first is when gamefish are chasing large schools of forage, such as the shad or the mullet. This occurs often in southern impoundments and tidal creeks, but it also happens periodically in large northern lakes when alewives and smelts are schooling. With clouds of baitfish in the water, the predators have plenty of targets, and the easiest way to get their attention is to put a popping plug in the area. For one thing, the lure looks like the helpless result of their feeding spree, and the sound will invariably command at least one fish to strike.

The second situation is more common. During periods of highwater, when the lake or river level is well up in the bank brush, a deftly placed popper sitting at the edge of the branches will attract fish from under their cover. Other types of baits would have to be in motion to get strikes, and this is one time when the sitting-and-talking plug has a tremendous advantage. The great majority of lunker bass caught on popping plugs are hooked in this fashion by casters who have the patience to work slowly. You must give the fish a chance to hear the lure, then allow enough time for the fish to find it.

Naturally, popping plugs work under a variety of conditions, such as night fishing, casting in the shallow-water holes of pad beds, and shoreline casting in the early morning and later-evening hours. However, other types of plugs can do as well and often better in these situations.

Surface Disturbers

Plugs of this type are more versatile than poppers and will often work when the bubble makers are ignored. The surface disturbers also float on top of the water, but unlike the popper, which must be fished slowly with pauses and jerks, these baits can be fished at varying speeds. Some surface disturbers can be *nodded*, or twitched in one spot; others can be worked from very slow to very fast and even skipped over the water; and still others have a regular swimming action at slow to moderate speeds. Surface disturbers are made in a variety of designs, incorporating metal arms, propellers, swinging legs, and even metal tails that flap on the water.

On calm days and even in bright sunlight, the nodding plug is often a killer on big bass. Nodding is pure fish psychology. It differs from popping in that you must assume that an old mossback is nearby and studying the plug. There is no need to attract his attention with noise. If the bass comes up for a look and swims

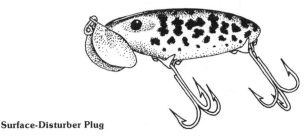

Surface-Disturber Plug

away—fine. Just leave the plug there, and after a while the fish will come back. Then nod your plug just a bit. The lure sits with its tail slanted down and its nose out of water, so when you move it slightly it tips forward like a paralyzed minnow. If the bass still isn't convinced, wait a bit longer and nod again. Do this often enough, and the bass will work up some real enthusiasm. You can also reel the plug along for 1–2 feet, and the rear propeller will make a wet purring sound. Then stop and nod. This plug should never be fished fast. It does its best work with a minimum of movement.

By contrast, the fore-and-aft-propeller lure works at all speeds. Its basic action is that of an injured minnow, when retrieved very slowly with long pauses and repeatedly directed with the rod tip from left to right. This is usually a good technique for evening bass fishing along rocky shores and lily beds. On days when the bass act like they went to sleep, you might try reeling this type of plug just as fast as you can crank. Skip it over the surface by jerking the rod tip. You will get the best action if you are using a long casting rod and standing on your feet. You have to keep a maximum length of line elevated from the water to make the plug act frantic. The idea is to convince the fish that something edible is hightailing for cover. This retrieve brings explosive strikes from logy summer gamefish. There are similar plugs, made without the propellers and with a longer and more slender shape, that are equally effective.

Many surface-disturbing lures have been created to resemble mice, frogs, and even ducklings. These all have to be fished slowly or at moderate speeds with short pauses. Such plugs are wholly imitative and give best results when a normal swimming action is duplicated. The proper way to fish a frog plug, for example, is to impart gentle kicking strokes with brief pauses. Allow the lure to stop occasionally, and, if possible, direct it toward a stump or lily pads. Live frogs are invariably heading for cover when they pass within reach of a gamefish.

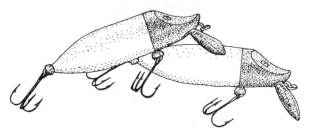

Floating-and-Diving Plug

Floating-and-Diving Plugs

Plugs of this type float at rest and dive when retrieved. They differ from the darters in having a more erratic side-to-side action, which is induced by a metal lip, grooved head, or flat front profile. Floating-and-diving plugs also work somewhat deeper, planing 3–7 feet down, depending on the length of your cast and the speed of your retrieve.

There are two ideal situations for floating-and-diving plugs. The first is when you are are casting toward a bank with a sloping shoreline; the plug can be reeled slowly in the shallow area and fished almost like a surface disturber, then speeded along to dive deeper as it passes over the drop-off. Naturally, this works in reverse for the bank caster or wading angler. The plug can be tossed far from shore, worked back deep, then, by slowing the retrieve, it can be steered over the inshore weed beds. Reflected light or water color will give some indication of the depth of various points, and the reeling speed should be adjusted accordingly.

The second spot is over a submerged weed bed in deepwater. Often you will find weed beds that come within 4–5 feet of the surface way out in the middle of the lake. Big bass, northerns, and muskies hide in the plant fronds and watch for food in the open area above. The floating-and-diving plug can be passed just over the weed tops when retrieved at the correct speed. Reel very slowly where the weeds are nearest the surface and faster as the plug approaches a deep hole. Rapid reeling causes the plug to dive deeper, but you can stop reeling in a fishy-looking pocket and twitch the plug with short pulls as it slowly rises toward the surface.

Floating-and-diving plugs are also very useful in early morning and late-evening trolling, when the fish are feeding in water of moderate depth. Unlike straight-sinking plugs, lures of this type are buoyant and will come to the surface when you slow the boat's speed or execute short turns. This prevents getting snagged and is ideal for the solo angler who is paddling or rowing his own skiff.

Sinking Plugs

Plugs of this type sink immediately upon contact with the water. Some sink slowly and can be worked at various depths according to how long you wait before beginning the retrieve. Inasmuch as the rate of descent is constant with any one plug, it's a good idea to count how many seconds it requires for the lure to drop to a fish-taking level. Although most sinking plugs have a slim profile and must be worked with the rod, others are fish shaped and have some incorporated action in the form of propellers. Fast-sinking plugs are designed for special conditions. One popular bait used in saltwater is exceptionally heavy for its overall size; the plug is 3¼ inches long, yet it weighs 1 ounce. On account of its nose design and location of the eye ring, the plug has a violent wiggling action.

The thing that makes a sinking plug valuable is that it can be handled in several ways. When casting on strange water, use different retrieves, starting with slow, steady reeling at various depths. After the plug has been worked from a few feet below the surface to near bottom without a strike, let the lure go down and bump gravel. If this doesn't produce, repeat the original casts in depth, but this time using a somewhat faster retrieve with short pauses every few feet. This causes the plug to dart ahead, then settle down. The sinking plug can also be pumped in short and long strokes at fast speed, which give it a very enticing action. However, the latter technique is more effective in saltwater than in freshwater. Actually, the practical distinction between a sinking plug and a deep diver is seen right here; the former can be varied

Sinking Plug

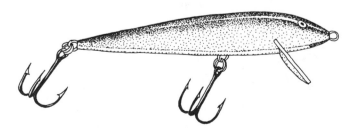

to a greater degree in speed and action. The strike-provoking, side-to-side wiggle of a disc-lipped deep diver, which must swim at a more or less constant speed, is not nearly as effective for species such as spotted sea trout, bluefish, snook, and ladyfish as the straight sinker, which has little, if any, lateral motion.

Midget sinkers are first-rate lures for river smallmouths. These plugs can be fished in fairly rapid water, whereas baits that have metal lips, hollow faces, or widely curved surfaces will not function properly. Water resistance would force them to the top or destroy their built-in action completely. The sinker with a propeller fore-and-aft has enough flash and motion to attract gamefish, and yet its streamlined shape keeps the plug deep. Naturally, midget sinking plugs can be used in lakes and for species other than the smallmouth. Remember that a sinking plug doesn't necessarily have to be used in water that is very deep.

Deep Divers

Deep divers are versatile lures and are used for black bass, pike, muskellunge, and walleyes. Most deep-diving plugs sink immediately upon contact with the water. However, some are designed to float before diving down to 30 feet or more. Unlike regular sinking plugs, whose depth is regulated by their specific gravity and by your retrieving speed, the deep divers have broad metal lips that cause the lure to plane downward as you reel. The depth attained depends on the design, length, and angle of the lip. Some plugs dive deeper than others; you should stock shallow, medium, and deep divers. To work these *crank baits* properly, start with a fast retrieve to get the plug swimming toward bottom, then reel at a medium speed.

The ideal situation for deep-diving plugs is in a lake or stream where the fish are holding below the 15-foot level. This generally occurs in July and August and on bright days when adult gamefish retreat to deeper water. Finding the right spot depends to a great

Deep-Diving Plug

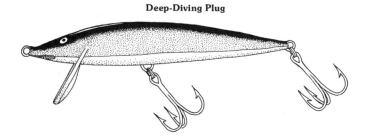

extent on the type of lake you are fishing. For instance, a rock-rimmed pond with little or no weed area inshore is usually more productive out where there are submerged beds of rooted vegetation or gravel shoals. You will often see yearling bass chasing schools of minnows along the pond margin, and, consequently, the natural impulse is to favor shoreline casting with topwater baits. But heavy bronzebacks feed beyond the drop-off in warm weather, and they can be reached with deep-running plugs. As a rule of thumb, topwater baits work best after the sun has touched the horizon and again from dawn until 9:00 A.M. Sinking plugs and deep divers fished over the drop-off adjacent to gravel points, shale banks, shoals, and submerged weed beds at the 15- to 30-foot level are productive midday lures. Black bass are often caught at the 40- to 60-foot level in southern impoundments during hot weather.

Fishing for River Smallmouths

The most important thing you can learn about bass fishing in a particular river is the seasonal "pattern" in fish behavior. Different types of habitats will attract and hold smallmouths at certain times of the year. To be sure, you will find young bass scattered over various parts of any good river, but their presence can be misleading, as the catchables of 12 inches or more (or from 1 pound up) are more selective in a territorial sense. Although river smallmouths do not undertake extensive migrations, they do move short distances—from shallow to deep riffles or from pools to pocketwater and even into backwaters and sloughs, according to the season. There is a variety of reasons for this phenomenon, such as the abundance or scarcity of specific foods, the loss of cover during lowering water levels, or the availability of new forage during rising water and correlated temperature changes (smallmouths begin active feeding at about 60° F., with the preferred range at 70°–80° F., but feeding ceases at about 50° F.). The skilled angler recognizes the productive spots; they may be shallow, rock-bottomed pools, with only a moderate current in the spring season; the main channel edges during summer, or the slackwater of deep pools, where there is no apparent current in the cooler temperatures of autumn. There is no universal rule, and it's difficult for the angler on a strange river to get an immediate "reading." In most cases, the substrate or type of bottom is a useful clue with which to begin working.

The least productive are bedrock and sand. These substrates are low in productivity, the bedrock being constantly scrubbed by the current, and the sand shifting with every change in velocity. Aquatic organisms will not thrive here. Coarse gravel and slab rock (as opposed to rounded stones or boulders) are usually most productive of bass foods, but ledges and long grassy banks often attract smallmouths for brief periods, regardless of the bottom composition. Remember that river bass, like their lake counterparts, are cover conscious and most commonly hide in rock crevices when not actively feeding. Normally, this is where the smallmouth remains during the winter months when water temperatures hit the low 40s. Once the possible lair is established, it must be fished slowly and carefully, with a minimum of casts. Throwing a lure out and bringing it back again and again is a habit that the trophy hunter cannot afford. The first cast should swing into the holding water at the proper depth and then be worked with all the art you can muster. Never be in a hurry. Sometimes a smallmouth will take a bait the instant it hits the water, but more often the area has to be covered carefully, and the fish may not make a pass until the fifth or sixth swim. If you are lucky and take a good bass, continue working the same area, as smallmouths are seldom alone, and frequently there will be a fair number of comparable-sized fish within a few feet of where the first one was hooked. Rest the area or change lures, but don't move too quickly to a new location. The active feeding area on that particular day may be a short stretch of no more than a 100 yards in a half-mile-long riffle, which is often the case on big bass streams. For this reason, the wading angler often has an advantage over the float-boat caster. When float fishing, it is profitable to anchor, or at least beach, the boat after hooking a big smallmouth and comb the surrounding water. A float trip should consist of at least 50 percent wading, whether the quarry is bass or trout. A boat is a great advantage, in that you can cover many more hot spots than can the angler traveling by foot.

When you begin to catch bass, make a mental note of the depth, type of bottom, and current velocity. If it's a gravel-bottomed shoal of 2–4 feet in depth with a moderate flow, look for identical situations along the river. Try other types of water if you must, but the chances of success are greatly enhanced at every similar location. This may go on for a week or even a month, then abruptly the pattern will change; the shoals are literally barren, and the bass congregate in stillwater along deep shores at drop-offs, or they may move into the deepest portion of the main channel and remain at depths of 12–15 feet.

The successful angling for stream smallmouths requires not only attention to details but a flexible method of casting. You must be able to work from top to bottom at various speeds and with light lures. Fly-fishing is dependent on the bass being in shallow water or at least rising to insects of some kind, and is based on the results of many seasons; it more or less boils down to those glorious periods in June and September—with exceptions, of course. Bait casting with a multiplying reel is somewhat more effective through the angling year, but some of the best smallmouth lures weigh less than the ¼-ounce weight, which is the practical minimum for revolving-spool outfits. The ideal tackle is a 6- or 6½-foot spin stick with a total weight of about 3 ounces, mounted with a light spinning reel spooled in 6-pound-test monofilament. This is plenty strong for river bassing (where 3-pound fish are exceptional) and permits long, delicate casts with ⅛- to ⅜-ounce baits.

Fishing for Walleyes

It is questionable whether any freshwater species has greater angling value than does the walleye. Wherever it is found in abundance, it is the primary target of most anglers. Walleyes strike readily, are generally concentrated in schools, attain a large size, and are unexcelled in eating qualities. They are especially easy to catch during their spawning period in the spring of the year. Jigs, spinners, deep-diving and sinking plugs, and small wobbling spoons are the basic lures on light-to-medium spinning, spin-casting, or bait-casting tackle. There are six basic facts that the successful angler should keep in mind: (1) Walleyes tend to congregate in schools; when you catch one, it is likely that there are others in the same spot or vicinity. (2) Except on rare occasions walleyes are found on the bottom of the lake or river, so the odds are with you if you keep your bait on or very near the bottom. (3) The primary food of walleyes is fish, and your lure should closely resemble a live fish. (4) Walleyes usually are found near or on a sandbar, reef, or other physical structure that provides a good feeding area in close proximity to deeper waters. (5) Walleyes usually are slow and methodical in taking food; keep your lure moving very slowly and give the walleye plenty of time to look it over. (6) After their spawning period, walleyes feed primarily during the evening and night hours, so you can expect the best results after the sun goes down.

Flies

Artificial flies are made in various styles. There are six general classifications: dry fly, wet fly, nymph, streamer fly, bucktail, and bug. However, there is some structural variation within each type of fly according to the kind of fish sought, as well as imitative requirements.

DRY FLY The dry fly is an artificial fly on which the hackle fibers project at approximate right angles to the hood so that the fly floats on the surface, imitating a floating insect of some kind. An ideal dry fly is made buoyant by its materials, but a chemical paste or liquid is applied for waterproofing. There are special dry flies made without hackles and with hackles that lie parallel to

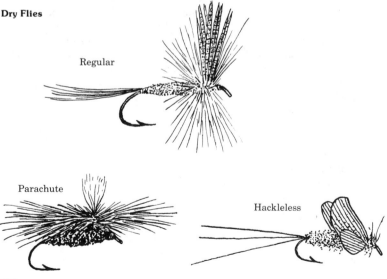

Dry Flies

Regular

Parachute

Hackleless

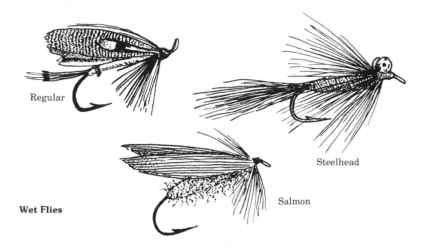

Regular

Steelhead

Salmon

Wet Flies

the hook shank. Dry flies are used for a variety of freshwater species.

WET FLY   The wet fly is a sparsely dressed artificial fly that is somewhat flat in appearance. It is fished under the surface and generally imitates a submerged insect. An ideal wet fly has "good entry" and sinks immediately upon contact with the water. Wet flies are used for a variety of freshwater species; distinctions in size and style of dressing are found between those used for trout, steelhead, and salmon.

NYMPH   A nymph represents the larval or nymphal stage of aquatic insects. Because of the similar angling techniques em-

Nymph Flies

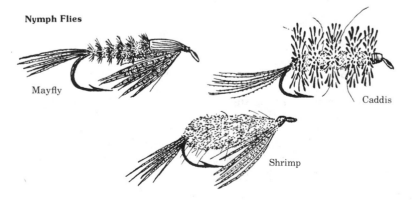

Mayfly

Caddis

Shrimp

ployed, it may also include other subaquatic forms, such as the freshwater shrimp. Like the wet fly, the nymph is fished under the surface. Nymph patterns lack wings but may have wing pads. Primarily a trout fly, a nymph can be used for other insect-feeding freshwater game- and panfish.

STREAMER FLY   A streamer fly is an artificial fly made with a long-feather or -hair wing and designed to imitate a minnow or other foragefish. Streamer flies are used in both fresh- and saltwater fishing.

Streamer Flies

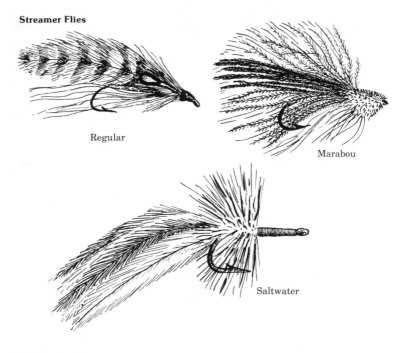

Regular

Marabou

Saltwater

BUCKTAIL   The bucktail is an artificial fly made with a long-hair wing and designed to imitate a minnow or other foragefish. The name is derived from the common use of hair from the tail of a deer for making the wing. Bucktails are used in both fresh- and saltwater fishing. Unlike the streamer fly, which is very similar in design and function, a bucktail is durable, and for that reason it is preferred by many anglers who fish where large or sharp-toothed species are common.

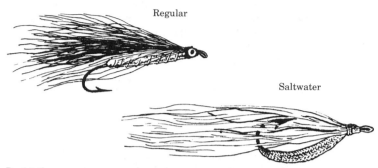

Regular

Saltwater

Bucktails

BUG The bug is a fly-rod lure designed to imitate a variety of aquatic and terrestrial foods, such as moths, mice, frogs, bees, and dragonflies. Although a bug floats on the water, it is distinguished from a dry fly in having a bulky body made of cork, plastic, balsa, or natural hair; hackle feathers may be used in making the wing

Bass Bugs

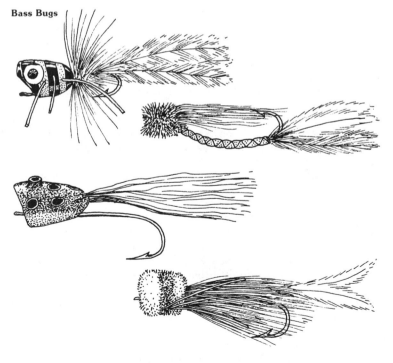

or tail, and the wings are usually turned down over the body or at horizontal angles. Bass bugs are usually tied on large hooks (No. 4 to 2/0); however, smaller and very similar versions are made for panfish. They may also be tied of durable materials for saltwater fishing, in which case the lures are identified as saltwater bugs.

How to Buy Artificial Flies

In an art form that demands strict adherence to the rules, one would expect all flies of one pattern to be exactly alike. But even with the same ingredients, no two fly dressers achieve exactly the same result. For one thing, it is difficult to tie a pattern correctly from a book description. You must have a model to work from; give one printed description to twenty different tiers, and you have roughly the same fly but twenty distinct styles. Some fly dressers use more hackle, longer wings or tails, or fuller bodies, and as a result, the angler generally develops a favorite professional according to what he (the angler) feels is ideal. However, quality does count, and the skilled fly tier will rarely stray from conventional patterns or materials. Naturally, he will dress some originals now and then, but if he runs out of prime hackles he will not substitute, say, a red-brown for a chocolate-brown, even though most people wouldn't know the difference.

Obviously, if you start out buying imitations of all the insects that hatch on American rivers, you will spend a small fortune. Even a basic collection can be an expensive project, and after the investment of several hundred dollars—sometimes an important one. For one thing, there's a tendency to collect patterns rather than types, and it's easy to wind up with dozens of flies that were all designed for the same job. Some anglers carry enough feathers to stuff a large mattress, and yet there are many occasions when they lack the right type of fly.

To begin with, regional conditions have a definite influence on your stock. A man coming from New England to fish a Rocky Mountain river, for instance, may not be prepared with the rough-hair flies that are so effective in western rivers. It's a good general rule to buy your flies in the locale you intend to fish. However, if you know a top-notch professional nearby, the chances are that he is aware of those patterns being used in other areas. At least, you can be sure of getting quality flies. You don't want hackle unraveling and wings snapping out, even if the pattern is correct. But no matter where you live, a basic assortment can be acquired that will stand the test of time and travel.

Nymph Fishing

Nymph fishing is acknowledged to be the most difficult phase of the fly-rod art. Yet, with some degree of casting skill and careful attention to details, it quickly becomes a reliable method of catching trout on artificials. Natural nymphs are providentially abundant at all seasons of the year, and, regardless of weather conditions, one can usually take enough fish to make the day successful. Some wet flies are really nymph imitations, and undoubtedly a great percentage of trout caught on sunk patterns are nymphing fish who made their error in the pursuit of subaquatic food. The difference between the wet-fly method and the nymph method is arbitrary, but broadly speaking, the latter eliminates patterns and techniques that would apply to the imitation of noninsect forms, such as fry or shrimp.

SEASONAL PICTURE   There is a great deal to be said for the study of entomology, whether it be a formal university course or simply reading a few good books on it at home. It's one of many subjects that can broaden your knowledge of the outdoors. The angler, however, needs no more than working familiarity with trout-hunted insects; he should be able to identify the most important groups and have a capsule idea of their life cycles. He should know which species are most abundant in his area and their expected period of emergence. Four of the groups are wholly aquatic, and it's particularly pertinent to know the size and color of their nymphs and larvae. Although mayflies are the most important insect as far as the dry-fly angler is concerned (with regional variations, of course), the underwater larder is more complex. The general picture is seasonal with mayfly nymphs, caddis larvae, stonefly nymphs, and the nymphs of dragon- and damselflies dominating at certain periods. However, their very abundance permits the angler a considerable latitude in his choice of artificials. For example, the complete cycle of a mayfly, from the time the nymph hatches from its egg until it emerges from the water as a winged adult, can require two years. Thus, the trout's larder is always full, and proof of that can be found on any stream-bottom rock. Turn it over, and you will discover speckled-brown or amber-colored nymphs clinging to the underside. They have a flattened contour, which, together with their strong clawed legs, enables them to hold their position in a strong current. As the weather warms, you will also find the empty shucks of skins of these same nymphs adhering to sun-dried rocks. When ready to emerge, many species complete their metamorphosis by crawling atop the stones to shed. On insect-rich rivers, the domes of boulders might literally be encrusted with shucks. All nymphs do not hatch in the same way, and a great many of them live in sand, mud, and silt. Although they are similar in form, nymphs are not always the same color and size. As a matter of fact, there are hundreds of different larvae that are common to American rivers. This is something of an advantage, because an artfully tied imitation is seldom questioned by a hungry trout. It's not unusual to catch a fish with an artificial mayfly pattern when its stomach contents reveal that it has been gorging on caddis larvae. In brief, there is more to be said for the method than for any preoccupation with what to use. Some patterns are superior to others, but, in general, any of the standards will work. Most important is your ability to present the fly properly and to use suitable tackle.

METHODS OF FISHING THE NYMPH   Trout feed very little during the winter months, but rising temperatures in the spring whet their dulled appetites for the abundance of nymph life that flourished even while snow banked the hemlocks. In the beginning of the season, when April rivers are still cold and before the hatches have started, an artificial nymph should be handled quite differently from the way it is fished later on. The fly must be presented at the trout's level, which, in the early days, is near bottom. You can't really fish too slow or too deep. The same condition may hold true of the hottest days in summer, when trout are gathered at the spring holes. By late August on eastern rivers, the currents grow quite stale; a few rings of dirty foam float apathetically around the eddies. Downstream fishing is often hopeless. Trout always lie facing the flow, and you can therefore approach them more closely from behind. The nymph also drifts more naturally when fished upstream. The basic attack in August is to work upriver with a long, 5X leader and a small nymph, keeping it as close to the bottom as possible. It's all "fine and far-off" fishing with drag-free drifts and careful wading. The fish strike very gently, and one must watch the water and any visible part of line or leader for the slightest movement that indicates a strike. Hooking a trout on the dry fly is easy by comparison. With floaters, the chief difficulty is striking too fast. Nymphs, on the other hand, are out of sight, and you must acquire an almost automatic reflex to tighten at just the right instant. And there's the additional hazard of breaking off if the strike is made too forcefully. But with experience you will find yourself hooking fish without even thinking about it.

Casting upstream is usually the most effective way to handle a nymph. You must put the artificial in places where trout are likely to feed and let the current carry it along at a natural pace. As with the dry fly, you should raise your rod slightly and strip line by hand to keep the nymph free of drag. Sometimes the best level to work is directly on the surface; there are periods when fish station themselves near the top to grab nymphs that are drifting with the current. On other occasions you'll find most of the trout foraging a few feet down, or, as it so often happens on opening day, they'll be directly on the bottom. If the river is very heavy and you can't face the current, then you can fish downstream by casting a slack line and allowing the nymph to sink deep as it drifts below your position. Don't recast immediately. Give the nymph a few twitches when it swings to a stop. There are runs and pools where you can take trout in both directions and other places where you must face one way to get strikes. But the importance of fishing a nymph at the correct depth cannot be overemphasized.

SINKING LINE VERSUS FLOATING LINE   To reach a wide range of depths, many nymph specialists carry an extra reel spooled with a sinking-type fly line. Although the more commonly used floating type is adequate to most stream problems, in water that is very deep or very swift it's almost impossible to work a nymph correctly unless the trout are actively feeding near the surface. There are a number of nicely balanced and smoothly finished lines of this type on the market that eliminate the need for split shot to pull a fly under. Depending on the height of the stream, either cast up or down; if the current is normal or at summer level, work up; but if it's high, work down. The trout may hold along submerged ledges 10–12 feet or more in depth. The problem in catching fish here is to get the nymph right on the bottom. To accomplish this, make a slack cast up and across the stream; then by shaking out more footage through the guides, the line sinks quickly as it swings downstream. You shouldn't miss too many trout this way. In deep, heavywater, fish take the nymph solidly, and it often happens that they hook themselves against the pull of the line.

In contrast, there are times when the artificial nymph must be fished at the surface. For one or two years, a mayfly nymph is subaqueous, but in the last stage of its existence it develops a hump on the part that would correspond to shoulders; this is the growing wings, which fly tiers refer to as the wind pad. When ready to emerge, the nymph rises to the surface, and while floating downstream, its nymphal shell is split and shucked off. The shriveled-looking insect that appears from the shell is a subimago, which anglers call the *dun*. Although the dun is at first unable to fly, its wings soon dry and become strong enough to carry the mayfly off to find shelter along the streamside. There it awaits its next metamorphosis to the imago. Two stages in this cycle that are of particular interest to the trout are when the nymph is floating helplessly on the surface, and of course, when the duns hatch. The latter is a dry-fly problem. The former, however, is a nymphing situation. During the period preceding a hatch, trout take position in the current where they can expect an abundance of nymphs, and without moving more than a few feet, each fish commences to gorge. In quiet runs, trout are often seen balanced on their fins just below the surface, turning left and right, as they sip their food. Under these conditions, a floating-type line is a necessity, and it's often advantageous to grease all but the last few feet of your leader to keep the nymph just under or on the surface film.

CADDIS LARVA   Next to the mayfly nymphs, the caddis larvae are very important. As a subaquatic food, the caddis probably surpasses the mayfly in many eastern rivers where the Ephemeridae are seasonally scarce. Although there is no actual nymph stage in the development of a caddis fly (the insect has a complete metamorphosis from egg to larva, and pupa to adult), the larva is taken greedily by the trout from the stream bottom even while wrapped in its case. As in a mayfly cycle, some caddis pupae have a vulnerable period when they drift on the surface. So from the angler's point of view he is imitating a caddis "nymph." The presence of these larvae in any stream is easily established. Caddis are the house builders, whose tiny sand, pebble, and twig cases are visable on the rocks. Some are cemented in place by the larvae, and others are portable; by means of strong hooks in its tail the caddis can drag its home about. But trout often eat the occupant, house and all. This accounts for the sticks and pebbles so often found in fish stomachs. Brook trout are especially inclined to gorge on caddis larvae. There are many good imitations available in white, cream, green, and dirty gray, which are the common colors of the naturals.

STONEFLY NYMPH   The stonefly nymph is next to the caddis larva in importance. It is generally similar to the mayfly in form and color but somewhat larger in size. Even old brown trout are inclined to get careless when stoneflies are abundant, and during a hatch, they take the adult voraciously. However, the significant emergences occur on relatively few midwestern, western, and far-northern rivers. In the eastern United States one does not find anything resembling these cloudlike "salmon-" or "willow-" fly hatches that create such remarkable angling. But stonefly nymphs are numerous in rocky, fastwater rivers throughout this range, and many good patterns are dressed to imitate them, such as Dark Stonefly, Golden Stonefly, Little Yellow Stonefly, Early Brown Stonefly, Large Stonefly, and March Brown. Generally speaking, and especially in the spring season, stonefly nymphs are most effective when fished close to the bottom. It is worthwhile to have at least a few artificials tied with weighted bodies. On turbulent rivers the stonefly nymph is usually fished up and across the current so that it sinks deep in the flow and swings downstream without drag. Quite often a nymph will be taken by the trout after it has settled to the bottom and been left there for several minutes. This is a good technique to use at the head of large pools where the current breaks.

The artificial nymphs vary in size from No. 4 down to No. 14 (many of the common nemourids are quite small, although they contribute greatly to the trout's food supply in some streams). As a rule, the large No. 4 dressings are most effective in heavy rivers such as the Delaware in the east or the Madison in the west. Most stonefly imitations are brown or tan in color, but these nymphs exist in variety and patterns in green, gray, and black with lighter colored undersides; bright yellow or orange markings are regionally effective.

MIDGE LARVA   Why trout should forage on this tiny wormlike creature when more substantial insect foods are available is a mystery. Winged adults resemble miniature mosquitoes as they swarm over the water during the emergence. Trout will roll, bulge, sip, and flash at the surfacing pupae, seldom more than ¼ inch long and usually much smaller. As with the caddis, we are not dealing with an actual nymph, but rather a stage in an insect's metamorphosis, one which requires nymphing technique to emulate.

There are two distinct ways of fishing a midge. If a dry pattern is called for, it is oiled and left floating on the surface. Let the fly sit quietly for some time before giving it a twitch. If this doesn't bring a strike, then retrieve the floater slowly with short pauses before picking it from the water. However, if the trout are feeding on the larvae and pupae of the midge, you will have to fish below the surface. The idea here is to cast and let the fly sink, then make it behave like the larvae coming up from the bottom. It should be drawn slowly to the surface; then after a sufficient pause to let the midge sink again, you repeat the process. Sometimes trout will strike the instant your fly hits the water, and occasionally they will hit a midge drawn across the surface.

There are times, also, when trout will seek midge larvae along the bottom, and you'll have to fish very deep for them. This takes a nice sense of touch, because the strike will be no more than a slight movement of the line. Using a sinking fly line, let the midge go down about 12–15 feet. Sometimes the strike comes when the fly is sinking, but usually it happens on the draw.

THE LEADER   It is seldom effective to present a midge on a leader tapered heavier than .006 inch. A thick point destroys the illusion of a natural and prevents the fly from moving freely with the current. If you have a delicate hand, you can work safely with tippets from 5X nylon (.006 inch) to 7X (.004 inch). These sizes are suitable for No. 18 to No. 22 hooks. At first glance, you make think that such light terminal tackle cannot hold large trout. This is a mistake, because the tiny, fine-wire hooks will slip in the skin of the mouth and bite firmly. As a matter of fact, you will often have difficulty removing the barb. There is also a trick to using 7X nylon safely; never make your leader with a short tippet section. Most anglers tend to believe that the less fine material they put in a leader the stronger it will be, whereas the opposite is true. You can feel the difference when unrolling a spool of, say, 1-pound test. If you take a few inches of the nylon between your fingers and pull, it snaps quite easily. Now roll off about 40 inches and pull (from both ends). The monofilament stretches, and it takes considerably more effort to break it. You should always add at least 3 feet of tippet, and on a 12-foot leader, do not hesitate to use between 40 and 50 inches of the 1-pound test for maximum elasticity.

ADVANTAGE OF LIGHT TACKLE   The tackle you use for midge fishing is important. You cannot work with a heavy line or a stiff rod because either one will snap a fine leader on the strike. The rod may be short or long, but it must be flexible. Some builders make extra-light wands specifically for delicate casting; one popular "midge" rod is 6 feet, 3 inches long and weighs 1¾ ounces, complete. In a specialist sense, these are the ideal dimensions for a very light fly rod. Your regular trout outfit might be perfectly suitable, however, and some idea of its ability can be judged by the line size used. The rod should not require a line much heavier than a No. 5. Any larger size will offer too much water resistance for smooth striking with fine leaders.

HOW TO STRIKE FISH   The real problem in using a fine leader is in striking the fish, and this requires a little practice. You don't really set the hook at all. Just tighten on the line and keep a steady pressure with no wrist jerk. This is difficult, particularly for experienced anglers with whom an instantaneous strike at the taking of the fly is reflexive. The strike in midge fishing must be firm, but it must also be calculated between the fine tippet and the weight of the fish. Fortunately, midge fishing is almost always done in waters that are relatively still, where you can see the trout rise and play the fish without the hazard of a wild current. Naturally, you will break off some fish ˙no matter how carefully you work, but if the number of breaks becomes excessive, then something is wrong with your tackle.

Wet-Fly Fishing

Wet-fly fishing is an important early-season method of angling for trout when the rivers are flowing high and cold. There is little surface activity at this time, and the fish forage on larval insect forms, which various wet-fly patterns may imitate. While the dry fly is usually fished upstream and allowed to drift in a natural manner, the wet fly is fished in a number of ways: upstream, down, across, and with or without some motion imparted by the rod. As a rule, the angler casts diagonally across the stream, letting the fly swing down in the current, and when the line starts to drag, the angler brings the fly to life with the rod tip. The line is retrieved in short pulls, and, ordinarily, a few trout will always find the swimming fly attractive enough to strike. Sometimes more fish respond if your retrieve is very slow, and on other occasions, if your return is fast.

THE WET FLY DOWNSTREAM   The wet fly fished downstream is perhaps the easiest method for the beginning angler to use in catching trout. For one thing, you will be wading with the current, which is physically less fatiguing than working upstream, particularly when wearing heavy clothing and waders. And whatever might be gained by getting the fly deeper in upstream casting is invariably lost when the neophyte handles the returning slack line. The role of the line hand is less important in downstream fishing. It won't be necessary to cast more than 30–35 feet. You may see some good-looking water along the far bank, but for the first day, concentrate on keeping your back cast high, and practice making short casts with a minimum of false casting. Each time a cast is completed, place the line on your rod-hand forefinger, so that when you retrieve, the line slides over it. You needn't squeeze your forefinger against the corks; keep your hand relaxed and your wrist somewhat stiff. By holding the line close to the rod, you will have complete control of the slack between the butt guide and your line hand, which makes it easier to hook a fish. If you simply pull line directly from the rings with your left hand, the rod no longer commands the situation. The forefinger hold also expedites handling of the slack with your line hand. When a cast is fished out, drop the line from your finger and cast again.

PRESENTATION   Tactically, you should try to modify each cast according to the speed of the current and the depth of the river. In a quiet pool you may be able to cast straight across the stream, and when your line begins to sweep around below your position the fly will almost be bumping bottom. In a swift, deep riffle you will probably have to aim the cast almost directly upstream to get the fly down to the same depth. In any case, you'll know when the fly is not being fished correctly because it will show at the surface. If you come to a place where the currents are varied and the line belly floats too fast, thereby pulling the fly to the top, you can correct the speed with slack. To adjust the drift of a wet fly, release a few yards of line just as the belly part begins to gather speed. If the current isn't strong enough to pull the line from your hand, give the rod a few shakes up and down, and it will slide out of the guides. The addition of slack takes the tension off the line and causes the fly to sink deeper. In time you will learn the many nuances of directing and mending your casts, but all you have to think about at first is putting that fly near a trout.

As you look downstream, you will see slick places in the bouncy water: boulder tops, and perhaps old logs or tree roots, and undercut banks. These all provide cover for the trout. Do not cast at them, however, because the fly won't be swimming deep enough when it passes these lies. Always think in terms of aiming your cast so that (1) the fly has enough time and slack to sink deep and (2) it reaches the fish just as your line completes its swing across the surface. If you are lucky enough actually to see a trout splash, follow the same rule of aiming a proper length of line upstream from its position and let the fly sweep around to it. What really happens when the line tightens in the current after the swing is that the fly comes to life. It rises like an insect from the bottom and moves toward the surface. This is a natural motion for an emerging nymph or larva that has left its gravel home and is swimming toward the top. So even if your wet fly passes several feet under a surfacing trout, it will arc up to the trout's level in a lifelike manner. You may notice, incidentally, that most of your wet-fly strikes occur at the moment your line has completed a swing.

THE STRIKE The strike is the only difficult part of wet-fly fishing. When a trout strikes the fly, you must hook it. Fish sometimes hook themselves on artificials, but the great majority mouth and eject the fly in a split second. This is countered by raising the rod up and back with enough pressure to sink the barb, yet not so forcefully that the leader might snap. You may miss quite a number of fish in the beginning and probably break off on a few more before a sharp reflex is developed. Eventually, it will become an automatic response to the strike, whether you actually see, feel, or sense the take. Fortunately, early-season trout usually strike hard because of hunger and the strong currents. A fish must act fast to seize its food—and you feel the impact as a rubbery *pluck* at the fly. If the trout misses and you see its flash or disturbance, don't draw the fly away, but give it a few twitches with the rod tip so that it darts forward a few inches and settles back. If nothing happens in the next minute, pull the fly from the trout's position slowly with continued twitching. Next, repeat the cast to the same place by aiming up or across the stream and letting the fly swing around again. If there are no further signs of interest after three or four casts, keep moving downstream. The fish is down for the moment, but mark the spot for later reference. After an hour or so it will probably be feeding freely again.

FISHING UNDERCUT BANKS One of the most productive spots for the wet fly is a long undercut bank, particularly one that has a run of whitewater at the head of it. Hollow banks are natural food collectors and also provide cover for big trout. Position yourself so that the fly can be cast slightly upstream into the ripply flow and can be left to swing down into the hole. Judging by the conformation of the bank, the stream is probably 6–8 feet deep at this point; so don't hurry the fly along. After making the cast, follow the line around with your rod (the tip should be at eye level) so that there is a minimum of drag and you are prepared for a strike. Depending on how the line point reacts, you can do one of several things. If the line twitches or jumps as though it hit a bump, set the hook. You won't often see a fish take in deep- or brokenwater. If the line sweeps around without a bump and stops its arc over deepwater, then just let the fly hang there for a minute or two. Sometimes trout will strike a perfectly motionless fly in the quiet part of a pool. Actually, the current gives the feathers a slight movement as the fly sinks very slowly toward bottom. Now lift the rod tip and gently twitch the fly to the surface. That should do the trick. If the current is deceptively fast and the line doesn't stop but continues its swing to a point directly below your position in the shallows, then make a new cast and adjust the drift with slack. Devote plenty of time to an undercut, because trout are certain to be there. The fundamental technique in exploring hollow banks is to let the fly sink to a level where the fish can see it, before twitching it past their dens.

Dry-Fly Fishing

Trout always position themselves with heads facing the flow. Thus, the easiest way to stalk them is by coming up from behind where their peripheral vision is limited. It's not only possible to get closer to the fish, but when presented upstream, the fly stands on the water quite naturally, twisting and turning with every subtlety of the current. Although it's difficult for a beginner to manage a cast carried back toward him by the flow, he soon learns to keep the line taut by stripping the slack without pulling the fly. There is much less chance of disturbing the water by fishing upstream. This is most apparent in small pools, where a trout hooked at the top will dash down and startle his neighbors with panicky acrobatics. By working up, nearly all hooked fish are drawn down with the current, which leaves the rest of the water undisturbed.

This is the whole argument for upstream fishing, and as a general stream tactic, it can't be beat. There are exceptions to every angling rule, however, and learning to recognize them is a valuable asset to the dry-flycaster. We know, of course, that on many whitewater rivers, downstream is the only possible direction in which you can wade. A floater tossed on the slicks and even skipped over a custardy surface can be amazingly productive.

DRY FLY UPSTREAM   Blind casting is a native art on nearly all American rivers. Unlike the food-rich, silky-faced chalk streams of Europe, the turbulent waters of American rivers do not always, and in some instances only rarely, reveal rising fish. The angler wades along slowly, reading the surface ahead to find pockets and current combinations that previous experience has shown to hold trout. His casting falls into a steady pattern, and often as not, he will catch many fish that way. Some anglers become very adept at the game and instinctively locate trout. However, we also have classic American dry-fly waters such as the upper Deschutes, the Firehole, Salt Creek, upper Madison, Ausable, and some of the limestone streams of Pennsylvania, where many fish will be rising visibly. These can be fished blind in their quick parts, but the studied approach is absolutely essential when fish are coming to the mayfly, caddis, and midge in quiet runs. Instead of holding deep and racing up and down like an elevator to grab passing insects, the flatwater trout has ample time to examine each and every fly. The three basic skills required of the angler for foolproof presentation under these conditions are:

1. Correct position of approach
2. Completion of cast in the air
3. Absolute accuracy

The correct position of approach to a rising trout is from an angle that will reveal only the smallest portion of the leader, no part of the line, and with the fly placed so that it will float without drag. The chief difficulty in blind fishing is that most casters tend to work directly upstream and thus place the leader over the fish. Of course, on a rough surface it doesn't matter too much, but on anything from moderate currents to flatwater, the best approach is generally quartering from one side of the trout or the other. At times your easiest approach might be almost at right angles to the rise. As a rule, aim about 4 feet above the trout and let the fly pass about 1 foot away from it. Try to get the fly on target as quickly as possible upon seeing the rise. The chances of a take are very much better if the fly arrives while the fish is still in a feeding posture. If the angle of approach is wrong, maneuver to a better position and *wait* for the next time it comes up.

When a trout has taken a natural and is still at the surface, it is most vulnerable. The vision of a fish is in proportion to its depth, and the deeper a fish rests, the greater its area of sight. Between the disturbance of rising and its limited area of visibility, it's perfectly safe to put the fly on its nose when it's at the top. If the trout is holding several feet down, try to drop a floater at least 4–5 feet upstream and let it drift into his view. All salmonids will grab the fly from almost any angle in the drift, with one exception—the grayling. These fish often strike after the floater has already passed their position. In any event, the ideal moment to present a dry fly is when fish are actually feeding, and the faster you can put the fly over them, the more strikes you will get. If you choose a spot where you can make a drag-free float without showing much of the leader or any part of the line, and, preferably, remain out of sight yourself, then a third of the problem is solved. Although the wading angler is often less visible than the man on the bank, in very quiet water or in shallow, running water, it's tactically sound to cast from some cover.

The second requirement in good presentation is to complete your cast several feet above the surface. By this time the line and leader have straightened in the air and the fly is dropping. For this reason, many experts prefer a very light, somewhat slow dry-fly rod, as the unhurried casting cycle permits *painting* the fly on the water at normal ranges up to 50 feet. With a fast-action rod, you are going to get a different kind of presentation. The casting cycle is fast and less accurate. Casting at the water is almost certain to result in a splashy presentation. If you do make a bad cast on a visible fish, it's advisable to go off looking for other quarry until that fish is feeding freely again. We can't predict what the "memory" period of a trout might be; it may be minutes or hours before it will rise again. If the fish felt the barb, it may be a day or so before you'll have another chance. This is a highly individual circumstance, but except for very large trout with a lot of experience, most fish forget our casting mistakes rather quickly. If you can lay the line on the surface with no forward momentum and place the fly accurately on the first toss, the possibility of a strike is excellent. It diminishes thereafter according to the execution of each succeeding cast.

Besides accuracy or the lack of it, there are three material things that make the job easier. From the instant of turnover, you can achieve a slow, no-splash descent of the fly for these reasons:

1. A balanced leader
2. A fine-diameter line point
3. An air-resistant fly

The balanced leader in basic design consists of 60 percent heavy diameters, 20 percent graduation, and 20 percent tippet. In other words, the butt section should be the longest part of a leader of any given length. This is contrary to the common commercial practice of making short butts, or sections of equal length. Secondly, the fly size must be proportionate to the tippet diameter. With the wrong leader, a tiny No. 20 midge can be as difficult to lay down quietly as an 8/0 salmon fly. Because of its minuscule dressing, the midge offers no air resistance and merely goes along with the leader for a free ride. For this reason, long, fine tippets are necessary, for they are air resistant in themselves. In other words, they absorb that final flea power at the turnover instead of whipping around as a short, heavy tippet does. The tippet length and diameter for proper midge fishing would collapse if you were to use it with No. 10 dry flies. Conversely, the idea of improving your presentation with a No. 10 by using an extra-fine tippet is not often practical. The larger fly is already air resistant. A fine-diameter line point (from .022 to .025) comes gently to the water. There's a wide gap between .022 and the common .037 plastic-coated nylon. Suffice it to say, refinement at the terminal end is going to pay off in more fish. A thick line point is splashy and creates a broad wake on flatwater, particularly when the fly must be activated with the rod. A thick line point is less flexible, contributes to drag, and requires the use of extra-heavy leader butts, and so on *ad infinitum*. In short, it's a messy thing to throw at a rising trout. If your quarry is a submerged salmon or steelhead that has no intention of looking for mayflies, the heavy diameter won't make a bit of difference. Bear in mind that in speaking of the "line point" we are actually considering the first 2 feet of a fly line and at least part of the front taper. For delicate fishing, the 10 feet nearest the trout must not weigh more than 30 grains, and the diameter should run from .025 to no more than .040 at the 10-foot mark. The first 30 feet must not exceed 120 grains. This more or less approximates a No. 4 line size. At distances of 50 feet, a light fly line almost guarantees lifelike presentation of the fly.

The third material requirement—an air-resistant fly—is seemingly a contradiction to everything we seek of our tackle, as the theorem reads that anything we do to overcome air resistance will increase the length of a cast. However, the rule is a relative one and doesn't apply to presentation of the fly. Remember, the cast is gone, the line straightened in the air, and the leader making its dying gasp. Until this instant, the size or type of dry fly (within normal limits) had no influence on the velocity or momentum of the cast. Now in harmony with line point and leader, the feathers may fall in a variety of ways.

At the extremes, a fly with a heavy hook or short, sparse hackles will not glide as smoothly to the water as a long hackled spider or variant-type fly; it's almost impossible to make a sloppy presentation with the disproportionately designed spider. At the last impulse, when the leader kicks over and the fly starts to drop, the long-hackled floater has all the flight characteristics of a dandelion seed. Spiders are not the only flies that are conveniently air resistant. The fabled Fan-wing Royal Coachman is another good example of sound design. Although most anglers worship the pattern for its appearance as it dances over a current, the bald truth is that many fan-wing patterns are effective because even a poor caster can lay them down quietly. The trouble with fan-wing flies is not only that they twist and weaken a leader, but also that their life-span is brief. After one good trout has mauled the feathers, the wings lose their cocky stance.

For general fishing, many anglers prefer dry flies that are tied slightly oversize for the hook number. So a hackle of standard diameter for a No. 10 dressing can be used on a No. 12, extra-light hook. This produces a modified spider effect with three and preferably no more than four turns of two hackle feathers. It may not look as correct as the stiff, bushy dressing of an orthodox dry fly, but the comparatively smaller hook sits the fibers on their tippy-toes.

Of course, there still are periods when windblown, meaty, winged foods, such as the grasshopper and stonefly, are literally whipped into the water and the trout are receptive to the wet *smack* of a natural, but the same rules apply insofar as the leader and line point are concerned. Dumping a fly on the water is easy— it's the neat delivery that earns fish over the greater part of the season.

DRY FLY DOWNSTREAM   One opportunity for downstream dry-fly work is created by head winds. A fierce downstream wind creates the conditions to move trout that wouldn't otherwise be caught. It limits their visibility by ruffling the surface, for one thing, and it also animates the fly. For best results, a long-hackled fly of the spider type is necessary. It will move independently of the current, because it stands away from the water without penetrating the surface film. A 10- to 12-foot leader, tapered to 4X or finer, is equally important, as the flexible length lets the feathers fly freely. If you are on the river with heavier tackle when a wind starts, it's possible to get some results, but the total score will only be proportionate to your gear; a heavy, weight-forward line won't raise from the surface in anything short of a gale, and a short or heavy leader will only anchor the dry fly in place. And bear in mind that big floaters tied on small, light-wire hooks do the most jumping.

The second opportunity for downstream work is provided by places that can't be reached any other way except by downstream casting. For the most part, these are awkward spots that anglers habitually avoid or pass by. On all streams, the fisherman should pay particular attention to bridge abutments, sharp bends in the riverbed, rows of boulders, and brush sweepers, such as old tree limbs that dangle in the water. These invariably form a blind side to the upstream caster. Brooks also provide a variety of tricky covers, such as tunnels under the willow, footbridges, and fallen timber. Cocked and floating naturally, a dry fly will take at least one good fish when sent with the current to hidden places.

The third opportunity for downstream casting is one that applies to individual fish: presenting the fly without showing leader or line. As a rule, all downstream casts put the fly in front of the fish before he can see more than a fraction of your terminal gear, but the problem we are solving here isn't concerned with wind or awkward places; the object is to hook a spooky fish in perfectly open, sunlit water. We all have experienced bright summer days when the trout vanish while the line is still hanging in air. Maybe you find one rising in a quiet pool, and before the taper has unrolled, it ducks for cover. Even though your cast is long with the line dropping like a cobweb and curved away from his position—the next fish flushes anyhow. This is the kind of day when you can catch trout on the downstream drift, not only because of the fly-first presentation but because of the fact that you don't have to cast into that aerial window.

Correctly executed, the slack-line cast is aimed directly down to the position of the fish, but it should float about half that distance. In other words, if the trout is holding 60 feet away, you should drop the fly about 35 40 feet downstream and cover the difference by shaking more line out. There are several ways of making slack-line deliveries. The oldest and perhaps easiest for most people is to false cast in the usual manner and, on the final stroke forward, stop the rod at a 45-degree angle; then, when the line begins to pull, simply wiggle the tip from side to side. This lateral motion will create little curves in the outgoing line. Play with this for a few minutes, and you'll find that you can make narrow or wide elbows of slack with no effort. For our purposes, 7 or 8 small curves should be enough. When you drift the fly down on a fish, you don't get slack concentrated in one big belly. It will get caught broadside in the current and cause drag. As a tactical advantage, the initial presentation should be made in a perfectly natural float. After the cast is fished out you can begin animating the fly against a dragging line. So the rod wiggling must be timed to distribute the curves through the length of the cast.

The fourth downstream opportunity is, as already indicated, when casting with the wind, a very productive method at times. Of course, a fly can be animated without borrowing the help of a breeze, and there are days, particularly in the late summer and the fall, when a few calculated strokes will produce exceptional fishing. There is a good solid argument for the success of a retrieved dry fly that many casters overlook. Ordinarily, a river surface is freckled with flotsam of various kinds, such as bark, leaves, twigs, weeds, and whatnot. With all these objects coming over the trout's head, the slightest movement from something alive draws its immediate interest. Both dragonflies and stoneflies push their abdomens through the surface when trying to get airborne. They also paddle frantically with their feet, and in the sunlight, this movement creates a sparkling trail on the water. The spasmodic kick of a caddis fly is hardly noticeable from above, but at trout level, it looks like an explosion. The big mirror is a world of in-animate and animate things, and the competitive fish must often make immediate decisions.

There is only a shade of difference between a natural and unnatural movement imparted to the fly. On rising fishing, an effort should be made to get a drag-free drift on the first cast. The fly will reach a point in its float when the trout either accepts or rejects it, and presuming the latter case, the angler must now draw his floater back for a new cast. When working directly downstream on a fish, this invariably requires pulling it over the fish—a motion that is either going to excite a strike or put the trout off. You will rarely get a second chance as you might in upstream casting when the fly dances away on tippy-toes. The retrieve must begin *before* the line comes near the fish. This is the moment when a fine line point, long leader, and correctly hackled fly make a critical differ-ence. On calmwater in particular, coarse terminal gear is going to create a wake and spoil the whole illusion. Raise the rod slowly, and begin twitching gently, bringing the skater upstream in short, pulsing strokes. If the fly is standing up on its hackles and the fish doesn't respond after it has moved a few feet, lower your rod and let the skater drift near it again.

Streamer-Fly Fishing

Angling success with streamer flies is dependent on the pattern and how it is fished. One factor may be more important than an-other under some conditions, but it is generally agreed that gamefish can be highly selective with respect to color and size and the speed and depth at which the streamer is retrieved. Despite the implausibility of some garish patterns, which seemingly have no counterpart in nature, the fact is that many foragefish are brightly colored, and this is particularly true of the males during the spring spawning period.

Streamer flies (including bucktails) have a high ratio of suc-cess in hooking big fish. However, if an angler devoted all of his time to casting minnowlike flies, he would not catch fish all of the time, nor necessarily very large ones. This apparent inconsistency is because streamers, like other types of flies, have a specific role in the seasonal picture of angling. Ideal situations for the streamer are in water where gamefish are conditioned to feeding on a periodic abundance of forage, such as the sockeye-fry migration in British Columbia, or the smelt runs of New England, or the candlefish and herring runs in the Pacific Northwest. But there are also important periods in suburban trout country—late in the evening, after dark, and immediately after a summer rain. Big browns are especially cautious about chasing minnows in bright sunlight. On rare occasions they will go on a daytime rampage, but in the protective cloak of night or discolored water they cruise the shallows looking for baitfish. There are no great clouds of fry to stimulate reckless attacks on hair and tinsel. More so than in other methods of fly-fishing, the streamer-fly angler is dealing with an art that may provoke strikes because of hunger, curiosity, excitement, or just plain pugnacity. The Mickey Finn pattern, for instance, is accredited with the power of exciting fish into striking. The White Marabou (often used as a locator fly) apparently arouses their curiosity, as otherwise cautious gamefish will follow the fluttering wing again and again. Nevertheless, knowing when and how to use streamer flies requires some knowledge of regional conditions.

STREAMER-FLY FISHING IN RIVERS   Under normal river levels, the streamer or bucktail is cast across the stream, and as the lure drifts with the current, a regular movement of the rod keeps the fly alive and the slack out of your line. The darting motion should be very short but spaced at regular intervals to simulate a minnow struggling in the current. Don't lift for a new cast too often. A deep-sunk fly left to be shouldered by the current and seldom fully retrieved can be tantalizing to big trout. In any kind of downstream casting, where the lure swings around and is retrieved directly up current, the angler always runs the risk of spooking his fish. After stalking the lure for some distance, the trout may decide to strike at the very moment his angler comes into view, and the result is an involuntary pass at the fly. This can happen with streamers as readily as any other lure, but the minnowlike fly can run through periods of refusal rises, even when you are well out of sight. The fish will boil short or even roll so close that you might foul hook several of them in a very short time. Such fish can sometimes be caught on a smaller-size or a darker-color streamer.

When fishing streamers it is important to vary the retrieve from time to time. Ordinarily, a slow, jerky movement will attract and catch trout, but there are situations where a rapid pull will provide more strikes. In general, the slow, bottom-scratching retrieve is effective in coldwater periods, and the faster, near-surface swim is better in summer weather.

MARABOU STREAMERS   One streamer that should be stocked in both the weighted and unweighted types is the marabou. Basically, a marabou is an attractor-type fly that depends on its quivering wing action to tempt strikes. It will often hypnotize cautious gamefish into rushing out of their dens for a close look, if nothing else. Even that can be helpful in locating big trout or smallmouth bass. But in big discolored water, a White Marabou dressed on a weighted body can be cast across the stream with telling effect. On deep pools, make a slack-line cast up and across the stream to let the streamer sink near bottom before tightening to retrieve. Then work the fly in short, rapid pulls so that it flutters over the gravel. This method will often get a few fish when nothing else seems to click. The marabou is particularly effective on overcast or rainy days, when the river level has come up a few inches. On miniature streams or in shallow water, the ordinary unweighted White Marabou is preferable; it is most effective when cast directly upstream. A fluffy, stork-feather wing is difficult to sink. However, that's an advantage when you are casting in knee-deep runs. The fly will hang just a few inches under the surface and come puffing back with the current.

Of course, marabous also attract lake-dwelling gamefish and can be applied here in much the same way. You might try the weighted fly in deepwater and use the unweighted kind in situations where you find cruising fish in the shallows and are in a position to drop the marabou 20–30 feet ahead of visibly moving fish. Dressed on a small, light-wire hook, the fly simply clings to the surface film until you begin twitching it at the approach of a trout. Cruising fish of any kind are usually spooked by a direct cast. This is also a favorite method of casting to bonefish on the grass flats. It solves the problem of frequent bottom snagging with orthodox types of saltwater streamers—many of which are too big and too heavy for proper fishing in shallow water.

SEMIDRY STREAMERS   The semidry streamer is epitomized by the Muddler Minnow pattern. The Muddler has another kind of versatility from the marabou. You can float it, sink it, skim it across the surface, or dive-and-bob it, depending on what you are trying to imitate. The Muddler contains the basic elements of both insect and minnow imitation. It can look like a stonefly, grasshopper, dragonfly, sculpin, stickleback, or a dozen other forage forms, when operated by a skilled caster. The Muddler is most effective where gamefish are conditioned to feeding on large surface foods. You can begin by fishing the pattern dry. Grease the hairs lightly, and pitch the fly under overhanging limbs and along the edges of grass beds. If nothing responds after floating it quietly for a minute or so, bring the fly back in short twitches, long hops, or whatever seems appropriate. Naturally, there's more fun in getting topwater strikes, but if the fish are holding deep, then it's a simple matter to tie on an ungreased Muddler and work at their level.

The easiest way to get a streamer fly down near bottom is with a sinking-type fly line. If you don't carry a line of this kind, then the next best thing is to have some of your flies dressed with slightly weighted bodies. Too much weight will spoil the action of the fly and make it difficult to cast; so get your patterns tied by a professional who knows how much lead the various hook sizes require.

MINIATURE BUCKTAILS AND STREAMERS   These are usually considered separately from the more commonly used large sizes. A good example of small, imitative patterns is the Blacknose Dace dressed on a 3X Long, No. 10 hook. The brown-and-white wing with a black stripe running through its center suggests various kinds of minnows. Many experts fish the bucktail on a 9- to 12-foot leader tapered to 4X. The fine tippet permits maximum animation even in quietwater. Miniature bucktails are overlooked by many anglers; yet the approximate 1½-inch wing that fits a No. 10 hook is comparable in size to most common minnows. During the hot summer months, when the water is low, try the Dace pattern dressed on a No. 12 hook. The spot to look for big trout at that time of the year is at the head of a deep pool where the whitewater begins to flatten. Cast the Dace across the stream with sufficient slack to let it swing around below; then feed more line out so that the fly drops back slowly into deeper water. The idea is to keep the bucktail swimming as long as possible without picking up for a new cast. Let the fly sink, then dart forward a few inches before changing its position by mending the line.

Tactically speaking, the miniature streamer should be suggestive of a tiny minnow and therefore dressed sparsely so that the fish doesn't have much to examine. This more or less limits the number of useful patterns to a few basic color combinations, such as black-and-white, brown-and-white, red-and-white, or whatever is most effective in your region. You might get a better imitation locally with striped badger or barred grizzly feather wing. However, the choice of materials is nearly as important as the size and translucent appearance of the fly. Needless to say, any collection of miniatures doesn't stop at the Dace pattern.

Bucktails tied on hook sizes larger than No. 6 are preferable for highwater fishing, night fishing, and in those situations where gamefish find an abundance of smelt, herring, golden shiners, or other large forage species.

BREATHER-TYPE STREAMERS   The splayed-wing, or "breather"-type, fly is generally made in two styles: the normal dressing with hook down, which is best known to western anglers in the Spruce pattern; and a weedless dressing with the hook inverted. The upside-down hook on a breather is especially useful for largemouth-bass, pickerel, and northern-pike fishing. The breather has wings made of hackle feathers tied back to back so that they curve outward. When pulled in short hops through the water, the opposing feathers close and open. The rhythmic movement of the wing doesn't imitate anything specific, but it suggests life of some kind, and that's ample reason to provoke a smashing strike from predatory fish. The inverted style can be cast ahead of a cruising fish and left to sink. As your quarry approaches, a few pulls will raise the streamer from the bottom with its wings kicking, whereas an orthodox hook-down fly is invariably snagged in the bottom. What makes the breather particularly effective, however, is the fact that it can be animated in a confined space. Just a few short twitches are enough to get the fly working in a small area between lily pads, for example, and the upturned hook can be slid across surface vegetation.

SALTWATER STREAMERS   The streamer flies used in saltwater fly-fishing are usually very much larger than those used in freshwater. In casting for coho salmon, striped bass, snook, or tarpon, the fly size often ranges from 1/0 to 6/0 with the streamer-fly wing to lengths of 5–6 inches. This poses certain limitations. Often, when projecting a standard pattern into the 0 sizes, it becomes overdressed and lacks action. It's usually best to avoid fancy patterns and select those with simple, durable materials. Streamers such as the Coronation Bucktail and Strawberry Blond are typical saltwater patterns, consisting only of a colorful hair wing and tinsel body.

Bug Fishing

Bugs are used principally in freshwater fishing for black bass and panfish. Larger versions of this type lure are also effective for a number of surface-feeding marine gamefish.

The standard bamboo bugging rod is 8½–9 feet long and weighs approximately 6 ounces. These dimensions are comparative, however, as many fiberglass and graphite rods in lesser weights and shorter lengths will cast air-resistant lures, provided the line is a WF-6-F size or larger. The important thing is to keep some sense of proportion among rod, line, and bug. A light outfit such as an 8-foot rod with the WF-6-F line is suitable for small bugs in the No. 6 and No. 4 dressing. But it would not function smoothly with the larger No. 2/0 bugs, which are virtually standard in big-bass country. Therefore, the ideal rod is somewhat heavier than usual, and the most popular lines are in the No. 8–No. 10 sizes. Bugging tackle must be powerful to overcome the air resistance of a bulky lure.

It's also important to use the correct leader with a bass bug. If you do not make your own, buy some of the knotless tapered kind in 9-foot lengths. A practical range would be in 8-, 10-, and 12-pound test. Although 12 pounds is heavier than you need to handle a bass, it requires considerable terminal rigidity on the part of the leader to turn over a big No. 2/0 bug. Bass are not leader shy to the extent that trout are; so tippets in the 8- to 12-pound class may be used successfully. The diameters should be selected according to the lure size; a No. 6 or smaller bass bug handles nicely on 8-pound test, while a No. 4 or larger requires a proportionate increase in diameter. If the bug falls back on the leader on your forward cast, it's either too long or too light. If the bug slaps the water, your leader is too short or too heavy. A little experimenting with various leader diameters will usually solve most casting problems. Bear in mind that tossing a bug is bound to be awkward at first, particularly if you've been practicing with little No. 10 dry flies.

Casting a bug differs in its rhythm from casting an ordinary fly. The strokes must be made more slowly to match the speed of the wind-resistant lure as it travels back and forth. You must wait until the line loop is properly straightened, by allowing a longer pause between rod movements. Beginners should try short distances first and watch the back cast instead of the forward cast, observing just how long it takes the lure to complete its rearward flight. On the forward stroke, start slowly, and gradually accelerate the forward speed of your rod. Successful bugging doesn't require extreme casting distances. A 30- to 40-foot cast is good enough for nearly all fishing conditions. Whether you cast from the bank or a boat or by wading, the knowledge of where bass feed is most important.

IMPORTANCE OF RETRIEVE   The largest percentage of bass taken on bugs are caught within 20–30 feet of the shoreline, among rocks, weed patches, downed timber, and lily pads. In fact, it's a good general rule to make your first few casts in knee-deep water. Bass hunt frogs, mice, and minnows along the marginal areas of a lake, and most insect life is blown there from the trees and bank brush. There are several ways of fishing a bug in these places, but the best tactic is to work slowly. The slower you fish a bug, the more bass you will catch. Covering a small section of the shoreline thoroughly will usually produce more strikes than trying to scattershoot the whole pond fast. This means you should allow 20–30 seconds for each retrieve. Working too fast is a common reason for poor results. Ordinarily, you just want to animate the lure enough so that it looks like a water-stuck moth. A bass will generally swim up to within a few feet for a closer look. While the bug rests motionless, the bass's appetite or curiosity should be sufficiently aroused to strike the next time it moves. There are times when a fast retrieve or a change of pace will get strikes from otherwise-indifferent fish. This happens more often in rivers, and especially with smallmouths that have been regularly worked over.

PRESENTATION OF THE BUG   Presentation is important in bass bugging. This type of fishing is generally done in shallow water, where bass are easily frightened at the sight of a shadow or a lure passing overhead. On a bright sunny day, particularly, the angler will often see the surface swirls of fleeing bass. The same thing applies to an unrolling fly line or a splashy presentation; more bass are frightened by the actual process of casting than by the appearance of any lure. For this reason it's a sound tactic to start with short casts and fish each one out, gradually extending your range, until the bug is presented at your maximum comfortable distance. For example, if you see a stump 40 feet away that looks like a good bet, make one or two short casts between your position and the real target. The bass may *not* be under the stump but wandering around looking for something to eat. If you put the line over it and the bug beyond it, there's very little chance of getting a strike. The progressive casting technique earns big bass. It's particularly valuable when you're working pocketwater among lily pads; often the most insignificant spot within a short distance of the boat will hold fish, while the stump is empty. By working short casts first, you will achieve clean presentation all the way out to the target. There's nothing that makes an angler feel more foolish than laying out a long cast and a pretty bug, only to have a hog-sized bass not 10 feet from the boat boil off for deepwater. So keeping your target in mind, show as little line or leader as possible both in the air and on the water. It's much better to undercast than overcast.

The same approach applies to bugging in rivers. Old logjams, leaning tree limbs, and boulders are the prime targets in a bass creek. Fish get under these objects to look for food, and when an attractive lure comes bobbing down with the current or drops on the surface nearby, a hungry bass seldom questions its edibility. Pay particular attention to places along the river where you can present the bug in a truly lifelike fashion by dropping it on the bank grass or on top of a log, then twitching it into the water. You can even cast a weedless bug directly into a low-hanging tree limb and hop it loose to drop on the surface. You will get hung once in a while, but not nearly as often as you would expect.

TYPES OF BASS BUGS   There are many kinds of bass bugs, and you should have a collection of at least three different types. Most experts use popping bugs about 50 percent of the time. A good popper has a hollow, dished-out face, so that when you give the rod an upward pull, the bug buries its nose under the surface and makes a hearty *gerblub* sound. If you get nothing but splash, or if the lure skids over the surface, then either you are not doing it right, or the bug is no good. The bass may not see a quiet moth-type bug, but its sensitive lateral line will "hear" a deftly worked popper. However, this type of bug is not always effective. If you are casting in heavy weed mats or pads, the broad bug face will get hung and pick up grass constantly. You can buy weedless poppers, but bullethead bugs are much better. Bulletheads have a collar of hackle and a skirt of streamer feathers. Actually, you can get some noise out of a lure of this type by pulling downward with the rod. But the long tail feathers dangling under the surface make it easy for the bass to locate a bullethead in thick pad cover, and the streamlined head doesn't hang up.

Fly-Fishing for Steelhead

On the western coast of the North American continent there are many rivers and streams with annual runs of steelhead. Some occur only in the fall and winter; others, unfortunately not as many, attract summer runs. These runs usually present ideal conditions for the fly-fisherman. Water that is extremely clear may require fine terminal tackle calling for exceptional skill to handle the bruising fighter. Fall will bring occasional storms that may raise and discolor the river for a short time, but one can usually depend on weeks of excellent water and good fishing. Winter presents a real problem to the dedicated fly man, since rivers are high and roily with only short periods of clearing or lowering water. Close contact by telephone with local tackle firms or anglers is essential. When favorable, get there immediately, as the river can change in just a few hours.

STEELHEAD TACKLE   Steelhead fly tackle is heavier than ordinary trout gear. Rods of 8½–9½ feet in length are standard. In bamboo, some of the favorites are made in fluted, hollow construction; these are extremely powerful for their weight and were responsible for many tournament distance records when they first appeared on the market. Fiberglass rods have, of course, captured a large audience, and one development in that construction is a method of joining the sections by using hollow glass as a ferrule to keep the total rod weight down and to produce an action very similar to one-piece blanks. Regardless of the construction, the emphasis is on power; the tip must not be soft, and the action must extend well down into the butt. The guides should be correctly spaced, and of large size to permit smooth shooting of the line. A screw-locking-type reel seat is essential.

The reel must be large enough to accommodate at least 100 yards at 15- to 18-pound-test backing as well as the fly line. If the angler plans to fish some of the Canadian waters where steelhead in excess of 25 pounds may be encountered, it is advisable to use a reel that will hold at least 150 yards of backing. A single-action reel with an adjustable brake is most popular, although some casters use automatic fly reels. In most models the 3⅝-inch and 3⅞-inch sizes (spool diameter) are suitable for steelhead fishing. Although brakes are usually of the friction type, at least one reel has a floating disc brake, which eliminates brake failure and heat distortion.

The virtue of a shooting head is that distance is easily accomplished with less effort. A single false cast is all that is necessary to shoot the fly to fishable distances. A regular, forward-taper line will handle much more satisfactorily in strong winds and is preferable under this condition. Also, beginners who are not skilled at casting will find a forward-taper line easier to use. It is essential to master the double haul (see Fly Casting, p. 51). The double haul requires considerable practice before the steps become reflexive. There is a slight difference in trajectory with shooting heads, and the general procedure is as follows: Grasp the line near the butt guide with the left hand (reverse the procedure if you are left-handed). As you lift the rod to throw the line up and to the rear, bring your left hand down smoothly. It must be timed perfectly with the lift of the rod. The movement of the left hand will vary in force depending on the distance required. A long cast may require bringing the hand beyond your hip. The next step is simplified when using a shooting head because of the fine diameter of the monofilament. As the line flows to the rear you will feel the pull of its weight as it begins to straighten out. Allow your left hand to follow the line up to the butt guide. Before the line loses its momentum, start the forward cast by bringing the left hand down sharply (as before) and timed exactly with the forward movement of the rod. Aim this forward cast *higher* than you would with an ordinary fly line. The shooting head differs from the regular forward-taper line in that perfect timing results in a long cast with no need for great power. Don't force the cast, or it will collapse and fall short of the distance required.

LEADERS   Leaders of 9–12 feet are used for steelhead fishing. On clear rivers, such as the Rogue in Oregon, leaders up to 14–15 feet have proven very successful in outwitting the extremely wary trout on that stream. For general purposes, the tippet should be 6- to 8-pound-test.

STEELHEAD FLIES   A good steelhead fly should be sparsely dressed so that it will sink readily. It must be tied to withstand hard use. Patterns are varied and range from gaudy to conservative hues. Minor changes are made occasionally in the dressings; the Skyomish Sunrise, for example, started as a red-chenille-body fly, and is now being used with red fluorescent chenille as well as yellow fluorescent chenille. However, the original pattern is often the best. Other steelhead dressings, such as the Boss, a Russian River favorite, differ from the standard steelhead patterns in having a very long tail of black hair. It seems out of proportion, but the Boss is highly successful, nevertheless. The somber Silver Hilton and the dull, crude-looking Burlap patterns rarely attract neophyte anglers; yet both flies are far above average and should never be neglected. You must also remember that a particular river may be influenced by a local fly tier who is an excellent angler. His selections will be used by more casters, and, hence, they will take a greater percentage of steelhead. It is wise to have a few of the local favorites, but do not neglect the standard patterns.

On any fly a quality hook is essential. It must be top-grade steel, and the points must be sharp. This is important. Many hooks used for this fishing are 4X- and 5X-weight wire, and usually Limerick bends. This type will tolerate considerable punishment against rocks on low back casts; however, the hook should be honed occasionally with a fine file. The forged 7957BX Roundbend Mustad hook is exceptionally sharp and is also popular. Flies tied on the latter hook should be weighted slightly. Another favorite is the Allcock W209 in sizes No. 2–8. This is a round-wire hook, sproat bend, 2X Stout, and also has an extremely sharp point. A round wire does not cut through the flesh as rapidly as a forged hook, which may result in more fish landed. However, this is a theoretical consideration. Double hooks are still favored on the lower Rogue River in No. 6–10. The local anglers believe that the fly rides better when tied on a double hook.

ANGLING TECHNIQUE FOR STEELHEAD   One must realize a basic fact in steelheading—the fish are only in the stream at certain periods of the year, and for many months the water may be barren or simply hold small trout. Steelhead move into the rivers in groups, and a stretch of stream that was productive last week may be empty until a new group arrives. Often, a riffle that produced a steelhead in the morning may have another fish in the same spot by late afternoon. The angler's ability to locate or anticipate good holding water is no small part of the charm of this kind of fishing.

As the fish travel upriver, they will follow identical routes through each riffle and pool, as they have for countless generations before. They will rest in the same spots, bunch up in certain pools, or stay in a favored 5- to 10-foot area in a riffle that may be 100 yards long. This will be repeated year after year unless a flood scours and alters the stream bed. Oldtimers learn these spots through constant fishing and by trial and error. Many experts can look at a strange river and instantly pick out the best riffles. Submerged ledges, changes in the bottom revealed by a slight variation in the surface flow, and the location of rocks—all of these have their special meaning. You can save a lot of time by avoiding the kinds of water that steelhead will not hold in and the places that cannot be fished properly even if the trout are present. For example, water that is extremely fast is not likely to contain steelhead. They prefer moving water, of course, but as a rule of thumb, if it is flowing too fast to wade comfortably, it is too fast to fish.

Deadwater is a poor producer on most rivers, although there are a few exceptions. The reliable places are the slicks above a rapid, which are usually created below big pools where the stream spreads out. Another kind of water that is consistently good is a long, uniform flow of moderate speed. Steelhead habitually lie in the channel of a run of the latter type, and it pays to study the deeper sections carefully.

The basic technique of steelhead fly-fishing is to wade in at the head of a run and cover the water with cross-stream casts until every portion of the riffle is reached. The fly will swing around in arcs, and you are most likely to get a strike between the time the line tightens as it quarters downstream and when it completes the swing directly below you. Keep your rod low and pointed toward the fly. You can let the fly drift dead or jiggle it a bit either by twitching the rod or pulling the line. Try both methods. Make three short casts in all; then, having covered the close water, extend the line 10 or 15 feet. Make three more casts and then extend the line again to reach the maximum distance so that the entire run has been covered from one side to the other. Now wade eight or ten steps downstream and repeat the procedure until the length of the riffle has been fished. This is the standard method. You can vary it, of course, by changing the direction of your casts, working the fly deeper by casting upstream, and running it near the surface by casting more directly downstream.

Catching steelhead is not difficult. The technique is quite simple compared to some other types of trout fishing. The ability to "read" the water and to cast a long line is most important. Wading ability also goes a long way in successful steelhead fishing because of the volume of flow typical of most coastal rivers.

Fly-Fishing for Atlantic Salmon

Although the Atlantic salmon may legally be taken with spoons, plugs, and live baits in some European countries, its chief angling value is to the fly-fisher. However, the quality of the sport varies with the location and the season. All salmon rivers do not fish well to the fly because of their size or turbulence or the prevailing weather conditions. Thus, a premium is placed on first-class water, and the cost of angling is often expensive. In the United States, only the state of Maine provides Atlantic salmon fishing, so the angler must travel long distances in the known periods that correspond with a run of fish.

The world of the salmon angler is in Norway, the British Isles, Spain, France, Iceland, the Maritime Provinces of Canada, Quebec, and the state of Maine. At its satisfying and productive best, salmon fishing is probably the most exclusive sport in the world. One must have leisure time to visit the famous streams, because there's no guarantee of success on any particular day or week. In fact, if you can average one salmon per day in a ten-day period the fishing would be rated quite good. If you average two or three salmon per day in the same time—it's exceptional.

SALMON TACKLE   There is no one fly rod perfectly suited to all salmon fishing. The variable factor is the conditions under which your fishing must be done. At the extremes, let's suppose that you are going to the Aaro River in Norway for big salmon. The Aaro is a chaos of whitewater that shoots into the head of Sogne Fjord. Near its mouth the stream gradient is 90 feet within a 200-yard distance. The biggest Aaro salmon weighed 76 pounds (4 feet, 8 inches long), but 40- and 50-pound fish are an everyday possibility. On the Aaro you must stop your fish at the very first run. This requires heavy tackle. Even with 14-foot rods and 60-pound-test leader tippets, Aaro anglers break off frequently. There is little point in working such a flow with finely calibered rods. On the other hand, if you are planning a trip to Iceland, don't hesitate to sample the delights of those miniature 7½-foot, 2½-ounce wands. There is very little opportunity of hooking a large fish in the treeless barrens, and the island is fissured by sparkling watercourses of an ideal size for light tackle. The average Icelandic salmon weighs about 6 pounds, and a 20-pound fish would be out of the ordinary. Although some of the Canadian rivers are still fished with big two-handed rods, the general trend today is toward 8½- and 9-foot lengths on most streams. Fortunately, maritime rivers lend themselves to the use of reasonably light tackle, and under normal conditions in the summer and fall, low water and small flies are the rule. As a general gauge, rods which handle No. 9 or No. 10 (floating) lines are best adapted for Canadian salmon fishing.

The fly reel for Atlantic salmon should be ample enough to hold whatever fly line your rod requires plus 150 yards of backing. For the most part, reels in the 3½- to 4-inch diameters are suitable.

The fly leader for Atlantic salmon fishing should test 6–12 pounds in the tippet section; it should be in 9- to 12-foot lengths. For dry-fly fishing in the summer you will also need fly leaders tapered down to 3X, or approximately 5-pound test.

THE IMPORTANCE OF FLY SIZE   The Atlantic salmon is among the heaviest fishes to be caught on artificial flies in freshwater streams, and as such, the angling represents, with few perceptible changes, a projection of the caster's art on a larger scale. Ordinary trout patterns may provoke salmon when the stream is low and clear, but, traditionally, the angler presents feathered extravagances that vary from thumbnail size to highwater patterns big enough to fill a man's palm. These include both wet and dry flies. In his fasting, *salar* becomes a whimsical Nero; so the size of the fly, its presentation, and, to a lesser degree, the color of the fly are critical factors in drawing a strike. Generally speaking, a well-rounded assortment should include all sizes from hooks No. 8 to No. 6/0 in the Silver Wilkinson, Silver Grey, Jock Scott, Durham Ranger, Dusty Miller, Green Highlander, Blue Doctor, Blue Charm, March Brown, Black Dose, Brown Bomber, Lady Amherst, Silver Rat, Red Abbey, and Nepisquit Gray wet patterns.

The choice of a wet fly on the stream depends on the stage of the water. Broadly speaking, the lower and clearer the river, the smaller the fly should be. A popular preference for summer conditions is a sparse low-water dressing on either a No. 6, 8, or 10 hook. The low-water fly is actually a small fly tied on an oversize hook. A No. 6 low-water pattern is about the same size as a standard No. 10. This hook has the advantage of greater hooking and holding power on big fish when a small fly is the only thing that will seem to interest the salmon.

In contrast, for early-season fishing, when the river is at flood stage, the most popular sizes are No. 1/0 to 5/0 hooks. These larger flies are more visible to the fish in discolored water.

THE LIE   Salmon differ from trout in their choice of stations in the river. A salmon will make its temporary residence in some of the most unlikely looking places. This "lie" may be nothing more than a slight depression in the bottom along the shallow edge of the stream—a spot where the trout fisherman would wade. Or it may be in a narrow slick at the tail of an empty pool. Most of the prettywater used by trout (which are conscious of feeding lanes) is meaningless to the Atlantic salmon. Furthermore, a salmon will not hold just anywhere in the stream. Comparatively long stretches are ignored. A mile of beautiful but fishless water may exist between one lie and the next. The salmon may stop to rest in certain pools for a short period in its upstream journey, but these are not the "taking" lies where it will rise to a fly. And as the water level drops with the approach of summer, the salmon will change its position once more to compensate for some deficiency in the current. Wherever it moves the most productive lies are apt to be fairly shallow. Three or four feet is the average depth.

Salmon utilize the same lies year after year, and unless you are familiar with the river, it's important to seek the counsel of a competent guide. Blind casting is seldom productive without some knowledge of the fish's location.

WET-FLY FISHING   The main difference between trout and salmon angling is that when we seek the former we are dealing primarily with feeding fish; our intent is to imitate their food. Salmon, on the other hand, do not feed at this time, or they feed so sporadically that for all practical purposes there's no reason why they should take a fly. In the endless debate, irritation, natural ferocity, memories of parr life, and various other theories have won some favor. So the artificial flies we use can be extremely fanciful as well as lifelike. The size and type to select depends on several factors, but presentation of the fly is of prime importance. It's generally agreed that the sunk fly should come to the fish sideways, so to speak, rather than hanging in a nose-upstream position. This doesn't mean a salmon won't hit the feathers at any angle, but the broadside fly usually draws more strikes, and because of its position, it almost automatically travels at the right speed. Whereas trout are sought by casting upstream with the dry fly, nymph, and often the wet fly, the search for salmon is almost wholly in a cross- and downstream path. This is not a rigid rule, but the trout fisher and the salmon angler commonly travel in opposite directions.

Ordinarily, the salmon angler casts the wet fly across and slightly downstream. Whether the line is perfectly straight or slightly slack as it touches the water doesn't matter too much. The important thing is to keep the fly from lagging behind the line and leader. By mending, or rolling the line so that it makes a curve upstream over intervening fast currents, he prevents the fly from dragging. How this can best be done varies with almost every cast. The experienced caster fishes with his mind as well as his hands. In slow water, for example, it may be necessary to lift the rod and strip line to put the fly under tension and keep it swimming at the correct speed. Conversely, the quick spots may require lowering the rod or paying out a few coils of line to decrease it. The thing to avoid is accelerating drag that ends with the fly whipping around like a cow's tail.

DRY-FLY FISHING   The time to use a dry fly for salmon is in stalewater under a blazing sky. All salmon regions do not provide consistent dry-fly fishing. Most European rivers are deficient in this respect. But in Maine and Canada the Atlantic salmon displays a keen interest in floating patterns. An angler could probably go through a whole summer season on Anticosti Island, for example, using nothing but the dry fly—an addiction that a Norwegian angler would never find practical. Fjord streams are bucketed with icewater right through August. To be ideal, the water temperature should be over 60° F. and its level somewhat on the droughty side. Under these conditions the dry fly is often superior to any of the sunk patterns. Occasionally, salmon are caught on floaters early in the season; however, it is the exception rather than the rule. Unlike the trout technique, which requires casting in an upstream direction, the dry fly for salmon is a more relaxed method. For the most part we work across quartering downstream. Salmon are not as easily disturbed by the sight of a man flailing the air; in fact, they often regard him with disdain. So the advantage of sneaking up behind the fish is unimportant. True, we use the longest casts possible and try to remain inconspicuous, but what we really want is to *see* the salmon. Knowing exactly where the fish is holding and what his reactions are to our presentation is the key to earning strikes. This doesn't imply that the salmon should be visible at all times; a flash, a stirring of the water, or some faint sign of its presence is all that we need to justify any series of casts. If a trout is hungry and the fly is presented nicely the first time, it will invariably rise to it. But the chance of taking that trout after a great number of casts decreases proportionately. This is not true of a salmon. It may rise to the first cast or the one hundred and first. Perhaps the chief mental hurdle an experienced trout angler must overcome is the fact that in dealing with *salar* we must often coax him into a strike.

THE SALMON STRIKE   Trout and salmon also differ in their strikes. Typically, a trout grabs the wet fly and ejects it almost instantly. We may see nothing more than a wink of bright color in the water or a stopping of the leader. Whatever the sign, it is brief, and our reaction must be fast. By contrast, a salmon takes with a heavy, almost dead pull. It often flashes under the fly and creates a commotion even before the feathers have been touched. Here a reflexive snap of the rod will simply pull the fly away. It's possible to let a salmon mouth the fly and turn downward before striking. We simply lift the rod to increase line tension enough to set the hook in the fish's jaw. When using the dry fly, it may require a bit more force to drive the barb home if there is any length of slack line on the surface. This requires some judgment.

The dry-fly rise is usually more spectacular and, perhaps for that reason, easier to miss. In a playful mood the fish may roll under the fly like a surfacing porpoise and lift it out of the water or even slap it with its tail. Such a fish can often be interested in some other fly at some other moment. But as a rule, the false riser is not ready to be caught. Grilse will also leap over the fly and snatch it on the way down. Big fish may come straight from below or in a roll half out of the water or, like a skilled gymnast, a fish will do a flip at the surface and nail the feathers within inches of his own tail. Visually, it's difficult for an angler to control trout-trained reflexes and adopt the deliberate strike. The important thing is to give the salmon time to get the fly in his mouth and close his jaws.

Hooks

There are many hundreds of hook patterns, which differ in size and shape according to their intended purposes. The parts of a hook are the point, barb, bend, shank, and eye; it is the design and position of these five parts that largely distinguish one pattern from another. Although not physical parts of a hook, the *gap* and *throat* measurements are also important features that further separate the various kinds.

Point: the sharpened end of a hook that penetrates the fish's mouth.

Barb: the projection extending backward from the point of a hook. The barb helps to keep the point imbedded by resisting reverse motion.

Bend: the bottom or curved portion of a hook.

Shank: the upper portion of a hook that extends from the bend on the side opposite the point to the eye.

Eye: a hole or loop at the end of the shank through which the line or leader is secured.

Gap: the distance between point and shank.

Throat (or *Bite*): the distance from the apex of the bend to its intersection with the gap.

Characteristics of Hooks

A quality hook is made of steel; it must possess a sharp point, a barb that is not cut so deeply that it threatens to break under pressure, sufficient plating to defeat saltwater rust and corrosion,

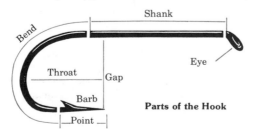

Parts of the Hook

and a smooth eye with no appreciable gap at the shank. The choice of the most effective hook depends on various factors: the strength of the tackle used, the size of the fish sought, how the fish strikes or takes a bait, how the fish's mouth is constructed, and the type of lure or bait that is used.

There are hundreds of hook patterns in use all over the world, and while many are simply minor variations of a previous model, each change was made for a practical reason dictated by local fishing conditions. To select a hook for your purposes, you must first understand the feeding habits of your intended quarry.

A fish doesn't masticate its food before swallowing. It isn't necessary, because the stomach has strong digestive enzymes that can accommodate anything the fish gets in his mouth. In some cases, such as in the mullets and sturgeon, the stomach is actually a food grinder. On rare occasions a bass, for example, will get a spinous catfish or bluegill stuck in its throat and literally choke to death. But the act of eating is brief, and it doesn't interfere with breathing. For instance, a trout normally "breathes" twice as fast as its angler. The fish closes its gillcover (operculum), draws water into its mouth, then closes its mouth, causing the gill arches to contract, and the rear edge of the gillcover is raised, forcing the water over the feathery red filaments that absorb dissolved oxygen. A trout may do this 40–50 times a minute while feeding. Any dental work a fish might apply to eating is literally accomplished between breaths. The jaw teeth, according to species, are designed to grasp, puncture, cut, or chop; these may be long canines, sharp and conical in shape for piercing and holding a slippery minnow or a kicking frog, as in the mouth of a walleye or northern pike. Or they may be short and fine in multiple rows—the cardiform dentation of a perch or catfish. Sharp-edged cutting teeth, or incisors, are found in bluefish, barracuda, and the classic piranha. But some fish lack jaw teeth and have comblike pharyngeal (throat) teeth, as in the sucker, which can vacuum algae from rocks with its soft mouth. Other fish may have molariform grinding plates, as in the bonefish, permit, or, for that matter, the redear sunfish, which also crushes mollusks. Others, like the porgies, have combination incisors and molariforms and can pierce or grind. To separate the inevitable mess of mud, broken clamshells, sand, or a detached crayfish claw from the function of breathing, a fish relies on its gillrakers. These are literally its napkin when dining. Gillrakers also come in various shapes and sizes according to the fish's diet; they may form a very practical sieve for straining plankton, as in the herring and gizzard shad, or appear as tough, stubby fingers that won't clog with odd bits of weed or minnow, as in the black bass. A fish, in any case, is well equipped to grab and ingest easily.

To select a hook you must know something about the mouth structure and whether your quarry chops, sucks, nibbles, grasps, or simply swallows its food. This is modified by the method of fishing—whether you will be using live bait or an artificial lure. It's perfectly feasible to use a long-shank hook for trout when casting night crawlers for example, but if using a bait such as salmon eggs, or an artificial like a salmon-egg cluster, which a steelhead would snatch quickly in a fast current, a short shank is essential. The same is true of a trout rising to a dry fly, where a standard or short-shank hook will "set" much easier than a long shank, which is inclined to tip away from its mouth. The barb penetrates when the forward movement of the hook, because of the pull of the line, is stopped by an obstruction at the point. The point halts while the remainder of the hook advances. Thus a cant is given to the hook as the point begins to catch. Each hook pattern is forced in a different direction.

Obviously, variables such as the speed of the fish's strike, the angle at which it takes, and the formation of the fish's mouth, to name a few, are going to affect your success. But in theory, we are concerned with the "rake" of a hook as it exists under a constant set of factors. If you attach a leader to the eye of the hook and stick the point in a piece of wood (with the shank parallel to the wood) and then pull, the hook will tip forward into a striking position. Although this may or may not indicate actual penetration, it should be obvious that the shank becomes a lever that causes the point to enter at an angle predetermined not only by the hook design but by the length of the shank.

Hook Patterns

The following are some of the more popular hook patterns used in fresh- and saltwater fishing:

ROUND BEND   Round bend is really a generic term, as the hook is given different names by various manufacturers, such as the Model Perfect, Gaelic Supreme, and Viking. It is the most popular hook for flies, especially wet, dry, and nymphs. The wide, round bend presents a large bite and quick penetration. It may not hold as well as the Sproat in a hard mouth but it's still the ideal for fast-striking, soft-mouthed fish when a small hook is required. It's also a good hook for panfish, when delicate baits such as crickets and grasshoppers are used.

SNECK   The sneck is also known as the square bend. This pattern originated in England during the nineteenth century. Sneck-bend hooks were popular in the United States for many years but nobody can recall why. The pressure on the hook point is severe and the sharp bends in the wire that create its square shape caused the hook to snap quite often.

SPROAT   The Sproat is a nearly round bend with a straight point. Size for size, it doesn't have as wide a gap as the round bend, and though it's used for the same general purposes, in my opinion it makes a better fly for *large* fish. In equal wire sizes it has less tendency to open. Many anglers favor the Sproat for bass bugs, streamers, and plastic worms, where fish of 4 pounds or more are possible.

LIMERICK   A half-round bend with a straight point, the Limerick's shape varies slightly according to its manufacturer. It requires slightly more pressure to sink the barb of a Limerick than that of a Sproat. However, the rakish design of a Limerick is so appealing to salmon fishermen, for example, that a classic salmon pattern doesn't look properly dressed when tied on any other hook pattern. The Limerick is not ideal for holding the fish with its relatively short bite, but it has good balance when swimming in the water, keeping the feathers upright when properly knotted to the leader.

CLAW   The claw is a generic team including the beak-type hooks but is also synonymous with Eagle Claw (a trade name). The claw-style hooks accomplish the theoretical ideal, in that the hook point is in direct line with the pull of the leader. These are made in many variations in shank length, wire diameter, type of eye, and finish, to make the design compatible to all types of bait fishing, where it succeeds admirably. This is a popular pattern with a sliced (bait-holder) shank to secure delicate whole baits like shrimp when bonefishing. Its off-balance design does not lend itself to flies, however.

SIWASH   Sometimes called salmon hook, the Siwash originated in our Pacific Northwest. It is used almost exclusively for salmon fishing, particularly in conjunction with spoons and other trolling baits. It's a round-bend pattern with an extra-long sharp point made 3X Stout. The point almost reaches half the length of the shank to give deep penetration in cartilage and membrane, and to prevent a jumping fish from throwing the hook. A salmon has a comparatively soft mouth, and the Siwash serves its purpose ideally.

KIRBY The Kirby has a round shape similar to the Sproat, but with the spear "kirbed," or bent to the side. The theory is that a kirbed hook will penetrate faster in a fast-striking, soft-mouthed fish, such as the black bass. Variations of the original Kirby, such as the Chestertown, were quite successful for certain kinds of fishing, although these have been replaced to a large extent by the modern claw-type hooks, which are also kirbed.

O'SHAUGHNESSY The O'Shaughnessy resembles the Sproat but is made from heavy wire and is usually forged or flattened to give it extra strength. For heavy-mouthed fish like the tarpon, striped bass, permit, roosterfish, or any of the large jacks and groupers, it's hard to beat. The O'Shaughnessy is one of the most popular hooks for big fish in saltwater. The spear may be straight or kirbed, but it's mainly used in the straight form. It's a good pattern for live baits or artificial flies.

Hook Patterns

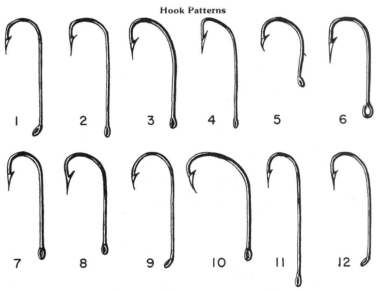

1. Round Bend	5. Claw or Beak	9. Aberdeen
2. Sneck	6. Siwash	10. Wide Bend
3. Sproat	7. Kirby	11. Carlisle
4. Limerick	8. O'Shaughnessy	12. Cincinnati Bass

ABERDEEN   The Aberdeen is a round-bend hook with a wide gap between point and shank. In fine wire this was a popular hook among live-bait fishermen in the United States for many years. It can hold a minnow without making deep punctures, and, in theory, the wide gap provides plenty of clearance to hook a swallowing fish, like the black bass. This has been modified in recent years by giving the Aberdeen a bent point, making it a half-claw-type hook.

WIDE BEND   The Wide Bend is an odd-looking hook with a slightly reversed bend with an out point and a turned-up ball eye. This is an excellent live-bait hook in freshwater, particularly when you're using minnows. It penetrates fast in membrane or cartilage.

CARLISLE   Another early English pattern, the Carlisle is a round bend with a short, kirbed spear; it differs from the Aberdeen in having less gap between point and shank. The Carlisle is essentially a long-shank pattern (longer than the Aberdeen, size for size) and is used mostly for minnows and night crawlers and especially on toothed fish, like the walleye or saltwater species such as the snappers.

CINCINNATI BASS   A century-old hook pattern designed for black-bass fishing, it has a round, curved-in point and is not kirbed. The Cincinnati Bass has some popularity among bait fishermen but has been largely replaced by the claw-type hooks for this purpose.

Wire Sizes

The diameter or weight of the wire used in a hook is specified by the letter X and the words *Fine* or *Stout*. Thus, a 1X Fine hook is made of the standard-diameter wire for the next size smaller hook; 2X Fine means that the wire is made of the standard-size wire for a hook two sizes smaller. Wire diameters are seldom made finer than 3X Fine. A heavy-wire hook has a reverse progression with a 1X Stout being the diameter for the size of the standard wire used in the next larger size hook, and a 2X Stout made of the standard diameter for a hook two sizes larger. Hooks are not regularly made with wire diameters greater than 4X Stout.

   The qualities of the various weights of wire must be kept in mind when making a selection, for many factors enter the equation. Light-wire hooks, all else being equal, penetrate a fish's mouth more readily than heavy wire but also wear through, or "buttonhole" quickly. Light wire tends to spring and bend. However, when fragile natural baits are used, the light-wire hooks are most practical because they do not tear the bait to pieces. Furthermore, if the bait is small and alive, lightness of the hook permits greater freedom of movement. Light-wire hooks are also important in the making of dry flies, because their lighter weight allows the fly to float well. For all practical purposes in this method, the light-wire hook is perfectly adequate for holding even large fish.

Heavy-wire hooks are stronger, do not spring when they strike hard bone or bristle, and do not bend or part under the impact of a strike from sharp-toothed species. Although they do not penetrate as readily, they are apt to hold more securely once they have been driven home. The stout diameters are most important in saltwater fishing but have broad application to streamers, bucktails, steelhead, and Atlantic-salmon flies.

Obviously, the angler must consider his tackle in relation to the hook. Where a light, limber rod can be employed, the hook

Variation in Wire Size

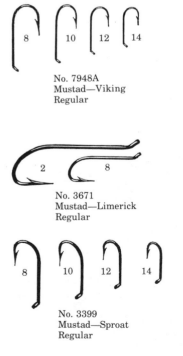

No. 7948A
Mustad—Viking
Regular

No. 3671
Mustad—Limerick
Regular

No. 3399
Mustad—Sproat
Regular

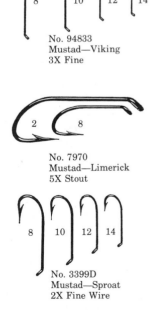

No. 94833
Mustad—Viking
3X Fine

No. 7970
Mustad—Limerick
5X Stout

No. 3399D
Mustad—Sproat
2X Fine Wire

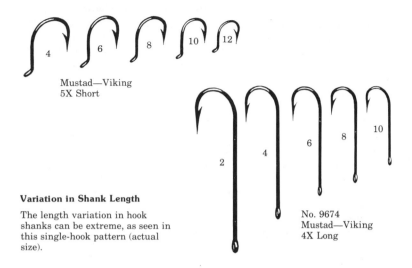

Mustad—Viking
5X Short

Variation in Shank Length

The length variation in hook
shanks can be extreme, as seen in
this single-hook pattern (actual
size).

No. 9674
Mustad—Viking
4X Long

must be of fine wire and possess a very sharp point if it is to be
set. Heavy tackle permits the use of more rigid, heavy-wire hook.

Shank Lengths

The difference in the length of a hook shank from the standard
length for its size is specified in *X* and the words *Long* or *Short*.
Thus, a hook of 1X Long is one that is as long as the standard
length of the next size larger; 2X Long means that the shank is
the standard length for a hook two sizes larger. This progression
continues to 6X, beyond which length hooks are not ordinarily
manufactured. In contrast, a hook of 1X Short is one that is as
short as the standard length of the hook one size smaller; 2X Short
means that the shank is the standard length for a hook two sizes
smaller. Hooks are seldom made that have shank lengths shorter
than 5X Short, but can be made to 9X Short.

The advantage of a short-shank hook is that it can be hidden
more easily in a small, natural bait, such as a salmon egg. It can
also be used for various small flies, such as midges and spiders, to
achieve high flotation without adding weight. The short shank has
good penetration on soft-mouthed fishes, such as grayling and
whitefish.

On the other hand, a long-shank hook defeats the sharp-
toothed fish, which may otherwise cut leader or line. In some cases,

such as that encountered by winter-flounder fishermen, the long-shank hook is preferred because it facilitates removal of the barb from the small, sucking mouth of the quarry. (One should not confuse the winter flounder and the summer flounder, or fluke. The latter has a large mouth.) Long-shank hooks are equally important to the fly-fisherman in making streamers and bucktails for both freshwater and saltwater fishing.

Types of Shanks

Hook shanks are manufactured in many shapes, but only six are commonly used.

Straight Shank: The hook shank is straight from eye to bend.

Humped Shank: A hump or humps are bent into the shank. The purpose of the hump is to prevent cork, plastic, wood, or rubber bodies from turning around the shank. This type of hook is used exclusively in making bass and panfish bugs.

Sliced Shank: A barb or barbs are cut into the shank. These projections will anchor a soft bait, such as a salmon egg, sea worm, or sand lance.

Bent-Down Shank: This type is designed to bring the line or pull closer to the line of point penetration. Although it takes a shallow bite, it is a good bait hook.

Central-Draught Shank: The shank is bent upward to give the hook a quick, raking penetration.

Types of Shanks

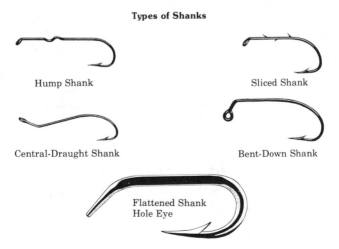

Hump Shank

Sliced Shank

Central-Draught Shank

Bent-Down Shank

Flattened Shank
Hole Eye

Keel Shank: The shank is bent to form a keel so that the hook point always rides upright in the water. This has many applications in making snag-proof or weedless flies.

Types of Eyes

There are six common types of hook eyes, which serve different purposes.

Ball Eye: An eye in which the wire diameter is constant and forms a circle perpendicular to the plane of the hook itself. The ball eye may be closed or open. The closed kind is tempered and therefore stronger; the open eye is usually found on cheap hooks.

Tapered Eye: In this type the shank of the hook directly behind the eye and the eye itself are tapered. This is done to reduce the weight of the hook and make it effective for dry-fly use.

Looped Eye: The wire in the eye of the hook runs back along the shank toward the rear of the hook. The end of this wire is usually tapered, although it can also be made untapered. Looped-eye hooks are traditionally used in making salmon wet flies.

Needle Eye: So called because it has an eye like that found on a needle. One advantage of the needle eye is that it may be easily strung through a natural bait without fouling. It is also strong.

Brazed Eye: The gap of the eye of this hook is brazed to the hook shank. It makes a very strong eye, and one that will not cut the leader or line. Big-game hooks are usually brazed to insure maximum strength.

Flattened Eye: In this type the end of the shank is flattened, and a hole is pierced into it. The flattened eye is used for medium-sized species in commercial fishing. Where natural bait, such as a sea worm, is used, a hook may possess no eye at all, but simply a flattened end. In this case, a monofilament, steel, or fiber leader is snelled to the hook shank and secured by the flat itself.

Eye Positions

The position of the eye is an important factor in improving the hooking potential of artificial lures. The four most common eye positions are the ringed eye (R.E.), in which the eye is parallel to the hook shank, the turned-up eye (T.U.E.), in which the eye is

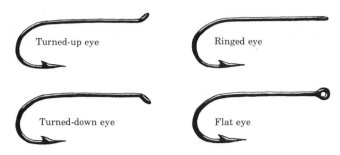

Eye Positions of Hooks

turned up from the hook shank, the turned-down eye (T.D.E.), in which the eye is turned down from the shank, and the flat eye (F.E.). The ringed-eye hook is most often used with lures that are used in tandem with other lures, such as a wet fly attached to a spinner. The turned-up eye provides more clearance between the hook shank and the point, which may be an advantage when using fully dressed flies or hooks with short shanks. The turned-down eye brings the hook point closer to ideal in the theoretical line of penetration, and in most cases is appropriate for hooks with standard or long shanks.

The flat-eye hook differs from the flattened eye in that the eye is formed separately and positioned perpendicular to the hook shank. It is confusingly called "ringed eye." This is an ancient design (Bronze Age) and still used on some large hooks for commercial fishing.

Types of Points

There are four types of commercial processes used today in the fashioning of hook points; by upsetting, by forging, by grinding, and by needle grinding. Through any of these methods the following types of points can be made:

Needle Point (N.P.): The process used in making this high-grade point is not a fast one. The needle point is ground on all sides, and when properly made, it has the best penetrating quality, although it easily becomes blunt.

Hollow Point (H.P.): This type, like the needle point, is designed for fast penetration, being hollowed or rounded out between the tip of the barb and the tip of the point.

Spear Point (S.P.): As this type of point can be readily manufactured in quantity, it is the least expensive one to make. The precise shape of a spear point varies with different manufacturers. The spear point does not have the quick penetration of a hollow-point hook.

Barbless Point (B.P.): Although one of the oldest known, this type has never become widely popular, as the lack of a barb makes it difficult to hold a fish after it is hooked. However, it is used by "catch-and-release" sport anglers.

Arrow Point (A.P.): Shaped like an arrow, this type is rarely used, because the point does not penetrate easily.

Knife-Edge Point (K.E.P.): This is a very sharp point used mainly for big-game fish. Four sides of the point are ground. The surface of the barb is flat and wider than normal, thus making it difficult for a big fish to throw the hook.

The finest hook loses much of its efficiency if the point is allowed to become dull or blunted. Carborundum stones may suffice to touch up small barbs, but a file is more effective in sharpening a large hook.

Point Positions

There are four common hook-point positions given below:

Straight Point: In this position the point is not bent in or bent out, nor is it rolled. It is in a position parallel to the shank.

Rolled Point: Sometimes called a rolled-in point, this type has the point bent in toward the shank of the hook. The rolled point is without peer for bait fishing in saltwater.

Bent-In Point: This differs from the rolled point in that the entire spear is bent toward the hook shank. Although such a point achieves a small bite, it is difficult for a fish to disgorge.

Bent-Out Point: In this position the hook point is bent away from the shank to achieve a quick penetration. A slight degree of out point is sometimes considered desirable in small flies and also on big-game hooks.

Kirbed Hooks

A hook point is normally positioned parallel to the shank. Some patterns, however, are kirbed, or offset, to the right or left, including a portion of the bend. Kirbed hooks are used principally for bait fishing with worms, minnows, or salmon eggs and to some extent with soft plastic lures. A kirbed hook is designed for quick penetration of membrane and cartilage in soft-mouthed fishes, such as the black bass or steelhead.

Hook Finishes

Some inexpensive saltwater hooks are blued, as are many cheap freshwater models. This finish is never satisfactory. Neither is japanning or the lacquering, which imparts a bronzed finish. All rust quickly when exposed to salt. Various alloys have been used to defeat rust and corrosion. The most efficient has been nickel alloy; however, it is soft, a deficiency that causes the hook point to become dull or blunt, and under heavy stress the hook bend will straighten. The most practical use of nickel alloy is in the fabrication of saltwater flies or small, light-tackle jigs. With lures of this type, rust is generally a greater problem than actual strength. But alloys have yet to match the all-around excellence of steel. The most popular heavy-duty marine hooks have been made of tempered steel and are heavily plated with cadmium or tin. When correctly tempered, stainless steel is superior, providing almost 100 percent resistance to corrosion.

Forged Hooks

Saltwater gamefish, pound for pound, are far stronger than their inland counterparts. For that reason marine hooks must be designed to take tremendous punishment. One way to increase the tensile strength of a hook is by forging. In this process, the hook is not just bent into shape and then tempered. After the bend has been made, the hook wire is hammered along part of the shank and all of the bend so that it is flat on two sides. After tempering, this process gives added strength where it is needed to prevent the bend from straightening under stress. Practically all big-game hooks are forged, and many of the smaller barbs used on medium-sized species are similarly treated to provide additional strength.

Hook Sizes

Unfortunately, there is no uniform system of hook measurements. Visual familiarity with the various manufacturers' hook patterns is the only workable gauge for the serious angler. Although attempts have been made to set a standard by measuring the hook in fractions of an inch, the system has never been successful, because it merely represents the length of the shank. A hook is really

Wright & McGill Eagle-Claw Hooks

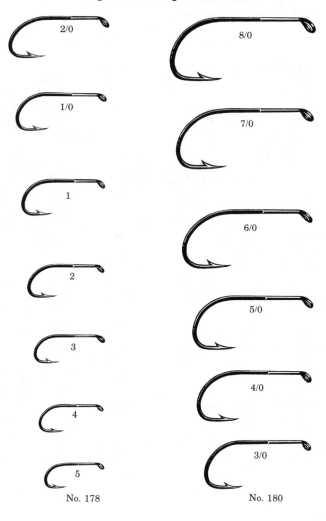

2/0

8/0

1/0

7/0

1

6/0

2

5/0

3

4/0

4

3/0

5

No. 178

No. 180

Mustad—Viking Hook Sizes, No. 7958 (Actual Size)

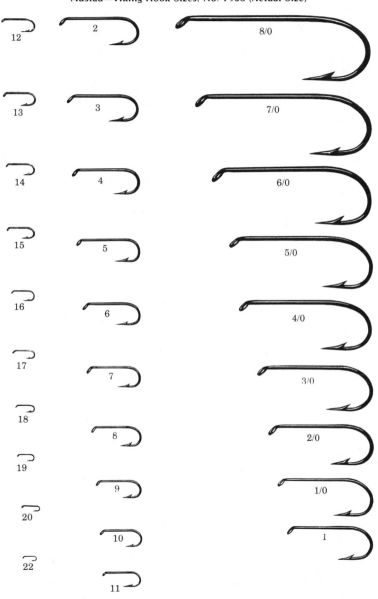

Double Hook   **Mustad Treble Hook**

two-dimensional, since the gap can vary greatly from one pattern to the next.

Double and Treble Hooks

Hooks are also made in double and treble styles. The double hook has two points on two separate bends joined to a single shank with a single eye. The treble hook has three points and three bends also joined to a single shank and eye. These are specialized hooks designed to engage fish striking from any direction (as in the case of treble hooks on a plug) and to provide balance on some small lures and flies. In general, single hooks penetrate faster and hold more securely.

Weedless Hooks

Weedless hooks prevent the point from becoming snagged and are essential to some kinds of fishing. The hook is protected by a light, single or double wire running from the eye to the point. These weed guards are an integral part of some spoon lures.

Weedless Hooks

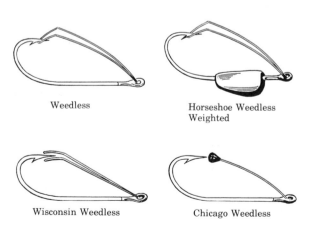

Weedless

Horseshoe Weedless Weighted

Wisconsin Weedless

Chicago Weedless

Knots

Tying knots is one of the most important skills of the successful angler. It need not be complicated; except for very specialized fishing methods, you can get along easily with a half dozen different ties.

The important thing about tying knots is to form and secure them correctly. They must be pulled slowly, steadily, and tightly. You might practice with heavy cord or even rope, so that you can see more readily how the parts are formed and joined. All knots reduce the strength of any material to a greater or lesser degree; therefore you should learn the ones that provide maximum security rather than easy or less-efficient knots. Any knot that retains 85 percent or more of the breaking strength of the material is generally useful, although some of the better knots are rated at 90 percent and higher in efficiency. However, due to the specialized requirements of angling and tackle, it is not always possible to employ the best knot for a particular purpose because of its bulk, rigidity, or tendency to slip when tied in various materials.

Blood Knot

The blood knot is used for joining two strands of material together, such as sections of nylon in making tapered leaders. The blood knot is efficient provided the diameters of both strands are reasonably comparable. If the variation is great (more than .015 inch) the offset nail knot would be more suitable. For most leader-making purposes, however, the blood knot is practical.

To form the knot, cross the two strands and hold between thumb and forefinger with about 3 inches of each section extended. Take the near-strand extension (whether right- or left-handed), and twist around the standing part of the opposite strand 5 times. Poke the end through the loop formed by the two strands, shifting the knot to the other thumb and forefinger to hold the crossing parts firmly together. Twist the other strand extension around the

191

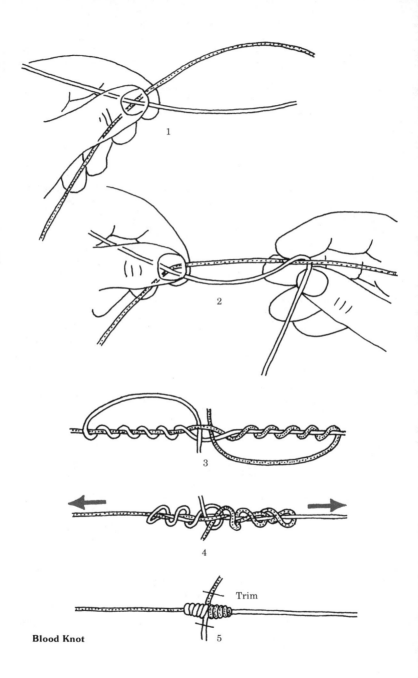

Blood Knot

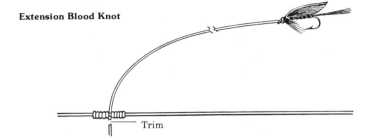

Extension Blood Knot

Trim

standing part 5 times in the opposite direction, and return the free end through the formed loop so that it enters from the opposite side. By holding both free ends between each thumb and forefinger, draw the knot together slowly by pulling on all 4 parts. When the knot is correctly formed, the strands can be pulled tight and excess material clipped from the ends.

Extension Blood Knot

This is used for tying dropper strands to a leader. A great many anglers use two or more flies at one time, so it may be necessary to create a dropper strand extending from the leader on which to attach the extra fly. For this purpose, the extension blood knot, which is tied in the same fashion as the blood knot, is ideal. The only difference between the two is that in forming the dropper you pull one end out 6–8 inches. You have to allow an extra-long overlap when you start tying the knot in order to get the proper length. This extension forms the dropper strand and is a permanent, strong tie.

Improved Clinch Knot

The improved clinch knot has many applications in tying flies, lures, bait hooks, and swivels to leader or line, or to tie a line to a reel spool. It is preferred by some fly-fishermen to the double turle, particularly when using straight-eye or ringed-eye hooks or when using very small artificials. In fine diameters it is more secure than the ordinary clinch knot (in which the free end is not drawn through the second loop) and will not slip. There are two things worth remembering about it: use 5 turns instead of the customary 3, and when fishing with delicate tippets below 4X, pass the monofilament through the hook eye *twice* before forming the

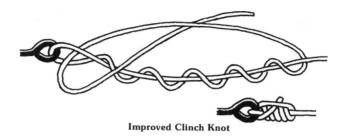

Improved Clinch Knot

knot. This is important if you have to use midges and tiny nymphs for big trout.

To make an improved clinch knot, pass the leader material through the hook eye (once or twice), and make 5 turns with the free end around the standing part. Next, pass the end between the eye and the first loop formed. Bring the end through the large loop just formed, and slowly pull tight while still holding the free end between thumb and forefinger to prevent its slipping out. Pressure should be applied gradually so that the knot is partially closed before securing against the eye.

Nail Knot

The development of plastic-coated fly lines has also been responsible for the acceptance of knots that would have had little value to anglers some years ago. For example, a nail knot simply cuts through a vacuum-finished silk line; yet it is eminently practical with a tough-coated, modern, plastic line. Actually, the harder you pull the knot, the better it "bites" and holds. So it's no longer necessary to knot a fly line to a leader loop. A knotted loop makes a bulky and not perfectly secure connection that always catches in the rod guides. The smooth nail knot, on the other hand, easily passes in and out, and you can leave the appropriate butt section joined to the line even if you want to change the leader's taper from time to time. By the same token, you can eliminate splicing a loop on the end of a line unless you are using a silk line. A loop is not only bulky but prone to come apart under heavy fishing pressure.

This nail knot can also be used for tying an extremely large-diameter section of leader to a small one, as in the case of a shock tippet; to join two heavy sections of material without creating a big lump or a dog's leg in the leader; and to attach a shooting head to a monofilament line. Although a carpenter's nail was originally used in forming the knot, anglers carry a section of hollow plastic or metal tube to wrap the material around. It doesn't matter, as long as the surface is smooth to allow the monofilament to slide off easily. The reason you will need something to work *around* is that all nail knots are finished by passing the free end through the center of the turns formed. This is awkward unless you can hold the shape of the knot until the tie is finally completed.

To make the basic nail knot, the heavier material, which may be either the fly line or a shock tippet, is first turned or bent back along itself for about 2 inches. Let's say you want to join a 1-foot-long, 60-pound-test shock tippet to the final 15-pound-test tippet of a 9-foot leader. A short, heavy-diameter shock tippet merely absorbs the abrasion of a hard-mouthed fish like the tarpon or big striped bass; you wouldn't have to use one for bonefish or redfish. Fortunately, large saltwater gamesters are not leader shy, so the thick strand is more practical than using wire. With the 60-pound

Nail Knot

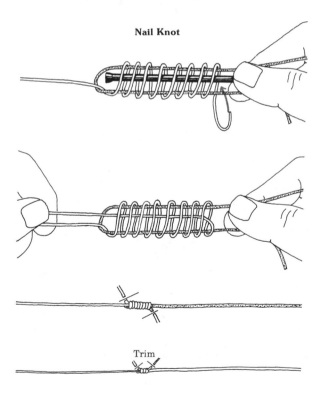

Trim

material turned back, pass the 15-pound tippet through the bend it has formed, and lay both parts against the nail. Pinch the free part in place with your thumb against the nail, near the base of the bend, and commence winding. Make 8 turns; then pass the free end back through the center, so that it comes out the same side it entered the loop. Do not *cross* the free end and the standing part. Remove the nail, and holding the four ends between thumbs and forefingers, pull the knot tight. Trim off the excess ends.

When making a nail knot to join a fly line to a leader butt, the nail knot alternate is easier to tie and forms a smoother connection. The tip of a fly line and the diameter of a leader butt are so similar that the monofilament gets a solid bite with only a minimum of winding.

Nail Knot Alternate

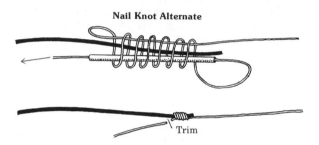

Trim

Nail Knot Alternate

An alternate method of tying the nail knot, which is practical for most kinds of fly-fishing when the diameters of the materials are not greatly divergent, is easily tied with the aid of any slender tube (such as a pump needle with the tip filed off). Start by holding the line, tube, and monofilament parallel, with the end of the tube and line even, and the leader material extending about 6 inches beyond to the left. Hold all three firmly; then double the monofilament back to the right and wind it 6 times around itself, the line, and the tube. Push the end of the leader material through the tube while holding the wraps in position between your fingers. Transfer the tube to your right hand, holding the wraps in place between thumb and forefinger, and slowly withdraw the tube. Pull alternately on short end and leader while turns are still held in position between fingers. When all slack is out, tighten the knot with strong, steady tension on the monofilament, then on line and monofilament. Trim ends close.

Double Nail Knot

Another variation of the nail knot is the double nail knot. The difference between the familiar blood knot and the double nail knot is that the latter is less bulky when using heavy leader material of 20- to 60-pound test. In these large diameters, it is difficult to form and secure a blood knot properly, because the free ends must be passed back through the loop first formed. The double nail knot is of prime importance in saltwater fly-fishing; however, it can also be useful in making heavy salmon leaders or trout leaders.

The double nail knot is used to join leader sections of the same or slightly different diameters, i.e., a normal progression such as 20-pound test to 25-pound test to 30-pound test, etc. If the diameters to be joined vary widely, an offset nail knot is superior. The double nail knot is made in two parts; the first end is formed with 4 turns around the nail, and the leader section is then passed through the center as illustrated. The nail is removed, and the knot formed is partially tightened. Form the other end in the same fashion, remove the nail, and tighten the knot. Slowly draw both ends together, pull secure, and trim excess.

Double Nail Knot

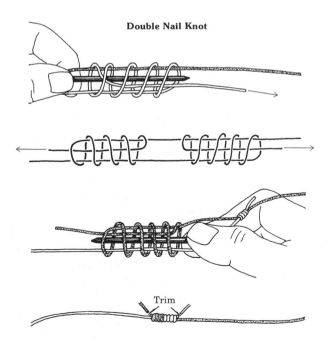

Trim

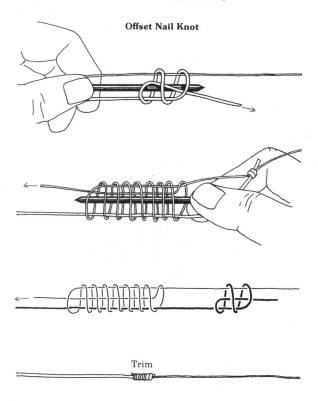

Offset Nail Knot

Trim

Offset Nail Knot

One of the problems in leader building is that we can't always progress smoothly with little variation in diameter between one section and the next. For instance, to make abrupt tapers for casting in the wind, or to help turn over a big-bellied fly line, it may be necessary to jump as much as 20 pounds in rated test between two strands. To tie light leader material to a heavy diameter, use the offset nail knot. While the double nail is perfectly secure on ordinary tapers, it won't hold well if you are going, for example, from 20 to 40 to 60 pounds, which is often necessary in a saltwater leader. To maintain a straight leader without the danger of a slipped knot, the bulk of one part of the double nail offsets the bulk of the other part.

To make the offset nail knot, form the heavy part first by making 2 turns around the nail and the leader section; then pass the end through the center. Remove the nail, and partially close the knot. Form the light material by making 8 turns around the nail; then pass the end through the center. Remove the nail, and close the knot. To close, pull the 4 ends tight; then pull on the long ends until the knot is secure. Trim off excess.

Nail-Knot Loop

It is not always practical to attach a lure directly to heavy (60- to 90-pound test) monofilament when using shock tippets. However, with plugs having a built-in action or with large streamer flies, when a knot is drawn tight against the hook eye the lure will not swing freely. The rigidity of the heavy material will destroy their action. This is particularly important when fishing for striped bass, tarpon, snook, bluefish, and other large gamefish. Thus, a loop is often desirable. This one can be used for fish up to 100 pounds or more with perfect safety.

Nail-Knot Loop

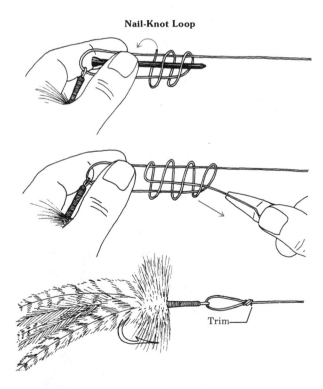

Trim

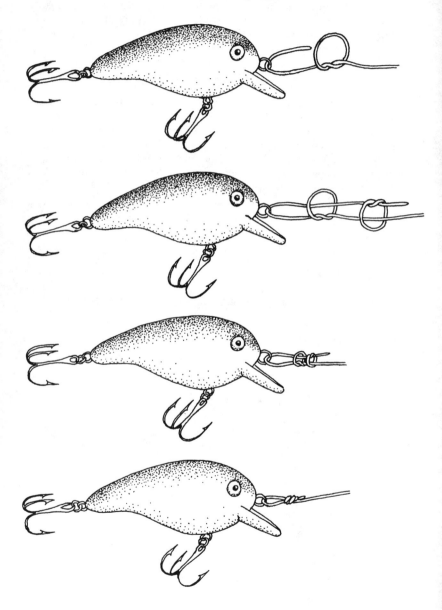

The nail-knot loop will slip under heavy pressure. However, when tied properly, it rarely does, and if it should, the knot merely jams against the hook eye and will not break. The important thing is that its purpose is served; even a big 5/0 bucktail will dance and flutter in a lifelike fashion when secured to a loop.

To make the nail-knot loop, pass the shock tippet through the hook eye and turn the monofilament back parallel to the nail. Make 3 turns around the nail and standing part, and pass through the center. Remove the nail. Hold one finger on the loop formed, and with a pair of pliers pull the knot as tight as you can. Trim off the excess.

Homer Rhode Loop Knot

This tie serves the same purpose as the nail-knot loop; it forms a loop through the eye of a lure, as opposed to a rigid knot secured to the hook eye, allowing the lure to swim more freely. It is easy to tie; however, it is not as strong as the nail-knot loop and should not be used in materials testing under 30 pounds.

To make the Homer Rhode, tie a simple overhand knot about 4 inches from the end of your line or tippet. Pass the end of the line through the hook eye, then back through the center of the overhand knot. With the free end of the line make another overhand knot around the standing part of the line. Slowly pull the two knots tight, sliding them together so that they jam one against the other.

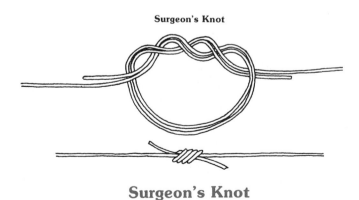

Surgeon's Knot

Surgeon's Knot

One of the simplest and most useful knots, especially in saltwater fishing, the surgeon's knot can be used to join monofilaments of

equal or unequal diameter or to join braided wire to monofilaments. It is commonly used to tie on shock tippets up to 60-pound
test. To make the knot, overlap the ends of the materials to be
joined and tie a simple overhand knot treating both strands as one.
Pass the two strands through the loop again and pull tight. For
greater strength, pass the strands through the loop 4 times to make
a double surgeon's knot.

Palomar Knot

This is a basic knot for tying a line or leader to a hook, lure, fly,
or swivel eye. It serves the same purpose as the improved clinch
knot, and some anglers find it easier to tie. Pass the line or leader
through the eye of the hook and return, forming a 3- to 4-inch loop.
Hold the line and hook with one hand and tie a loose overhand
knot in the double line with the other hand. Now hold the loose
overhand knot and pull the loop around the hook. Pull on the
doubled line to draw knot tight.

Palomar Knot

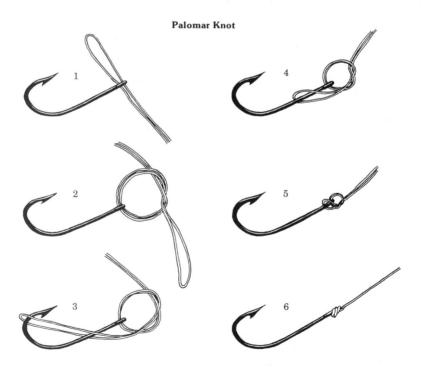

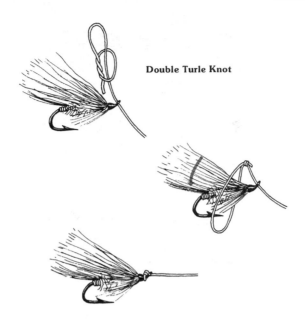

Double Turle Knot

Double Turle Knot

The double turle knot is compact, strong, and comes out straight
through the eye of the fly. To make it, pass the end of your leader through the hook eye from the front and slide the fly up the
leader and out of the way. Make a slip knot in the end of the leader
bringing the end around twice. Pass the end through both turns
so that the extension is parallel to the standing part. Draw tight,
and pass the loop thus formed over the fly so that it closes snug
around the head of the fly and not in the eye or on the leader itself.

Spider Hitch

The spider hitch is used to make a double line or to form loops in
monofilament when making saltwater leaders. This is a very simple and a secure tie. First double the line and form a reverse loop
toward the free end. Hold the base of the loop between your thumb
and forefinger. Wrap the double line 5 times around your thumb
and the reverse loop. Pass the closed end through the reverse loop.
Pull the closed end so that it unwinds slowly off your thumb until
the knot tightens.

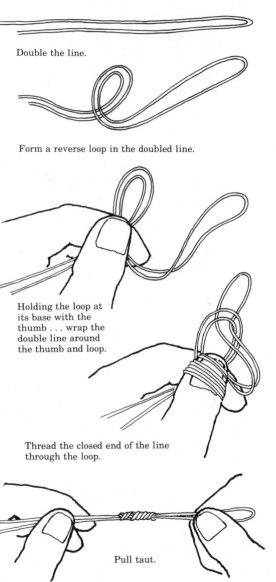

Double the line.

Form a reverse loop in the doubled line.

Holding the loop at its base with the thumb . . . wrap the double line around the thumb and loop.

Thread the closed end of the line through the loop.

Pull taut.

Spider Hitch

Perfection Loop Knot

The perfection loop knot is used to tie a loop at the end of a synthetic leader, such as a nylon leader used in fly-fishing. The loop serves the purpose of joining the line and leader together. Hold the nylon between thumb and forefinger with about 4–5 inches extending upward. With the other hand, form a loop behind the stem and hold the crossing part between the fingers. Make a second loop in front of the first loop, and bring the end around between the two thus formed. Holding it with slight pressure at the base, bring the second, or front, loop through the first loop with the fingers of your other hand. Continue pulling the second loop slowly upward while holding the free end of the nylon and simultaneously drawing the knot portion closed.

Perfection Loop Knot

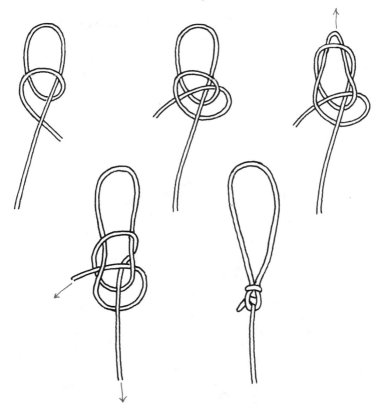

Improved End Loop

Improved End Loop

The improved end loop is used for making loops in leaders or heavy lines. It is stronger than the perfection loop knot but bulkier, and is used to best advantage when security is of prime importance. The knot is easy to make. Form a double strand of 4–6 inches in length by folding the end of material back parallel to itself. Next, turn the double strand around itself 5 times, and insert the end through the first loop formed. Pull the knot as tight as possible.

Salmon Hook Knot and Bumper Tie

These two knots are popular among West Coast salmon and steelhead fishermen. The hook knot is used for snelling and permanently securing monofilament to the shank for whole and cut-bait rigs. Generally, this requires two hooks, tied in with the same knot on the same leader and spaced to fit the bait. In the bumper tie, the large, adjustable loop is snugged down to hold the bait in place.

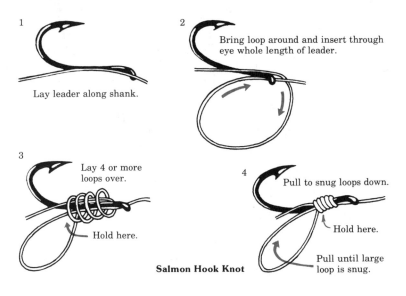

1 Lay leader along shank.

2 Bring loop around and insert through eye whole length of leader.

3 Lay 4 or more loops over. Hold here.

Salmon Hook Knot

4 Pull to snug loops down. Hold here. Pull until large loop is snug.

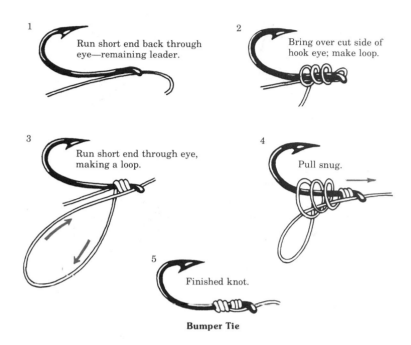

1 Run short end back through eye—remaining leader.

2 Bring over cut side of hook eye; make loop.

3 Run short end through eye, making a loop.

4 Pull snug.

5 Finished knot.

Bumper Tie

Bimini Twist

This is a difficult but useful knot, used to create a double line with the full strength of an unknotted line. A long loop takes two people (see illustration), but a short loop—placed over spread knees to keep the line apart—will work. First double the line to form a loop somewhat longer than what you want to finish with and, holding the loop at one end, twist the loop 20 times, keeping the index finger in the loop and making circular motions with the wrist. Tighten the twist by separating the two strands of the loop at one end and working back to the other end, which should also be firmly held apart. Bring the loose end of the line toward the loop while placing a forefinger on the twist, continuing to open the loop. Now the twist begins to rotate. As it rotates, the open end is automatically wound around it. Be careful that the open end does not wrap over itself. Continue wrapping until you reach the end of the twist. Stop the rotation by holding the wrap carefully, and at the same time make a half hitch around the right base of the loop. Continue to keep the two lines of the loop separated. Then tie another half

Bimini Twist

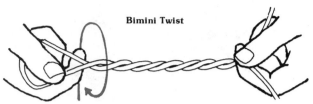

Double the line and form a loop longer than the one you want to end up with. One person holds the end of the line, the other holds the loop end and proceeds to twist the loop 20 times by keeping his index finger in the loop and making circular wrist motions.

Next, separate the two strands of the loop and work back toward the open end to tighten the twist. The person holding the loose ends then pulls the line apart.

The person holding the loose ends puts his forefinger on the twist and brings the running end of the line toward the loop, as the first person at the looped end continues to open the loop. The twist begins to rotate.

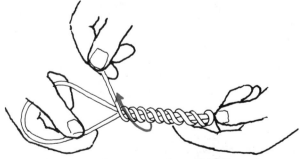

As the twist rotates, the running end automatically winds around it. Be careful not to let the running end wrap over itself. The wrap should continue until the end of the twist is reached.

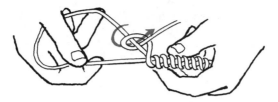

Stop the rotation by holding the wrap carefully, and at the same time make a half hitch around the right base of the loop, while the two lines of the loop are kept separated.

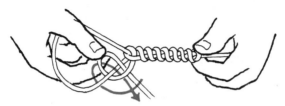

Tie another half hitch about the left base of the loop. You can now let go of the wrap.

Finish the knot with a clinch knot tied about both lines of the loop at the base. Do this by placing the lines of the loop together while taking 3 or 4 wraps around both lines and coming through the line. Pull the knot tight.

The knot is completed when the clinch knot is pulled tight and clipped.

hitch around the left base of the loop. You can let go of the wrap at this point and finish the knot off with a little clinch knot tied around both lines of the loop at the base. To do this, place the lines of the loop together while taking 3 or 4 wraps around both lines and coming through, as in the illustration on the previous pages. Pull the knot up tight and clip it.

Wire Leaders

Generally speaking, some type of metal or synthetic leader is essential to saltwater casting. Almost every oceangoing gamefish is either peculiarly equipped for cutting a casting line by nature—as in the scissorlike mouth of the barracuda, the razor-edged operculum of the snook, or the bony scutes of the jack crevalle—or by habitat—as in the coral caves of the grouper or the oyster bars of the spotted weakfish. Inasmuch as refined terminal tackle seems to be comparatively unimportant in saltwater fishing (although there are notable exceptions), the angler has a somewhat wider choice of leader sizes and materials.

Piano Wire

Straight piano-wire leaders are popular among saltwater casters. These are made of high-carbon steel that has been galvanized or tinned and stainless steel. The advantage of piano wire is that it's relatively cheap, easy to loop for attaching the lure or hardware, and strong per diameter. However, wire kinks readily, and the kinks break. Its inherent stiffness also spoils the lure action. These drawbacks are evidently minor considerations, as the material is still preferred by many experts when casting for big fish. If you use piano wire for densely packed schoolfish, like the Spanish mackerel, bluefish, or king mackerel, be certain to buy the kind that's colored tobacco brown rather than the bright, tinned finish. When one fish hits the lure, others will slice a reflecting wire with the precision of a switchblade. Of course, plain wire rusts more quickly than tinned, but in saltwater fishing, metal of any kind cannot be trusted for prolonged periods. The same applies to swivels and snaps, which should be black or brown. Piano-wire leaders can be bought ready-made with twisted loops or with swivels attached. Some anglers obtain the raw material in coils and make their leaders on location.

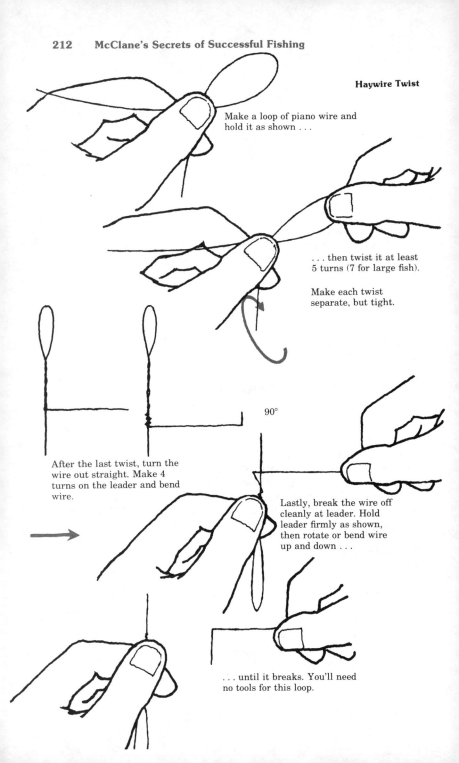

Haywire Twist

Make a loop of piano wire and hold it as shown . . .

. . . then twist it at least 5 turns (7 for large fish).

Make each twist separate, but tight.

90°

After the last twist, turn the wire out straight. Make 4 turns on the leader and bend wire.

Lastly, break the wire off cleanly at leader. Hold leader firmly as shown, then rotate or bend wire up and down . . .

. . . until it breaks. You'll need no tools for this loop.

Haywire Twist

To make a secure loop in a wire leader, twist both ends of the loop at least 5 times. Then, by holding steady the loop thus formed, wind the free end tightly and uniformly around the standing part 4 turns. Do not cut the free end with pliers; bend the section to be removed at a right angle, and rotate it in a circular motion. The wire will break cleanly at the base where the winding is completed.

Piano wire usually comes in ¼-pound coils and 25-foot coils, and the sizes that are of interest to casters run as follows:

Size	Diameter (inches)	Carbon Steel (test pounds)	Stainless Steel (test pounds)
2	.011	28	27
3	.012	34	32
4	.013	39	38
5	.014	46	44
6	.016	60	58
7	.018	76	69
8	.020	93	86
9	.022	114	104
10	.024	136	128
11	.026	156	148
12	.028	184	176
13	.030	212	202
14	.032	240	232
15	.034	282	272

Braided Wire

Braided- or twisted-wire leaders are more flexible and less liable to kink than straight wire, but they are somewhat heavier in diameter for comparable strengths. They also require a crimping tool and metal sleeves for forming swivel connections if you make your own. However, none of these disadvantages outweighs the advantage the flexible leader has when you are hooked to an active jumping or rolling fish. Braided wire is also made with nylon cover, and this kind is most popular in both saltwater and freshwater fishing. The nylon-covered braid has great flexibility, seldom kinks, and the wire strands do not fray. These come ready-made in various sizes; most popular are the 6-inch and 9-inch lengths in 20-pound test for freshwater, and 12-inch and 18-inch lengths in 30-pound test for saltwater.

Waders and Wading

Waders

Waterproof footwear is generally divided into two types: boots, or hip waders, and chest-high waders. Both types are important in many kinds of freshwater and saltwater fishing. Although the foot portion of most waders is made of rubber, the remainder or pants portion is usually made of a lightweight material, such as rubberized cloth, to allow greater freedom of movement.

HIP WADERS Hip waders (hip boots) give ample waterproofing to wade small streams or shallow water. In warm weather they are more comfortable than chest-high waders and often the better choice for that reason. Quality lightweight hip waders with cushion insoles and nonslip, cleated rubber outsoles are standard equipment for the stream angler. These should have reinforced toes and edges to prevent foot bruises when wading on rocks. Hip waders may also be obtained with felt outsoles, or felt sandals or spiked creepers may be slipped over the feet for greater security on moss-slippery stream beds.

Hip waders can be decidedly dangerous if the angler is not cautious and goes over their tops in swift deepwater. They will become extremely heavy and almost impossible to lift against the force of a current. Chest-high waders, on the other hand, have a greater safety factor, particularly when they are snugly secured at the top with a belt (the pucker string is inadequate). Contrary to the popular belief, a "spill" is not necessarily a serious affair— so long as the waders do not fill with water to drag you down. If snugly drawn at the top, there will be enough air imprisoned actually to help float you. This knowledge should not encourage reckless wading, for common sense tells us that swiftwater can always be dangerous.

CHEST-HIGH WADERS Chest-high waders permit wading in deeper water and are essential on all big streams. In the early season or during cold-weather periods, they also provide more warmth. Chest-high waders are divided into two types: stocking-foot waders, which require the use of brogues or wading shoes, and boot-foot waders, which are made with regular boot feet. Both types are popular, but the older stocking-foot waders are preferred by many experts. One advantage is that the lower leg, being small and of thin material, presents a minimum of resistance to the current when it is folded around the calf and held snugly at the ankle by the brogue. And the stocking wader, of thin, flexible material including that of the feet, can be easily turned inside out for drying. However, while the brogue is comfortable enough on the foot, it is rather heavy and clumsy, since it must be worn at least a size larger than your shoe size to permit wearing a pair of heavy, wool socks over the wader foot to protect the rubber from abrasion by sand and gravel. The feet will wear out comparatively quickly. If you prefer this type of wader, wear only felt or hobnailed brogues for safe footing. The felt may be had on a canvas shoe, much like the standard basketball shoe, which is a bit lighter than the standard wader brogue with its heavy leather sole, and is more easily dried out.

The boot-foot wader may be slightly heavier, but it also has advantages. You do not have to remove and dry the wading shoes after each trip. The semistiff boot leg comes about halfway up the calf, where it is cemented to the lighter wader material, and it thus protects the shins during the many inevitable stumbles over logs and boulders. The heavier material of the lower leg also resists snagging on sharp underwater rocks and other hidden hazards. Some anglers think it difficult to dry out the boot-foot type when the inside is wet from perspiration, but this is easily accomplished by turning the tops down as far as possible, spreading the boot top, and either placing the waders out in the sun or hanging them upside down to catch the warm air rising from a stove or campfire.

It is wise to always buy waders of a generous size. In cold weather you may want to wear extra underwear or trousers inside them, and it is better to have the legs wrinkled and crotch loose to permit unhampered climbing over fences and logs. Waders too tight will bind your every movement, and the strain will cause undue wear at the seams.

SOCKS   All outdoor footgear should of course be purchased large enough to allow for heavier socks and also to permit your feet to "work" and spread naturally without cramping. Some dampness always occurs inside hip boots and waders. Your skin constantly perspires, which is not noticeable when you are inactive but is obvious when you're at work. It is even more noticeable when you are wading in coldwater, and at times waders feel as if they are leaking, because the warmth of your body causes condensation. Water removes heat from the body about twenty-seven times faster than air does, so the temperature of your feet, which have a relatively limited blood supply to begin with, can drop quickly. In very cold climates it is advisable to wear insulated boots designed to trap air without compressing moisture in your wool socks. There are some hip boots that have been designed for a comfort range from 0 to 20 degrees. This is ideal for arctic wear in the fishing season, as well as for most ice fishing. Wool socks are essential for both warmth and comfort. The maze of fibers in wool yarn forms tiny air cells that delay the passage of heat from the body. It is also wise when wading ice streams to wear a pair of light-wool socks inside a pair of heavy ones, because the air space between provides insulation.

Wading

The first rule in wading is to know where you are going. Some people get so intent on their fishing that they have no idea where they can make an exit. It's easy to find a safe place to enter a river, but after an hour or two of casting, you might be a half mile downstream in a cul-de-sac of wildwater and perpendicular banks. Dunkings usually occur when the angler tries to walk along the bottom as though he were strolling down a street. Aside from the fact that rocks are not always resting securely on the bottom and can roll or tilt, they are invariably covered with some algae, so the expert wader is, above all, methodical. Even if a bottom looks perfectly stable, he treats each stone as a booby trap and always has an escape route in mind.

Actually, it becomes reflexive, by surveying the visible part of a river, to know immediately just how far one can wade in any direction. Bear in mind that expert wading consists not only of being able to traverse a deep stream but also of the ability to select the best position for casting, then stalking fish without disturbing the water. Often as not, beginners wade where they should be fishing and fish where they should be wading. Like so many sports, the technique starts with footwork.

If you are a beginner, stay in the shallows and invade any deep places cautiously. When wading upstream or down, move slowly, placing one foot ahead of the other and keeping your weight on the back, or anchor, foot until the front, or lead, foot is planted firmly on the bottom. However, when wading across a strong current (and this is where nine-tenths of all spills occur), keep your feet spread apart, and, with knees slightly bent, proceed in short, shuffling steps.

The technique is similar to the footwork of a fencer in the *en garde* position. No sport demands a keener sense of balance than fencing. In taking the basic guard position, the foil man stands with heels together and feet at right angles so that the front foot points at his opponent; then he moves the front foot about 1½ lengths forward, bends both knees to distribute his weight evenly on the legs, and keeps his body erect. From this position, the fencer is able to advance (front foot first), retreat (rear foot first), jump forward or backward, and lunge and recover smoothly. It takes years of practice to do it well, but the principles of balance in motion are the same, and when they are modified to suit your needs, you'll find yourself perfectly at ease in fastwater.

Assuming that you are crossing a current coming from the left, place your left foot ahead of your right foot; slide the left foot forward about 1½ lengths; then bring the right foot forward the same distance. Repeat these half steps so that your right foot never passes your left foot. You can move along quite rapidly in this fastwater shuffle, which has the virtue of maintaining perfect balance with your body weight evenly distributed on both feet. Consistent with good balance in either sport, the lead foot should be pointed in the direction of travel and the anchor foot pointed at right angles from it; in other words, with the current coming from the left, your left foot is pointed cross-stream, while the right foot is pointed downstream. With the current flowing from the right, your right foot becomes the lead foot pointing cross-stream, and your left foot is the anchor foot pointed downstream.

Surf-Fishing

Although a variety of tackle can be used in surf-fishing—even the fly rod when conditions are right—catching inshore marine gamefish is an art form in itself, requiring specialized gear. A two-handed casting method is necessary, with either a large spinning reel or a multiplying reel.

Surf Tackle

The conventional surf rod is a casting instrument designed to hurl heavy lures or sinkers to a maximum distance. Casts of 250 feet are not unusual for a skilled surf-fisherman. Obviously, manufacturers of surf rods find it necessary to strike a delicate balance between power and flexibility, so that an angler can make the long cast, then set the hooks and play a strong fish without breaking the line. With such a rod, all surf-fishing experts recommend and use the wide-spooled squidding reel fitted with free-spool and star-drag features. Reel size and line test will depend on the rod's action and the type of surf-casting contemplated. The reel should always have a 150- to 250-yard capacity.

A one-piece rod is always preferable to the two-piece model, and such rods can be manufactured with ferruled spring butts for those who anticipate difficulty in transporting the longer stick from home to fishing grounds. Standard spring butts usually measure 30 inches from butt cap to reel seat. This is correct for a person of average height, but may not fit the shorter individual or the caster with exceptionally long arms. A one-piece rod with a generous portion of the butt section cork-taped permits an angler to clamp his reel at the proper location. Guides should be the best obtainable, with strong bridges and quality rings. Agate rings offer the least friction; Carboloy is hard, but the friction factor is somewhat increased. Cheap, plated rings are to be avoided; they crack and, subsequently, fray the line.

Most popular of the conventional surf rods is a medium-action

stick that measures 9½–10 feet from butt to tip-top and is calibrated to handle lures in the 2- to 4-ounce weight bracket. Lighter
and heavier lures may be cast, but performance falls off on either
side of the optimum. Three of the major variations are listed below.

The Tidewater Anglers Club of Virginia tournament rod, a
10½-foot, heavy-duty stick that is designed to cast lures in the 4-
to 6-ounce weight range to maximum distance. This rod currently
holds all major East Coast tournament records; yet it is a practical
fishing stick in areas where heavy lures or heavy bait-sinker combinations must be cast to extreme range. It is, understandably, a
fatiguing rod for the fisherman to use.

Cape Cod's Production Rod, so-called because many of the rod-
and-line commercial striper fishermen of that area use it to take
big bass in the surf, also measures 10½ feet, and is calibrated to
cast lures and baits weighing 3–5 ounces. The rod is popular only
in New England and along the Outer Banks of North Carolina.

New Jersey's Jetty Rod is a cut-down version of the standard
surf-casting stick. Overall, it measures 8–9 feet, and butt length
is shortened (to 20–24 inches) to facilitate snap casts when the
angler is precariously balanced on a barnacle-covered rock. This
rod is also used by many boat fishermen who steer their craft just
outside a breaking surf and cast in to the shore. Its lure-weight
bracket is similar to that of the standard medium.

Popping rods are still popular on all coasts. These are simply
short, light, squidding sticks, the link between a saltwater bait-
casting rod and a surf rod. Calibrations would fall at 1–2½ ounces
of lure weight. The rod is ideally chosen for light plugging and for
short-range surf-casting for such species as the northern weakfish
and small channel bass. It is also effective on school stripers.

Spinning is essentially a light-tackle technique. Hence it does
not supersede squidding but adds a new and efficient weapons system to the angler's arsenal.

With certain exceptions, the heavy surf-spinning rod is similar
to the two-handed conventional surf rod. Its guides are much
larger, diminishing from a relatively huge gathering guide down
to a standard tip-top. Lengths run 8–9 feet overall, and rods usually boast "fast," i.e., whippy, tips. These big fixed-spool outfits are
calibrated to cast lures in the 2- to 4-ounce weight range. The
heavy surf-spinning reel, an open-face type with smooth, adjustable drag, should hold 200 yards of 15- to 18-pound-test monofilament line. Heavier tests are impractical. The combination is specialized, popular in some areas of Massachusetts and Rhode Island,
along the Outer Banks of North Carolina, and on some sections of
the Pacific Coast.

A more popular outfit is the medium-weight rod, which is favored by a great many surfmen on all coasts. This two-handed stick measures 8–9 feet, and is calibrated to cast lures or baits in the 1½- to 3-ounce weight bracket. Again, the reel should hold at least 200 yards of line, with tests running 12–15 pounds.

The Correct Line

To insure optimum results, a surf-fisherman must choose the proper line for his tackle combination and method. In spinning, the problem is simply that of choosing a monofilament of the correct pound test to match rod action.

Linen, or Cuttyhunk, once considered the classic line for surf-fishing, no longer sets the pace—having been superseded by nylon braid, Dacron braid, and nylon monofilament. Each of these synthetics offers advantages and disadvantages.

Nylon braid is the most effective in the casting of heavy artificial lures. The line is smooth; it picks up enough water to provide some measure of "coolant," for the caster's thumb, has a good knot factor, and is not excessively elastic. Squidders consider 36-pound test the classic weight but often use lighter lines—and heavier. Where big channel bass or stripers are sought, 45-pound test may be a good choice.

Dacron braid is finer in diameter per rated pound test than is nylon and has far less stretch. This increases the angler's chances of hooking fish but contributes to a slightly inferior knot factor. For casters with tender thumbs, Dacron is a "hot" line. On the credit side, again, Dacron's fine diameter and lack of buoyancy make it an exceptionally good choice for the angler who plans to fish with bait on the bottom.

Nylon monofilament is well chosen for certain phases of surf-fishing. Round monofilament in the lighter tests, say, up to 30 pounds, vies with Dacron in bottom fishing where wave action, current, and wind tend to handicap the angler. Flattened or ribboned monofilaments in tests up to 30 pounds are effective in the casting of artificial lures. Heavier monofilaments become unmanageable—and all of the single-strand lines are excessively elastic by comparison with the braids.

Leaders

While rod, reel, and line comprise the heart of a surf-fishing outfit, leaders are sometimes necessary. These may be made of heavy monofilament for the taking of gamefish that lack sharp cutting teeth, or wire or nylon-covered wire if the quarry is sharp-toothed. When using artificial lures, the leader should be encumbered with a minimum of hardware. One terminal snap is sufficient, and this only to facilitate the rapid changing of lures. Swivels of various kinds, together with sinkers, are necessary only when bottom fishing is the method used.

Surf-Fishing Lures

Artificial lures will tempt any of the gamefish coveted by surf-fishermen on the Atlantic, the Gulf, or the Pacific coasts. Even cod and flounder find it impossible to resist a properly fished lure. Success for the angler lies in presenting the right tempter at the right time—and in the strike zone.

Five major types of artificial baits (one actually a natural bait rigged for casting) are used by the surf caster: metal squids; weighted bucktails or feather lures; plugs; rigged eels and eel-skin rigs; and a variety of soft plastic lures.

METAL SQUIDS   A widely effective range of metal squids are available to the surfman. Originally cast of block tin, which has a soft and almost translucent glow, many of the modern squids are made of stainless steel or baser metals that have been chrome plated. In type they range from the old, bent sand eel through keeled and diamond jigs and spoon-shaped creations. All are intended to simulate the flash and frantic swimming action of small baitfish, and all are at their best in the froth of a breaking surf.

Metal squids are produced with single and treble hooks, with and without bucktail or feather dressing. Often they are improved by attaching strips of pork rind to their hooks. These lures are popular in 1½ to 5-ounce sizes. Metal squids are most effective during daylight hours but sometimes tempt fish at night.

WEIGHTED BUCKTAIL   Called bugeye, doodlebug, and weighted streamer on some sections of the coast, a weighted bucktail is a lead-headed jig, usually dressed with natural bucktail or synthetic fibers, feathers, plastic, or rubber strips. It is manufactured in a variety of weights and sizes. This lure is most effective when cast up and across a strong current, then retrieved in a series of hops. The bucktail is an excellent nighttime bait and often produces as well in daylight hours. Like the metal squid, its fish-taking potential may sometimes be increased by impaling a pork-rind strip on its single hook.

PLUGS Squidding at one time reigned supreme as the province of the surf-casting purist. Today, the plug caster often scorns any other method and maintains that his lure and technique are most sporting, most spectacular, and most effective.

These claims are open to debate, but the treble-hooked plug certainly catches tons of surf-running gamefish. Sporting-goods shops offer a wide assortment of these lures in 1½ to 4-ounce sizes, and the selection ranges from large surface swimmers and sub-surface wigglers, through poppers, darters, and torpedo-shaped types with no action other than that imparted by the angler's rod. The lures are manufactured of plastic and wood, and, for heavy saltwater use, the treble hooks are strung on end-to-end rigging. Plugs are effective on day or night tides.

RIGGED EELS Rigged eels and eel-skin rigs are most familiar to the striped-bass and bluefishing enthusiast of the North Atlantic Coast. The whole eel, a 10- to 14-inch specimen preferred, is strung with heavy nylon or linen when striped bass are the quarry. If bluefish are present, chain is used to keep these sharp-toothed marauders from chopping the bait into small pieces. Two or three single hooks are sewed in at the appropriate locations—one at the head and one or two protruding from the belly.

To differentiate between weighted and unweighted eel rigs, that with a lead head is called an eel bob; the unweighted version is usually referred to as a whole eel. These baits are most effective at night when they are cast and retrieved slowly with a periodic pulsing of the rod tip.

EEL-SKIN RIGS The eel-skin rig is a far different lure, in two basic types. One, used in canals and estuaries where the current is strong and the lure is fished close to a hard bottom, is simply the skin of an eel fitted over a double-hooked, hollow-headed lead jig. Water, passing through the jig's hollow head, inflates the skin and gives it action.

On sand beaches the eel-skin is often used in conjunction with a keeled squid. Here, a ring is soldered to the jig so that the skin can be attached. This lure rides higher than the hollow-headed type and works above the sandy bottom. Both lures are most effective during the hours of darkness, although they often take fish in broad daylight. While famous for execution on striped bass and bluefish, eel rigs will take other inshore gamefish.

SOFT PLASTIC LURES Soft plastic lures are relatively new on the surf-fishing scene; yet they have succeeded in catching fish and may soon become as important as the old favorites. Plastic eels and sea worms, some of them fitted with wobble plates to insure swimming action, have earned the admiration of saltwater anglers.

All of the artificial lures favored by surf casters are manufactured in a wide range of weights and sizes. Many simulate specific bait species, and others (among them some of the most effective) rely on action alone.

Rigs and Baits

The striped bass, that unpredictable surf fish with a host of admirers on America's Atlantic and Pacific coasts, will eat just about any marine tidbit that happens along. The striper's bill of fare includes herring, menhaden, anchovies, mackerel, bullheads, sand launces, and any other small fish—including baby stripers. In addition, no crab, clam, shrimp, squid, worm, eel, sand bug, or small lobster is safe if a bass is hungry. Channel bass are nearly as catholic in their tastes, although, as they grow to trophy size, the big reds are primarily bottom feeders. Bluefish have been likened to animated chopping machines; they seem to kill for the sheer love of killing and will attack a wide variety of marine bait species. Obviously, the fish that frequent inshore waters may be baited with many natural offerings. It is the angler's task to determine which of the tempters is most in demand at the moment. Most of the various gamefish tend to be selective.

Among common and useful bottom rigs for bait fishing, first on the list is the fishfinder rig. This is a simple, sliding sinker arrangement that permits the biting gamester to move off with the hook and line while the sinker remains anchored. The rig is most effective on bottoms that are not swept by heavy currents; there the pressure of water on the line creates considerable drag and cancels out the benefits of the fishfinder.

Anglers seeking red drum or black drum, neither of which species is particularly adverse to dragging a sinker attached to a bait, use a three-way swivel with the hook attached to a short leader and sinker to another and even shorter trace.

Choice of sinker shape and weight is of major importance in surf-fishing. On sand or mud bottoms the pyramid type, with its sharp, angled edges, is most likely to hold. Where rocky outcrops or coral are obvious, use the dipsey or bank sinker, which is rounded and, so, less likely to foul. Sinker weights will range from about 1 ounce, on up to 4–6 ounces, with the heavier rigs necessary wherever pounding surf and strong currents predominate.

A Selection of Surf-Casting Lures

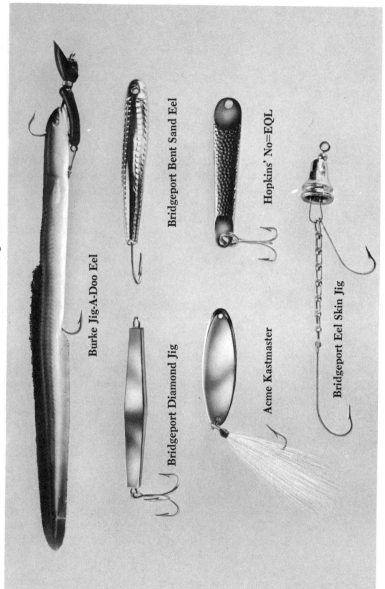

Burke Jig-A-Doo Eel

Bridgeport Bent Sand Eel

Hopkins' No=EQL

Bridgeport Eel Skin Jig

Bridgeport Diamond Jig

Acme Kastmaster

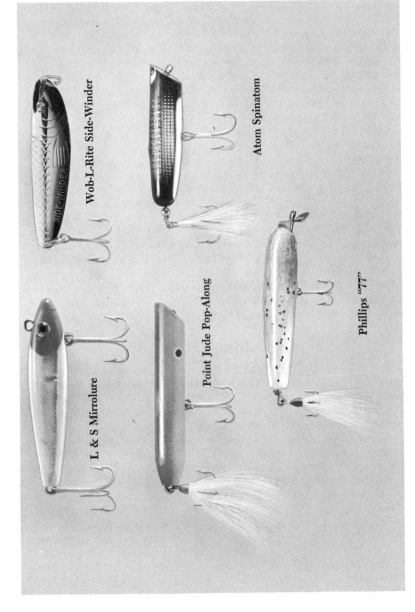

Wob-L-Rite Side-Winder

Atom Spinatom

L & S Mirrolure

Point Jude Pop-Along

Phillips "77"

Baits can be lifted off the bottom—out of the range of bottom-feeding trashfish, or to lure gamesters feeding several feet over the bottom—by attaching a small float just ahead of the hook. Sometimes the cork or balsa-wood float can aid in luring a hungry fish, and for that reason it is often painted bright red or yellow.

A technique that often produces strikes is the presentation of a live baitfish on a fishfinder rig. Hook the baitfish through the tough skin just ahead of the pelvic fins, so that it will be able to maintain balance in the water, even though held in one place by the restraining line and sinker.

Proper choice of hook patterns and sizes is important in bait fishing, with size often most critical. The angler who is seeking school stripers, for example, will be most successful if he uses a hook in the 1/0–3/0 size range. If large bass are expected, choose hooks ranging 6/0–8/0—depending also on the type of bait employed.

Natural presentation is of major importance. Sea worms bunched on a hook may take a hungry fish, but the wary and selective gamester is more likely to accept a worm that has been threaded well up on the hook shank so that it streams naturally in the current. Always use fresh bait. Remember that a stale, bleached-out offering discharges little of its fresh, basic scent into the surrounding water. Most gamefish rely on their sense of smell as well as their eyes to locate food.

Surf-Fishing Technique

The surf caster must be both hunter and fisherman. Whatever his quarry, it will be necessary for the angler to search for the most promising locations and then take due notice of signs that indicate the presence of feeding gamefish. Tide, wind, weather, and water conditions must be taken into account.

Upon visiting an unfamiliar beach, the experienced surf-fisherman launches a quiet reconnaissance. If possible, he surveys the area during a period of low tide when the location of inshore holes, gullies, and sloughs are easily determined. These will serve later on as the aquatic highways of gamefish when the tide begins to flood back in. The points and bars that produce clashing rips at specific stages of the tide are worth particular attention, for here the baitfish and other sea creatures will be tumbled, and predators will lie in wait. Inlets or openings that pour water into the sea are potential hot spots, since they discharge hordes of bait as the tide ebbs. In such a spot the falling tide may be more productive for the fisherman than the flow.

Evidence of feeding fish is often graphic. You may see them breaking the surface, or perhaps they will be betrayed by sudden, swift flurries of harried bait. Terns, herring gulls, and other sea birds gather in over feeding fish. Indeed, a single tern may pinpoint the quarry by pausing in its straightaway flight to dip down and then to swing around in a tight, exploratory circle.

Even at night, the surf caster looks for a "sign." A half dozen flopping baitfish on the beach may mean that predators are feeding close to shore. The slap of a gamester's tail can be distinguished through the hiss and crash of breakers. Some of the popular gamefish betray themselves to the angler who has a sensitive nose. Striped bass smell like thyme, bluefish throw off an aroma of fresh-cut melons, and channel bass exude an acrid, chemical scent.

Surf fish often run close to the beach, searching for food right in the wash of the breakers. For that reason it pays to work a lure or bait all the way to the rod. The speed of retrieve may be varied until the ideal pace is rewarded by a strike. Note that retrieves are slowed to a minimum after dark.

In squidding, particularly where the lure is fished through the whitewater of breaking waves, the cast should be timed so that the artificial drops right behind an onrushing breaker. Begin the retrieve immediately, and keep the squid swimming in the water behind the tumbling wave, which is relatively clear. Gamefish have a chance to see it there.

Most gamefish prefer to feed in "live water"; that is, where there is some current to stir bait. For that reason, look for action when the tide is rising or falling. The old rule is to fish "two hours before and two hours after the top of the tide." Don't leave it at that, though. A flurry of bait can produce sport at any time, and natural conditions may create ideal fishing at any stage of the tide. Every successful beach fisherman is an opportunist.

Wind is no foe of the surf caster. In fact the angler's chances are always brighter when the surface is disturbed. Some species will feed in tremendously rough water. It rarely gets too turbulent for striped bass, but it can be too calm and bright.

Since gamefish are selective, a change of artificials or of bait may trigger fast action. Sometimes a plug of one color will be scorned, while the same lure that is painted a different hue will draw immediate strikes. Fish feeding on the bottom are likely to ignore a surface-swimming lure but may pounce on a jig bounced along on the sea floor.

Where fish are concentrated in a specific area, say at the edge of a rip or in the turbulent water piling up on a bar, it may be unnecessary to impart motion to fresh bait. Usually, though, it pays to cast the bait well out and then bring it back toward the beach to cover a greater area. This should be done slowly, with appropriate pauses, so that a striped bass, channel bass, surf perch, or any other inshore gamefish will have an opportunity to examine the offering.

Surf casting from a small boat is profitable in many areas. While this should not be attempted unless the angler is familiar with sea conditions on the fishing grounds, or is casting from a boat skippered by a competent local guide, it is a highly effective method. Often lures or bait cast in toward the beach and retrieved through the onrushing waves generate a greater percentage of strikes than the same tempters cast from shore.

Sinkers

Sinkers are molded in various shapes and sizes, each according to its purpose. Sinkers are used to lower, anchor, drift, or troll baits at a designed depth. They also are used in conjunction with artificial lures in fresh- and saltwater fishing.

Bottom-Fishing Sinkers

Weights designed to take a bait to the bottom and to hold it without fouling are of two basic types: the angular, sharp-edged sinkers designed to dig into a soft bottom, best represented by the pyramid; and those that are rounded, and, so, less likely to foul on rocky or coral-encrusted bottoms, represented by the dipsey.

Where tidal currents and wave action are not excessive, the egg sinker is a popular shoalwater type. Tropical anglers use this one on the flats, as it is ideally suited as an anchor for a bonefish or permit bait.

At the opposite extreme, for angling in water that is exceptionally deep, and when seeking such bottom feeders as cod and haddock, the heavy, swiveled drail is a favorite.

Double and triple pyramids are designed to insure greater holding action by the presentation of more edges and flat surfaces. Similarly, multiple-cone sinkers are used to defeat the action of currents and waves, the theory being that one sinker counteracts the movement of another.

Freshwater anglers generally favor the dipsey types for bottom baiting and find that egg-shaped or round weights are ideally suited to many purposes. Split-shot, ranging from BB size up to 00 Buckshot, are effective in light-tackle bait fishing. Wrap-on and clinch-on sinkers often are practical.

Bottom fishing must take into consideration the ground that will be baited, depth of water, strength of currents, and effect of wave action; therefore, sinker types, shapes, weights, and terminal rigs are important.

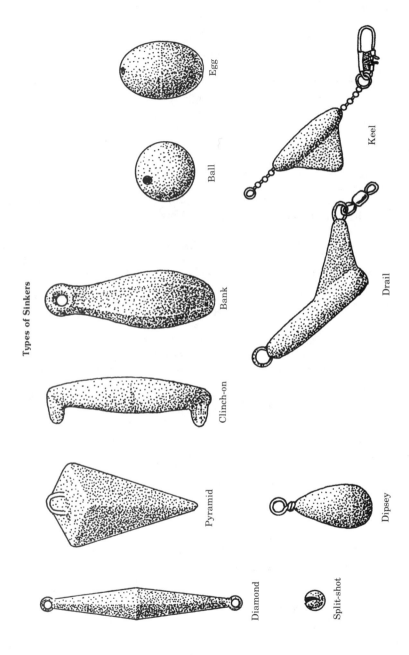

Types of Sinkers

Egg

Ball

Keel

Bank

Drail

Clinch-on

Pyramid

Dipsey

Diamond

Split-shot

Fishfinder

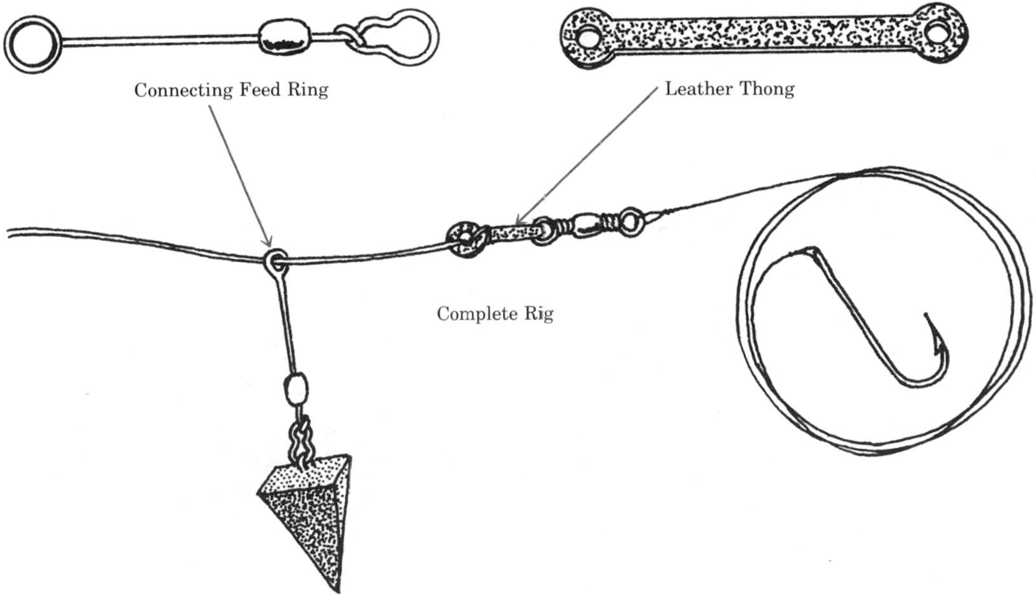

Leather Thong

Connecting Feed Ring

Complete Rig

The required sinker weight depends upon angling technique and the tackle employed. Where trophy striped bass and channel bass are sought in the surf, pyramid and dipsey sinkers weighing 3–6 ounces are most practical, and 4 ounces is probably an average weight. On the offshore grounds, particularly where it is necessary to lower a baited hook to the 100-foot level, 8- to 16-ounce weights are necessary. Here the dipsey or bank and the drail are most practical.

The standard terminal rig for wary gamefish found in the surf or in shallow water is the fishfinder. This is, simply, a sliding-line arrangement. When the fish takes the bait, it is able to move off without disturbing the sinker itself. Fishfinders are available at sporting-goods shops but can be made on the spot. Use one barrel swivel, one snap swivel, and a practical sinker. The snap swivel, to which the sinker is attached, is threaded over the running line. Tie the barrel swivel to the end of the line and then attach a leader and hook to the opposite eye of the barrel swivel. Leather thongs, often specified, are not essential.

Obviously, the egg sinker, with a hole drilled lengthwise, is in itself a fishfinder type, but is employed in shoalwater or where scouring currents and pounding waves are no problem.

Many gamefish seem insensible to the drag of a sinker; where these are sought, leaders may be attached to the weight itself. Numerous rigs are employed, among them the "high-low" combination, in which the sinker is attached to the terminal end of the leader, and hooks—on dropper loops—are secured above at intervals so that the baits will tempt bottom feeders as well as those cruising somewhat above the bottom.

A rig often used for channel bass consists of a three-way swivel to which is attached a heavy monofilament or wire leader and hook, with a sinker suspended below.

The swiveled drail, shaped something like a distorted banana, often features two hooks, each attached to droppers. The rocking action of the drail makes it possible to feel the slightest strike.

Trolling Sinkers

There are several sinker designs that are primarily for trolling with natural or artificial baits. These include the torpedo or cigar-shaped sinkers, keeled sinkers, diving sinkers, and ball sinkers; the latter are often used in conjunction with release devices.

Most popular are the torpedo types. These are produced in a variety of weights and are attached at the junction of line and leader. Swivels are optional.

Keeled sinkers also serve anglers employing a wide range of tackle combinations. Most of these are swiveled, for one of their purposes is the elimination of line twist.

Diving sinkers of several types are available, some with diagonal, inclined planes forward; others are fitted with line-connecting eyes at the balance, so that they normally tend to drop into the depths.

In some areas, particularly on the Pacific Coast and the Great Lakes, cannonball sinkers are popular. These often range up to 3 or more pounds and are molded of cast iron. When a fish strikes the ball sinker is freed by means of a quick-release swivel.

With the exception of the cannonball sinker, most trolling weights are carefully streamlined. The object is a minimum of resistance to the flow of water and prevention of air bubbles, which might detract from the appeal of the following bait.

A "hidden-sinker" rig, first developed on the Pacific Coast and currently used in many areas, is worth noting. Here, the sinker, a ball or dipsey type, is encased in the sewed-up body cavity of a baitfish that will be trolled. The same general principle is employed in the eel bob, a natural eel with a lead weight attached to the head.

In freshwater trolling, the keel sinker is most often used. The clinch-on can be substituted when it is necessary to take a lure or bait a short distance below the surface, and a split-shot may serve the same purpose.

Drifting and Live-Lining

Ball, clinch-on, wrap-around, and dipsey sinkers all are used by anglers who drift or live-line natural bait. In most cases the weight is used to maintain a natural buoyancy or to keep the bait suspended below a float at the desired depth. The weight selected depends on the force of currents and, of course, on depth. Shape is dependent upon the angling technique employed.

Where it is deemed advisable to roll a bait along in a current, egg, split-shot, and wrap-around weights prove most useful. The wrap-around tends to foul in weeds or on the bottom, so it is effective when used in a strong flow where the bait will be presented just below the surface.

The bullet-shaped cone sinker is also used in drift-fishing with artificial lures that are "worked" in the current, such as plastic-worm rigs. It is very popular for casting in freshwater lakes.

Trolling

Trolling is a method of angling whereby an artificial lure or natural bait is drawn behind a moving boat at any depth from the surface to the bottom and at varying speeds according to the species of fish being sought. Some gamefish in both fresh- and saltwater, such as the walleye, lake trout, sailfish, wahoo, marlin, and tuna, are ordinarily taken by trolling rather than by casting or still-fishing. This may be necessitated by the depth at which the fish are located or by the size of the bait (up to 6 pounds in some forms of big-game angling). Trolling is accomplished in all types of craft, from a canoe to a sportfisherman, and with many types of tackle, from a handline to heavy big-game gear. As a rule, motor power, either outboard or inboard, is used, but freshwater anglers often operate their craft manually with oars or paddles, and in some inland states, motor power is prohibited by law.

The Lead-Core Line

Trolling is a complex method of fishing. The tackle, rigging, and techniques vary as greatly as the number of species sought, which encompasses almost every fish found in fresh- or saltwater. In its simplest form the angler may troll for bass or pike in a shallow lake with his regular casting outfit and monofilament line, using his favorite spoon, spinner, or plug. But an elastic monofilament with a specific gravity of 1.08–1.15 (light enough to float) is hardly suitable for deep trolling. If the lake is deep and the fish are below the 30-foot level, it will be necessary to use more specialized equipment, such as a stiff "boat rod" with a Dacron braided lead-core line and trolling reel. The lead core, which is normally used in 100- to 300-foot lengths, varies in diameter and density (.020- to .034-inch diameter and 13 grains per foot to 33 grains per foot), is heavy, and requires a larger reel. This is spliced to 150–200 yards of finer-diameter braided line. A lead-core line is very satisfactory for intermediate trolling depths and is popular for lake trout and landlocked salmon in New England, where the 60-foot level is considered deep. Most lead-core trolling lines are color coded at 30-foot intervals. Thus, with a new color at every 30 feet, after dropping back, say, green, red, blue, white, and yellow, the angler knows he has 150 feet out, and a ½-ounce lure at normal trolling speeds is between 15 and 20 feet down. In regions where gamefish hold at extreme depths, a thinner wire line is preferable. For example, to get a lure down to 300 feet it may be necessary to pay out about 450 feet of line, since it makes a long arc in the water behind a moving boat. This can be controlled with a downrigger (see page 237); nevertheless, a lead core has its depth limitations because of line diameter.

The Wire Line

Wire line is made of stainless steel, bronze, copper, or Monel (nickel alloy), designed for deep trolling. The basic problem in many kinds of trolling is to get a lure to extreme depths. A wire line will sink unencumbered, and, being inelastic, it allows the fisherman to impart movement to his lure by jigging the rod. Wire lines are made in a wide range of sizes; the most popular for general saltwater and freshwater fishing are 14- to 45-pound test (.016- to .024-inch diameter).

The disadvantage of all wire lines is the fact that they are not easy for the beginner to handle. Unlike lead-core line, wire kinks very easily, and the angler must be careful when paying out and spooling the line back. Most kinks are caused by letting the line spin out too fast behind a moving boat. Never, under any circumstances, throw the reel into free-spool without engaging the click or placing the thumb firmly on the spool to prevent an overrun.

Wire-Line Tackle

The reel is an important component of wire-line fishing. The best type is a saltwater star-drag model with a fairly wide, shallow spool. Deep, narrow-spooled reels have been designed for wire-line fishing, but it's easier to pick a backlash out of a wide spool than a narrow one. The spool should never be completely filled but should have a clearance of at least ¼ inch between the line and the crossbars. When retrieving wire line, always level-wind it across the spool from side to side; never let it pile up at one point. This greatly reduces the chance of backlashing.

It is not necessary to fill the reel with wire line. Most of the reel can be spooled to about two-thirds capacity with a Dacron or

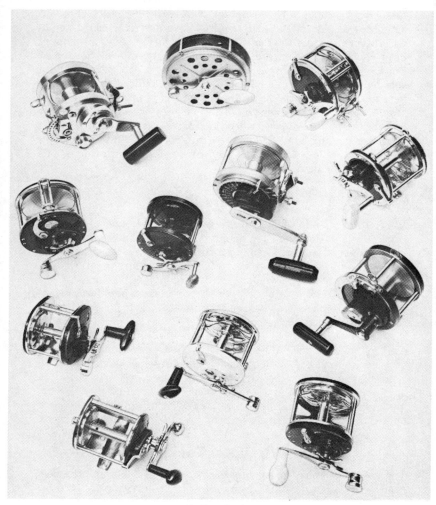

Trolling Reels

monofilament line; then the appropriate amount of wire is spliced to it. For general purposes, 300 feet of solid Monel is sufficient in fresh- and saltwater. The braided and twisted Monel lines, being especially suitable for lesser depths, do not ordinarily require more than 300–450 feet, but they do require more yardage than the solid Monel lines to go down to equal depths. This is the important point to consider when substituting braided and twisted lines for solid Monel. The boat speed and lure weight, as well as the sinking coefficient of the wire itself, are highly variable factors (a 300-foot length of solid Monel line will seldom attain more than a 50-foot depth at an average trolling pace). It is useful, therefore, to mark the wire line at 50- to 100-foot intervals with nail polish, adhesive tape, or masking tape to determine just how much line should be dropped back when fishing in specific areas. Experience counts in this type of angling.

Wire line has no elasticity; therefore a suitable rod is one with some flexibility in the tip. Quick-taper, 6-foot fiberglass trolling rods with a fairly stiff butt are ideal for this purpose. To minimize the tendency of wire to cut through the guides, select Carboloy rings or roller guides.

Trolling in the Great Lakes

Ever since the successful introduction of coho and chinook salmon in the Great Lakes, sport fishermen have upgraded not only their boats and motors but trolling tackle as well. New methods and techniques were developed, the most notable being the use of recording fathometers to spot schools of fish and the use of an entirely new piece of equipment to facilitate what came to be called "depth-control fishing." This technique developed because of the habit of the salmon to stratify at specific water-temperature levels. Here, most salmon schools are found "suspended" at the 50° F.–55° F. temperature range, regardless of how deep the water may be. An ingenious piece of equipment called a downrigger was developed in order to depth-control fish. The downrigger is a rather simple mechanical device that utilizes a heavy weight (usually 7–10 pounds) attached to either braided or solid wire line wound on a large wheel. The lure and leader are attached to the weight by a breakaway coupling and lowered to the depth required (either by counting the turns of the wheel or by a metering system mounted on the wheel). When a salmon strikes, the angler's line is pulled free of the sinker.

Trolling has proven to be the most efficient method of taking salmon in this fishery. Medium to heavy-duty tackle is needed, particularly as the salmon near maturity. Large-capacity spinning or revolving-spool reels with at least 200 yards of 20- to 30-pound line are popular. The lures used differ somewhat from those favored on the Pacific Coast in that bright colors predominate. The basic types are: trolling flies and dodgers, wobbling spoons, swimming plugs, and spinners. Lures that have a built-in action are usually trolled behind "cow-bell" type of flashing attractors that simulate a school of baitfish. Productive trolling depths depend on water temperature and may vary all the way from the surface to water in excess of 100 feet deep, but normally fall in the 30- to 70-foot range. The most productive trolling speed is usually 2–4 miles per hour—much slower than the 6–8 miles per hour used by most saltwater salmon trollers.

The lake trout forms a more static population in the Great Lakes, particularly in the northern areas such as Grand Traverse Bay. Fish are taken from April through November, using techniques and equipment similar to the coho fleet, although the trout are usually found in deeper water. They follow a slightly lower temperature range of 48° F.–51° F., and it's not unusual to troll over 100 feet down to find them.

Trolling for Salmon in the Pacific

Chinook and coho salmon differ in several respects from the Great Lakes fish when caught in their native habitat. They are not "temperature suspended." Here, the chinook may be found near the surface at dawn, but mature fish are invariably found below the 30-foot level throughout the day. Cohos, on the other hand, are most common from the surface down to 30 feet. Ocean cohos are very successfully caught on fly tackle with trolled streamer flies. Chinook prefer a slow-moving lure worked close to the bottom. Trolling is by far the most popular method of taking either fish. The standard tackle consists of a conventional 7½- to 8-foot fast-taper trolling rod or boat rod, with a star-drag reel and 20- to 45-pound-test line. The line capacity should not be less than 200 yards. Dacron, nylon, and monofilament are popular line materials, but many anglers prefer solid Monel wire. Both downriggers and diving planes (made of aluminum or plastic) are popular for deep fishing.

Salmon trolling is practiced in the ocean near shore, in large protected straits or sounds, or in river estuaries. Ordinarily, more fish over a longer period will be taken in the ocean, but there are local exceptions. Ocean trolling can be done with large plugs, spoons, or plastic squids, but most salmon are taken on herring, anchovies, candlefish, or, when available, Pacific sardines. The herring or other baitfish must be presented to the salmon in a particular way, dependent upon the method of bait attachment or use. In trolling, two hooks are ordinarily used. They are small, about No. 2/0, the upper one being free to slide on the line but not so free as to lose the position at which it may be set. Usually both hooks pass through the snout and down through the "chin," the upper hook remaining in that position, and the other is passed through and inserted near the tail in such a manner as to bend the body of the herring slightly. If the hooks are properly positioned the bend will cause the fish to gyrate slowly as the lure is trolled.

HOW TO RIG HERRING   There are three methods in common use for rigging herring and other baitfish for salmon trolling:

Using a treble hook with wire or monofilament leader attached, thread the leader through the herring with a large needle so that it passes from the mouth and out the vent; the hook should be drawn tightly so that one prong can be inserted in the body and the other two prongs exposed at the vent. The mouth of the herring is tied closed with a short string or length of leader material.

Using both a treble and a single hook on monofilament leader, secure the treble hook in the herring just forward of the tail and put the single hook through its mouth.

Using two single hooks on monofilament leader, secure one

Herring Hookups
(top to bottom): whole hookup, plug-cut hookup, and cut-spinner hookup.

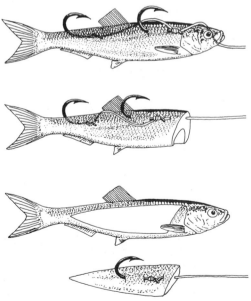

hook in the side of the herring on the lateral surface just forward of the tail and put the other hook through its mouth.

THE HERRING DODGER   As a variation, a Herring Dodger or a large, shiny metal flasher may be placed between the sinker and the bait. The attractive, side-to-side gyrations of the Dodger will in part be transmitted to the bait, and with such a rig the bend in the body of the herring is not as critical. However, the baitfish must be at the correct distance from the Dodger, and the Dodger at the correct distance from the sinker. Most anglers prefer to use a small baitfish—usually not over 5 inches in length— for coho or silver salmon, although chinook can be taken on larger baits. The trolling speed differs with location and, sometimes, species. The coho will often take a bait at speeds of 4–8 miles per hour. The chinook will usually be picked up at a speed of 1–2 miles per hour. In the early part of the day a 4- to 6-ounce crescent sinker should be tried, and larger weights, later in the day. Sinkers up to 32 ounces are used. In river estuaries, salmon will take a brass Bear Valley No. 2–No. 4 or other similar types with a 3/0–5/0 hook, a single Siwash or treble. The trolling speed is slowed to 1–2 miles per hour. For silvers the weight is attached to a 6- to 8-inch dropper line that is about 4 feet above the lure, and the smaller blades are used. Use larger spinners for chinooks.

TERMINAL RIGGING   With medium- or small-size herring the following leader lengths are best:

LEADER LENGTH

Herring Dodger	Distance Sinker to Dodger (inches)	Distance Dodger to Bait (inches)
No. 3/0	20	12
No. 0/0	24	16
No. 0	26	20
No. 1	30	22
No. 2	36	26

Any variation from suggested leader lengths should be on the short side. Longer bait leader cuts down action to bait; longer sinker leader prevents the Herring Dodger from having snappy action; shorter sinker leader tends to prevent it from spinning. Shorten the bait leader when using extra-small herring or baitfish. The amount of line to let out will vary with the weight of the sinker and the depth at which the angler wants the herring to be. For cohos the bait can often be trolled with success 8–10 feet behind the boat in the propeller wash.

THE ROTATING FLASHER   The rotating flasher differs from the Herring Dodger in that it's designed to rotate rather than wobble in the water. Rotating flashers can be trolled at faster speeds than the Herring Dodger, although the optimum is reached when the moving flasher transmits a steady beat to the rod tip. Flashers are usually fished with 50-pound-test Monel wire line and 20-ounce sinkers trailing a plastic squid bait. At greater speeds, larger areas can be covered, which aids in locating salmon schools.

HOW TO LOCATE SALMON   Locating the fish can sometimes be difficult. Often the success of other anglers can be noted. Birds may work on small fish at the surface to give an indication of the possible presence of salmon nearby. The surfacing, feeding fish may be obvious. There may be a traditional trolling "slot" that seems to have fish in it consistently. The mouths of rivers are usually most productive. Tide rips are also favored fishing spots. They are easily located by the floating eelgrass or other debris that strings out in a narrow line over the surface. Sometimes a rip is marked by foam on the surface. Under the worst conditions the angler may have to prospect for fish with no signs to offer help, and this may be particularly true when fishing for deep-running chinook.

The time of day can be significant. The early angler who is on the water at daybreak will be usually the most successful in taking salmon. At that time and until the sun has been up for a while, the wind may be at its lowest activity, providing more pleasant fishing conditions.

In a seaway the angler with a tendency to mal de mer will find it advantageous to keep his eyes at horizon level and to avoid stopping the forward motion of the boat. On the Pacific Coast, ocean fishing is safest when the winds are below 20 miles per hour. The double-ended, wide-bottomed, 20-foot dory of the Oregon coast is probably the best all-around craft for the salmon angler. With a 10- to 15-horsepower outboard engine in the well, the design will handle beautifully in a difficult situation.

Big-Game Fishing

Big-game fishing is a general term covering a number of large marine game species. Specifically, big-game fishing encompasses the black, blue, white, and striped marlin; swordfish; wahoo; sailfish; bluefin and yellowfin tuna; tarpon; and the more active sharks, such as the mako, hammerhead, tiger, white, and bronze whaler shark. Other species usually of smaller size (less than 100 pounds) and often caught incidental to the quarry sought, such as the dolphin, African pompano, amberjack, king mackerel, tanguigue, albacore, and great barracuda, are included in the general definition. In common all are taken by trolling or drift-fishing.

Until the 1950s the sport was limited to anglers who had the time and money to travel and charter the expensive craft that typifies big-game fishing. With the development of fiberglass hulls, collapsible outriggers, inboard-outboard engines, and modern trailers capable of transporting and launching boats up to 30 feet in length, the sport became financially feasible for the average man. Today there are thousands of avid sportsmen prowling the Gulf Stream off Florida, the Bahamas, the Gulf of Mexico, the Caribbean, the Pacific Coast, and the Montauk–Block Island area with well-equipped craft in the 19- to 28-foot class and capable of subduing almost any big-game fish. The mobility of these boats, plus the development of more sophisticated rods and reels and miniaturized electronic gear have resulted in a whole new breed of ocean anglers.

Big-game fish are predators. Their food consists of baitfish of many species—depending upon the part of the world in which they are feeding. Whether it is a sailfish "balling" pilchards off Florida's east coast or a black marlin pursuing a school of bonitos off Panama, the technique is the same. Big-game fish have voracious appetites and will chase almost any number of species from cruising singles to schools of hundreds. It is enough to know that they are vitally interested in rigged baits skipped on the surface or trolled just below or allowed to swim alive and close to the surface while kite fishing.

There are a number of methods of rigging baits for trolling. From slices of small baitfish, such as mullet—called *strip baits*— to the rigging of large mackerel or bonitos there are only slight variations. The speed of trolling depends on the species of fish sought, but generally trolling is done at a rather rapid rate, enough to keep a rigged bait of a pound or so skipping on the surface. The trolling speed of the boat depends on the current, wind direction, and wave action. For instance, fishing the Gulf Stream off Florida or the Bahamas might require a speed of 10 knots while traveling north to keep a mullet bait skipping correctly. This is because the Stream moves in a northerly direction at about 5–6 knots and the boat is moving with the current. Heading south, however, would be against the same current and would require less speed to keep the bait in proper action. Professional charter-boat captains learn the correct combination of speed and engine revolutions in various sea conditions that produce strikes.

The Boat

Basically, a boat for big-game fishing should meet certain requirements. It should be seaworthy enough to withstand fairly high seas. It must have enough power to get to the fishing grounds— regardless of how far out—be able to cruise while trolling all day, and return to port at night. It should be maneuverable enough to speed up when necessary or to make tight turns. Preferably it should allow the skipper some altitude to spot fish ahead of the boat, feeding seabirds, and gamefish coming up from below the baits. In addition, it should be equipped with a fighting chair, if possible, although many big-game fish are fought with a rod belt. Fighting chairs may come in all shapes and sizes, from the folding, lightweight chairs used on small boats to the intricate and sophisticated fighting chairs on the big sport-fishing boats. Ideally the chair should contain a gimbal or socket in which to place the butt end of the big-game rod. The best chairs provide a footrest (so that the angler can utilize the strength of his legs in battling a fish), armrests, an adjustable backrest, provisions for a fighting harness, and should be capable of swiveling in a 360-degree turn upon a pedestal mounted solidly on the cockpit deck.

The adequately equipped sportfisherman should also carry two outriggers. The smaller boats can mount collapsible fiberglass or aluminum outriggers that extend out about 15–25 feet, while the

Sportfisherman (Boat)

1. Antenna: mainly for radiotelephone use but also for some electronic navigating aids.

2. Tower or Tuna Towers: welded tubular aluminum structures installed to give fish guide maximum height of locating fish and also provides third control station.

3. Outriggers: anodized aluminum tubes that are rigidly based for the purpose of towing along heavy baits.

4. Ladder: for access to bridge from cockpit with steps for quick access from deck.

5. Bait Box: refrigerated storage for fresh or frozen bait.

6. Fighting Chair: with integrally mounted footrest, gimbal and rod holders allow angler to fish with heavy tackle from any quarter, as chair can be turned to line up with fish.

7. Cockpit or Lower Control Station: auxiliary station located near angler so guide can assist in boating fish without leaving controls.

8. Bow Rails: installed to allow safe handling of anchor or dock lines on forward deck.

9. Flying Bridge: the principal operating station for the boat, with all the necessary controls and electronic gears centered here; also makes an ideal observation point for the boat owner.

10. Transom Door: for taking larger gamefish aboard without need for lifting over rails.

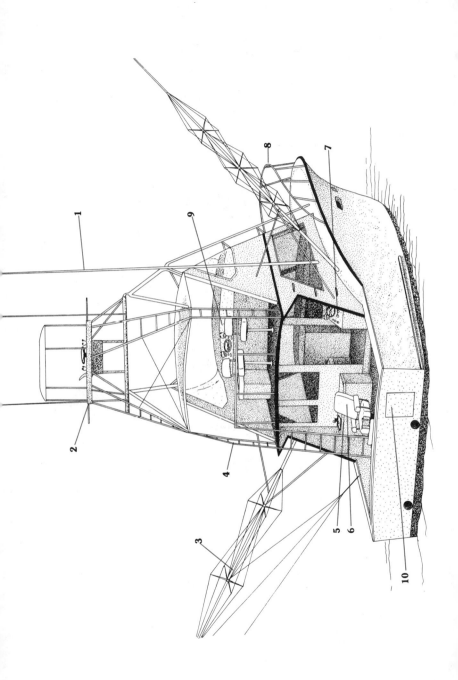

Small Sportfisherman
The small sportfisherman has revolutionized big-game angling. These outboard and stern-drive rigs have become tremendously popular in regions where weather and sea conditions are normally favorable.

larger boats generally mount more sophisticated outriggers of aluminum, capable of extending out 45 feet from the port and starboard gunwales. Obviously the farther out the baits can be trolled on either side of the wake of the boat, the better the chances are for attracting the attention of cruising gamefish. The boat should have at least four solidly mounted rod holders—preferably two in each gunwale at the sides of the cockpit—in order to run two outrigger lines and two "flat lines." The two flat lines are positioned at different distances behind the boat in the wake, but closer to the boat than the outrigger baits.

A fish box is necessary, and the larger boats usually have no trouble installing one across the inside of the transom or below deck in the cockpit area. Smaller boats may have to improvise, but many fish boxes today are built into the hull of small sportfishermen. The tuna tower of the large sportfisherman provides a place from which the captain can run the boat high above deck level. Small sportfishermen do not provide as high a platform, although lightweight towers may be installed on small boats. In many of the smaller boats the center console-steering system enables the angler to get considerably higher over the surface of the water than older steering methods. A transom door that swings open close to water level is ideal for sliding large fish into the cockpit. Many of the large sportfishermen are equipped with these. On smaller boats anglers must rely on hauling the catch over the transom or gunwales after it has been brought to the boat and subdued. A gin pole may be mounted on both small and large boats, and provides the best method for raising large fish above the water surface with a system of pulleys. Many gin poles today are made of lightweight aluminum and can be mounted in smaller sport-fishing boats. Bait boxes can be and usually are portable ice chests where both rigged and unrigged baits are kept cold to be used when ready. There should be storage room for big-game rods and reels while underway.

Equipment considered absolutely necessary on a big-game sport-fishing boat consists of a long-handled gaff and a wooden billy club, preferably weighted, and a tail rope. In addition, a flying gaff can prove invaluable for larger fish. The gaff is necessary for every species of big-game fish. Billfish, in addition to being gaffed and hopefully tail roped, can be killed quickly and cleanly, if wanted for mounting purposes, by a solid whack between the eyes with the billy club. Cloth gloves are also advisable not only for grasping the wire leader used in big-game fishing but for grasping the rasplike bills of marlins, sailfish, and broadbills.

Communication equipment on the larger boats may include sophisticated marine radios, ship-to-shore radiotelephones, radar gear, and Loran for bad weather and long-distance navigation. Somewhat more refined depth-finding and fish-finding equipment can be carried on the bigger boats, but—with the miniaturization of equipment prevalent in the space age—many small sport-fishing boats today carry excellent small marine radios, including citizens band sets and depth and fishfinders.

Angling from a Sportfisherman

Fishing equipment need not be elaborate on a small sportfisherman. Although hulls (less than 25 feet) lack the stability for a flying bridge, short, demountable outriggers and a lightweight fighting chair with gimbal are all that's necessary for most kinds of angling, including sailfish and white marlin.

Tackle

There is considerable leeway in this day and age for selection of big-game tackle. Fifty years ago most big-game anglers had to rely on the huge, stout, wood rods, such as those built by Hardy, and heavy, big reels, such as the Vom Hoff. But today, with the excellent tubular glass rods and lightweight reels with precision braking systems, an experienced angler can subdue a big fish with relatively light tackle.

Big-game rods and lines are rated in pound classes: 12-pound, 20-pound, 30-pound, 50-pound, 80-pound, and 130-pound tackle. This is the breaking strength of the line, and each class has a matching rod of suitable length, weight, and flexibility. These trolling rods are usually from 6 to 6½ feet in overall length (including tip and butt section) and are mounted with at least 5 roller guides to reduce line friction. Corrosion-proof guides of stainless steel or Carboloy are preferable. The butt section may be made of wood (solid ash), aluminum, or fiberglass; it will also have a notched end ferrule to secure it in the fighting chair gimbal or rod belt. Rods in the 80- and 130-pound class usually have curved aluminum butts to provide greater leverage when pumping very large fish. The reel seat is generally made of chrome-plated brass and should be hooded with strong locking rings to keep the reel from working loose under pressure.

Monofilament is the most popular line in the 12-, 20-, and 30-pound tackle classes. Its elasticity is an asset with light tackle. In the 50-pound class many anglers prefer Dacron, with its minimal elasticity for pumping larger fish. In the 80- and 130-pound classes Dacron is almost essential.

Big-game trolling reels are designated by the 0 (for ocean) system. The largest reel is a 12/0 and the smallest a 2/0. The best and most expensive reels are made of solid bar aluminum and have a precision-engineered drag. There are two types of drags in wide use: one is the star drag and the other is a quadrant lever. Unlike the star drag, the quadrant lever is separate from and does not rotate with the spool drive shaft. The advantage of the lever-action drag is that the striking drag can be preset, giving the angler a distinct advantage in that the exact tension can be set or reset instantly under a number of varying conditions. Drag tension is of great importance in fighting large, fast-moving big-game fish—whether in setting the striking drag just before a strike, resetting it after changing damaged baits, or upon bringing a heavy fish to the boat. Many big-game reels (and most of those from the 4/0 size up) have harness lugs in the top of the end plates. A shoulder, or kidney, harness is essential when playing large fish, and the harness belts can be secured to the reel; this permits the angler to free his hands while using his back muscles or legs to put pressure on the fish. Leg pressure is of paramount importance when working giants of 500 pounds or more.

The following chart gives the generally recommended weights in ounces for big-game rods. It also shows the suggested reel size and line test (in pounds) for various species of big-game fish. Rod weights are given at the tip of modern glass rods.

BIG-GAME FISHING TACKLE

Light

Species	Reel Size	Line Test (pounds)	Rod Weight* (ounces)
Atlantic Sailfish	2/0–4/0	12–20	6–9
Pacific Sailfish	2/0–4/0	12–20	6–9
White Marlin	2/0–4/0	12–20	6–9
Striped Marlin	4/0	12–20	6–9
Blue Marlin	6/0	20–50	9–16
Black Marlin	6/0	30–50	12–16
Swordfish	6/0	30–50	12–16
Bluefin Tuna (Giant)	9/0	50	16–20

Medium

Species	Reel Size	Line Test (pounds)	Rod Weight* (ounces)
Atlantic Sailfish	4/0–6/0	20–30	9–12
Pacific Sailfish	4/0–6/0	20–30	9–12
White Marlin	4/0–6/0	20–30	9–12
Striped Marlin	7/0	30–50	9–12
Blue Marlin	9/0	50–80	16–24
Black Marlin	9/0	50–80	16–24
Swordfish	9/0	50–80	16–24
Bluefin Tuna (Giant)	9/0	80	16–24

Heavy

Species	Reel Size	Line Test (pounds)	Rod Weight* (ounces)
Atlantic Sailfish	6/0	30–50	16–18
Pacific Sailfish	6/0	30–50	16–18
White Marlin	6/0	30–50	16–18
Striped Marlin	9/0	80	18–20
Blue Marlin	12/0	130	24–30
Black Marlin	12/0	130	24–30
Swordfish	12/0	130	24–30
Bluefin Tuna (Giant)	12/0	130	24–30

*The rod weight as given is for the tip only in tubular glass construction. When using monofilaments the heavier rod weights are suggested, because of the elasticity of the line.

Bait and Rigging Bait

The mullet is found over much of the world and it is one of the best all-around trolling baits. Although the mullet rarely enters the actual diet of big-game species (for example, during an extensive study of sailfish stomach contents, the only mullet remains found were "split" for baits), it has the durability required for ocean trolling. In areas where mullet are not abundant or do not occur at all, there are a number of good surface baits available. In the Florida, Bahamas, and Caribbean areas the balao is an excellent bait for sailfish, white marlin, and small blue marlin. It can be purchased in fresh and frozen form and is easily stored. However, it is not effective in taking the larger blue and black marlin and that is where the bonito, bonefish, mackerel, and even small dolphin come in. Also, live or frozen squid can be used, as well as artificial squid lures. In addition, many other baits are manufactured today (herring eels, for example) as artificials. There are as many ways to rig bait as there are methods to use them on the commonly accepted methods of rigging baits for trolling. Strip baits are popular for some of the smaller billfish.

Leaders and Hooks

Wire leader comes in shiny and dull finishes and it is a matter of choice which one uses. The main thing to remember is that any kink in wire leader can weaken it to the point where it will easily break. As far as test strength is concerned, each roll of wire gives the breaking test on the package, and it is wise to base the size of wire leader you are going to use on the size and species of the fish sought. It is best to overguess your fish's weight when deciding on the wire leader. Many a big fish has been lost because it hit a bait being trolled on leader meant for a smaller fish.

Big-game hooks must take a tremendous strain, so it is wise to purchase good hooks if one is to succeed in taking fish of several hundred pounds or more. The best hooks are made of high-carbon-steel-alloy wire and are plated with cadmium or tin to prevent rusting. The wire is hardened at 1550° F. and tempered at 750° F.; the ring at the eye is formed by cold swagging, which reduces bulk at the eye. All large saltwater hooks today are forged; that is, after the hook has been made, it is hammered flat along both sides of the bend, while still hot, to give it additional strength. The appropriate hook size and pattern depends not only on the fish but the type of bait or rigging used. The table on p. 254 is a general guide.

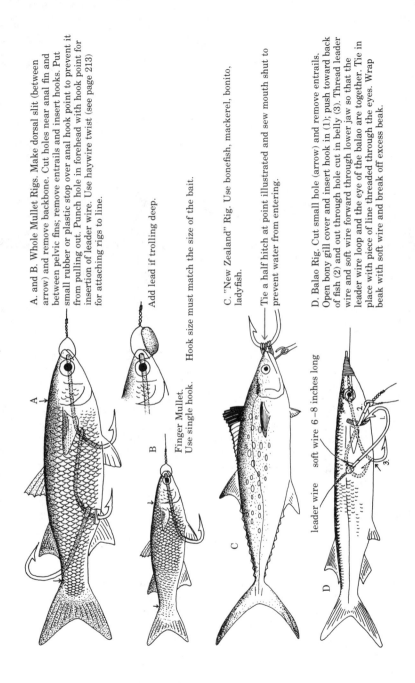

A. and B. Whole Mullet Rigs. Make dorsal slit (between arrow) and remove backbone. Cut holes near anal fin and between pelvic fins; remove entrails and insert hooks. Put small rubber or plastic stop over anal hook point to prevent it from pulling out. Punch hole in forehead with hook point for insertion of leader wire. Use haywire twist (see page 213) for attaching rigs to line.

Add lead if trolling deep.

Hook size must match the size of the bait.

Finger Mullet.
Use single hook.

C. "New Zealand" Rig. Use bonefish, mackerel, bonito, ladyfish.

Tie a half hitch at point illustrated and sew mouth shut to prevent water from entering.

leader wire   soft wire 6–8 inches long

D. Balao Rig. Cut small hole (arrow) and remove entrails. Open bony gill cover and insert hook in (1); push toward back of fish (2) and out through hole cut in belly (3). Thread leader wire and soft wire forward through lower jaw so that the leader wire loop and the eye of the balao are together. Tie in place with piece of line threaded through the eyes. Wrap beak with soft wire and break off excess beak.

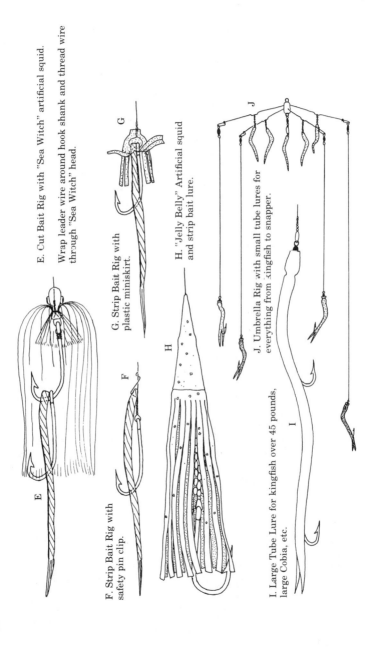

E. Cut Bait Rig with "Sea Witch" artificial squid.

Wrap leader wire around hook shank and thread wire through "Sea Witch" head.

G. Strip Bait Rig with plastic miniskirt.

H. "Jelly Belly" Artificial squid and strip bait lure.

F. Strip Bait Rig with safety pin clip.

J. Umbrella Rig with small tube lures for everything from kingfish to snapper.

I. Large Tube Lure for kingfish over 45 pounds, large Cobia, etc.

TERMINAL TACKLE

Fish	Hook Size	Pattern	Leader Wire Size	Mono (pounds)
Atlantic Sailfish	7/0–8/0	O'Shaughnessy	No. 5–No. 7	50
White Marlin	7/0–9/0	O'Shaughnessy	No. 8–No. 9	80
Pacific Sailfish	8/0–9/0	O'Shaughnessy	No. 8–No. 9	80
Striped Marlin	8/0–9/0	O'Shaughnessy	No. 8–No. 10	80
Blue Marlin	9/0–10/0	Sobey	No. 11–No. 13	
Swordfish	8/0–12/0	Sobey	No. 11–No. 13	100–180
Black Marlin	9/0–12/0	Sobey	No. 11–No. 13	
Bluefin Tuna	10/0–12/0	O'Shaughnessy Sobey	No. 14–No. 15	

The Fishing Chair

Originally, fishing chairs were simply office chairs bolted to the cockpit floor and served more as a secure place to sit than as an aid to fishing. Leather cups were later attached to the front of the chair to help hold the butt of the rod. The fishing chair as we now know it was originated by Harlan Major in the early 1930s. His chair had a gimbaled rod socket, removable back, and a locking chair base; all fittings were bronze, and chairs were heavily built of teak or mahogany to give years of service.

Fishing chairs today could be grouped into several general classes. The most common is a portable, lightweight chair, usually made of tubular aluminum with a gimbal secured to the front chair frame. This chair is not of the swiveling type; so it can only be used for very light fishing.

The type of chair originated by Major is now used with medium-weight tackle, and while it has been improved, it's still a chair with a simple locking base that allows the angler to turn to face the fish. This chair is installed in the boat at a standard chair height, since the angler will have his feet on the deck. It may have a simple rod holder attached to allow the angler to rest the rod between strikes, and occasionally a holder is furnished to keep a glass or bottle near at hand.

The third type of chair and one that is a must for the angler using medium and heavy tackle is the fighting chair. This is a very heavily built chair with attached footrest that can be adjusted to suit the angler, and an oversized stanchion and mounting plate. This chair is mounted quite high. It should be approximately level with the cockpit coamings so that the angler can get full use of his rod, particularly to raise a fish that has gone deep. The chair must have a spindle, which is carried on antifriction bearings so that the chair can be kept in line with the fish even when all of the angler's weight is on the footrest. A hand brake must also be provided to hold the chair securely when not in use. It should have a gimbal that can be adjusted to several positions up and down to allow for different-length rod butts. It must have integral rod holders so the rods are always on the chair in case of a sudden strike. The back must be either hinged or movable to several positions, ranging from almost upright for comfortable sitting during the long periods between strikes to an almost-horizontal position to allow the angler to pump a heavy fish in using his whole body and not just his arms. While this chair might appear massive, long years of experience have proven that there is no alternative to size, because it must accommodate a person with a harness and be strong enough to withstand a downthrust of as much as 400 pounds on the extended footrest.

Outriggers

In their simplest form, outriggers may consist of short sections of almost any rod or tube that projects outward from each side of the boat. Outriggers used by commercial trollers are often only 5–10 feet in length; however, these have no value to the angler. In sport fishing, the outriggers are used to accomplish one or all of the following purposes:

To spread the baits far apart
To make it possible to fish more than one line
To present another kind of bait; i.e., skipping as well as swimming
To fish the baits at a long distance behind the boat out of its wake, without strain on rod or angler
To allow the angler to troll heavy baits for large fish

Ordinarily, the offshore boat will troll two stern or "flat" lines. These baits skip or swim astern in the wake of the boat. With the addition of outriggers, four lines can be fished, which make a different presentation in that the baits ride clear of the wake. There

Fighting-Chair Technique

1. Main purpose of fighting chair is to let fisherman use powerful muscles of legs and back against fish. Here, boat's mate adjusts length and tilt of footrest.

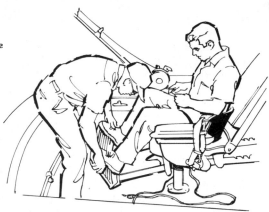

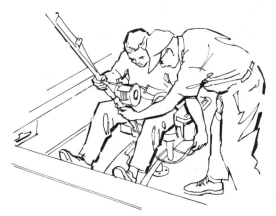

2. Butt of rod rests in gimbaled socket at front of chair, main harness goes around angler at small of back. Thongs around thighs complete harness rig.

3. Action of pumping, with fish on, consists of quick drop of rod from vertical to horizontal, and swift reeling in of slack gained. Then, using legs and back . . .

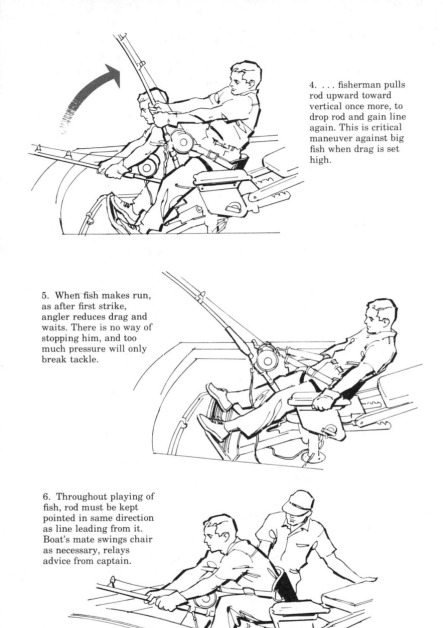

4. . . . fisherman pulls rod upward toward vertical once more, to drop rod and gain line again. This is critical maneuver against big fish when drag is set high.

5. When fish makes run, as after first strike, angler reduces drag and waits. There is no way of stopping him, and too much pressure will only break tackle.

6. Throughout playing of fish, rod must be kept pointed in same direction as line leading from it. Boat's mate swings chair as necessary, relays advice from captain.

is also the "automatic" drop-back feature provided by the slack line needed to go from tip of rod to tip of outrigger. This is a distinct advantage in billfishing since it gives the angler a little time to reach his tackle at the strike. Furthermore, the fish could, and often does, hook itself.

The outrigger for most fishing need not be over 30 feet in length. The outrigger pole itself can be bamboo, wood, metal, or, more recently, fiberglass. There are numerous methods of supporting the outrigger, but some arrangement has to be made to keep the outrigger inboard for laying alongside a dock or another boat as well as strong enough to support it in its fishing position, which is generally at a 45-degree angle. The outrigger pole must have guides secured to it so the halyard can work freely and the outrigger pin to which the fishing line is attached can be hoisted to the tip of the outrigger.

Trolling heavy baits requires an outrigger that is solidly braced. The most successful have been made of anodized aluminum with aluminum spreaders and stainless-steel guying wires. This is the workhorse and can troll almost any bait, from mullet or ballyhoo used for sailfish up to baits weighing 8–10 pounds for large marlin. Depending on the size of the boat, and again the requirements of the angler, these outriggers will range in size from 30 feet in length with one spreader, up to 45 feet with four sets of spreaders. Whereas the smaller outrigger can be base mounted only, these larger outriggers require well-engineered attachment fittings to spread the loads properly both to the boat and the outrigger. The strain on a long outrigger in a rough sea is almost unbelievable, even without towing a bait.

The Strike

Perhaps the most crucial instant in all of big-game fishing is when the fish strikes the bait. Many times the fish will hit with such force—brought on either by hunger or anger—that it will hook itself. In that case it removes any problem of whether to drop back or speed up the bait. The angler in this case is simply concerned with handling the fish properly, now that it is hooked. But all fish do not strike the trolled baits instantly, preferring to inspect them closely before deciding to take one. It is this situation that can cause problems. The angler may choose to free-spool the reel, allowing the bait to drop behind the boat and sink, and the fish will swallow it "dead" in the water. On the other hand, when a fish can't seem to make up its mind to hit one of the baits, either speeding up the boat slightly or rapidly cranking the handle of the reel will excite the fish, causing it to strike. Sometimes neither method works and the fish simply departs without striking at all.

One thing is certain on the strike. It is wise for the angler to be watching the baits and preferably either be seated in the chair or standing close to it when the strike comes. In this way the fisherman can either grab whichever rod contains the line the fish hits and get ready to strike the fish himself—in order to set the hook properly—or a mate may hand the angler the proper rod, and the butt can be quickly fitted into the chair gimbal. Many big-game fish are missed because the angler is too far away from the rods or chair when the strike comes. Big-game fish do not occur numerically as often as smaller species, and an angler may go many hours or even days and not get a strike. But when a big-game fish does strike, there is very little time in which to make the correct moves. It is best to be ready.

If the crew is certain the fish has taken the bait, there are several options open to the angler. If he is inexperienced, it is best to take the advice of the skipper or mate. In many cases, knowing their own waters and the habits of the fish, they will slow the boat down almost to idle, and allow the fish to take the bait and circle down to a depth where it will turn the bait around and swallow it. It is an unnerving experience for a novice to have a crew tell him to wait for a 10- to 15-second count before striking, but occasionally this is best. Big-game fishing crews in many parts of the world use this system, particularly off the west coast of Mexico. At the end of the count the skipper will gun the engines of the boat to take up slack. The angler then lowers his rod tip almost horizontally and strikes once, or twice, hard; by bringing the rod up sharply to the vertical position he sets the hook.

In other areas of the world crews may use a different system. For example, some Bahamian skippers seem to prefer to speed up the boat as soon as the slashing bill of the fish has struck the bait and the line has fallen to the surface of the water from the outrigger clips. Many of them feel this will succeed in hooking the fish at the instant it swallows the bait. In contrast, many sportsmen prefer to see the skipper put the engine in neutral as soon as the fish is hooked, feeling that an angler should fight his fish on more equal terms. This is somewhat academic, but is the method required in the Palm Beach Masters' Tournament, for example. At any rate, most conventional techniques of fighting big-game fish today include the use of the boat as much as the rod and reel. It has been said by many of the "pros" that more big-game fish are caught by the man at the wheel of a sportfisherman than by the angler in the chair. There is no arguing that a good combination of skipper, mate, and angler is hard to beat when it comes to landing big-game fish.

Many skippers and mates have their own opinions about the preferred striking drag for different reels, lines, and species of fish, but a rough chart can be made up that will serve generally for most cases. A general rule could be that the striking drag should not be set to less than 20 percent of the line's maximum test strength or more than 40 percent of that same breaking strain. A simple pocket-sized fish-weighing scale can be used to measure the pound test of the line at the tip, after the rod has been set in a gunwale rod holder. The chart would look approximately like this:

Rod Class	Line Test (pounds)	Reel	Capacity (yards)	Species	Striking Drag (pounds)
Very light	12	2/0	475	Atlantic Sailfish	4
	20	3/0	500	Atlantic Sailfish	5
Light	30	4/0	500	White Marlin	7
Medium	50	6/0	575	Blue Marlin	20
Heavy	80	9/0	600	Black Marlin Swordfish	25–30
Very Heavy	130	12/0	750	Giant Tuna	40

TERMINAL TACKLE   That tackle that exists between the snap swivel at the end of the line and the hook is of the utmost importance in fighting large oceanfish. Considerable importance should be attached to the selection of good swivels, for a cheap, weak, or defective swivel has caused the loss of many a fine fish. The ideal swivels are those made of stainless steel and operating on small bearings. They are slightly more expensive than the conventional brass or black swivel, but hold up better and prevent line twist.

DOUBLE LINE   Just above the leader, this should be constructed and tied with a Bimini twist knot, allowing approximately 10–15 feet of double line for lines of 50-pound test and under and up to 30 feet of double line for the heavier line tests, such as 80- and 130-pound. It should be tied every 24–36 inches with a few twists of dental floss, which will keep it together so that it can easily pass through rod guides. Wire leaders come in both braided cable and stainless steel. Both are about equal in strength for the length and weight. What the braided wire makes up for in less tendency to kink over stainless steel is lost in its tendency to rust more easily, especially in saltwater. It is up to individual skippers to choose. A simple guide can be followed as to which wire size should be used with classes of rods and line tests. It also gives the suggested monofilament leader and its breaking test.

Tackle Class	Species	IGFA Line Class (pounds)	Mono Test (pounds)	Stainless Steel (pounds)
Very light	Atlantic Sailfish	12–20	30–50	#3 (32)
Light	White Marlin	30	80	#8 (86)
Medium	Blue Marlin	50	120	#10 (128)
Heavy	Black Marlin	80	200	#12 (176)
	Swordfish			
Very heavy	Giant Tuna	130	300	#15 (272)

Using stainless steel leaders or nylon monofilament is optional. Wire leaders have a tendency to kink and break at that spot where monofilament does not. Yet the wire has advantages, such as being almost impervious to cutting by sharp teeth. Mono is made in so many grades and sizes that tables of diameters and breaking strains mean little. The breaking strain of monofilament leaders is marked on the packages, as is also the case with steel leaders.

Playing the Fish

Big-game fish, almost without exception, will make their most frantic and longest run right after being hooked. Depending on the size and condition of the fish, it may take out anywhere from several hundred to more than a thousand yards of line in a matter of minutes. With marlin or sailfish one can expect a heart-stopping series of acrobatic jumps as the fish clears the surface repeatedly in an effort to get rid of the hook. In the case of the bluefin tuna there will be no jumping but a tremendous burst of strength as the fish streaks away and downward. In both these cases the angler is advised to keep the rod tip up to let the bending rod absorb the shock and—as the fish gets farther out from the boat, still speeding—slightly reduce the drag to prevent the line from breaking. This is the moment, as the pressure on the line increases progressively when more of it leaves the spool rapidly, where most fish are lost. They are lost because the lines break from too much strain alone or because the angler becomes too worried about his fast-disappearing line and increases the drag, hoping to slow it down. It is better to have a lot of line out. The drag of the line being pulled through the water will do more than anything else at this time to slow down the fish. When the fish has stopped its initial run and begins to swim, then the angler can begin to regain lost line. The fish may jump any number of times after that, but always remember that the slight decrease in drag as it makes its runs will lessen the chances of losing a fish. Regaining line on a fish is a matter of pumping properly. The rod is raised or pumped when the slack is taken up. It is quickly lowered while the reel handle is turned to gain slack, then pumped or raised again. The reel handle should not be turned while the rod is being raised to regain line. It will simply cause the drag to slip unnecessarily, losing, rather than gaining, line.

The mate will have reeled in the other three lines to give the angler room to fight the fish without becoming entangled in other lines. The advantage of the swiveling chair becomes apparent to a novice big-game fisherman when he feels the mate constantly turning the chair so that the angler is facing the direction where the line slants out to the fish at all times. This permits the equal distribution of weight on the part of the angler fighting the fish. It is during this time that the captain of the boat can help or hinder a fisherman by the way he handles the boat. If the angler is tiring and the fish is either swimming down and away from the boat or sounding, the skipper may "back down" on the fish by putting the boat into reverse, thus taking considerable strain off the back and arms of the angler and allowing him time to gain line on the fish. Other skippers follow a different battle plan and may turn the boat and run parallel to the swimming fish, allowing the angler to slightly reduce the drag and causing a billow to form in the line between the boat and the fish. This exerts tremendous pressure on the fish, causing it to tire far more rapidly than the backing-down method, which is really more to spare the angler than to tire the fish.

It is at this stage, particularly if an angler is a novice at the game and is feeling the strain in his back and arms, when a harness can ease the pressure. Slipped under the angler, it fits snugly around the lower back in the kidney region. It has canvas or leather straps that can be snapped to rings on both sides of the reel. This allows the angler to absorb the powerful pull of the big fish with the back and leg muscles rather than taking all the pressure on the back and arms alone.

As the fish gets closer and closer to the boat, the angler can

Rod Holders
Rod holders serve a twofold purpose: for storage when not in use
and for providing a mount when lines are attached to outriggers.
This also permits multiple use when trolling.

roughly judge its depth by the angle of line slanting from the rod
tip to the fish. As the angle (from the vertical) lessens quickly, one
can expect the fish to surface and jump. It is then that the rod tip
should be held high to absorb the strain of the thrashing jump
and also to prevent slack from forming, allowing the fish to throw
the hook.

Usually big-game fish will sound toward the end of a battle,
going as deep as the thousand-foot level or more. They may even

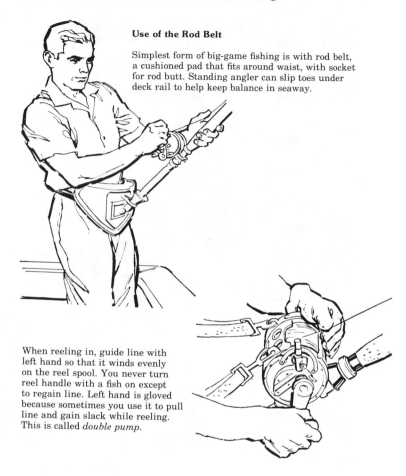

Use of the Rod Belt

Simplest form of big-game fishing is with rod belt, a cushioned pad that fits around waist, with socket for rod butt. Standing angler can slip toes under deck rail to help keep balance in seaway.

When reeling in, guide line with left hand so that it winds evenly on the reel spool. You never turn reel handle with a fish on except to regain line. Left hand is gloved because sometimes you use it to pull line and gain slack while reeling. This is called *double pump.*

die down there from exertion or from pressure or the combination of both. There are two options for the angler. He can have the boat move directly over the fish and try to pump it up, depending on the angler's physical condition, the size of the fish, and the length of the fight. This can and many times does require hours of very difficult work, particularly if the fish is large and dead. This often attracts sharks, particularly if the fish is bleeding. The only alternative is to move the boat several hundred yards ahead of the fish, preferably with the drag reduced to avoid putting any additional stress on the line. Then the angler resets his drag higher and begins to pump the fish up again. The new angle of the line (rather than straight down) tilts the head of the fish up as it is pulled, planing it up rather than pulling it. Many sport-fishing skippers utilize this method.

If the fish is not dead, or if it did not sound for long, and is now obviously tired and coming into the boat, a series of things can take place that will greatly affect the angler's chance of boating it. Most billfish are extremely strong fighters and will make last-minute jumps quite close to the boat when the novice angler least expects it. This is the time when most billfish are lost, because the angler allowed slack to form in the line and the fish was able to throw the hook. At this point the rod tip should be held as high as possible. A fish jumping close to the boat is also more likely to get itself tail wrapped by the wire leader.

The snap swivel marking the place on the single line where it joins a short length of double line, which is in turn fastened to the wire leader, will finally appear. This is the signal for the boating process to begin, because the snap swivel cannot pass through the roller guides at the rod tip. That is as close to the boat as the angler can bring the fish with the rod. It is then up to the mate to reach out, preferably with gloved hands, take the double line or leader, and lead the tired fish close to the side of the boat near the stern. There he will grasp the bill or use his gaff. If the fish is very large and/or it is wanted for mounting, the skipper or another member of the crew will either whack it across the forehead with a weighted wooden billy club or stun it temporarily while a tail rope is passed around the head, snapped closed, and slid down the length of the body until it is pulled tight at the slender area at the base of the tail of the billfish or tuna. The skipper or other crew member may also have gaffed the fish to prevent it wrenching itself free from the man holding the bill. If the fish is to be tagged for migration studies or is not wanted for mounting, it will be released. In that case it is not gaffed or struck with the club nor is a tail rope fastened to it. The tag is inserted in the musculature at the base of the dorsal fin and the wire leader is snipped off close to the eye of the hook. A combination of saltwater and stomach acids will erode the hook in time and give some other big-game angler a chance to battle the fish another day.

If the fish is to be boated, it is either taken aboard through the transom door; pulled over the gunwales if it is small enough; or the tail rope is fastened to the snap of the gin pole and the fish is hoisted, tail first, above the surface.

The moments of boating a big-game fish can be very dangerous for anglers and crew members who are not experienced. The slash of the bill or the swipe of a large sickle-shaped tail can seriously injure people. It is better for the angler to stay in the chair—even if he is experienced—while the crew is going about the business of boating the fish. Crew members and anglers in the cockpit should be extremely careful not to step into any coils of the line or leader while the fish is being held alongside. Serious injuries can occur if a big fish breaks loose from the man holding the bill or the gaff. It is for that reason that an angler should set his drag on the very light position during this time. If the fish does get loose and make a last-ditch run, it will have less chance of snapping the line than if the drag is on full position.

Recording the Catch

If the fish is to be entered in a tournament, there are several factors to remember. No one on the boat was to have assisted the angler during the fight by touching him in any way or helping with the rod or reel. The mate may turn the chair for the angler and other persons may hand him the objects if he asks for them, such as a cold drink or a seat harness or rod belt. These rules have been long established by the International Game Fish Association. The angler is to fight the fish alone until the mate reaches out to take the leader wire.

Also, upon reaching the dock or marina, the fish should be weighed by an official weighmaster or dockmaster. The proper forms should be filled out and signed by the weighmaster and a witness. The fish should also be measured for length and girth to insure proper mounting. The test of the line should also be recorded and the type of bait used. It would not be too bad an idea to have a few pictures taken during that moment. It may not happen many times in an angler's lifetime.

Reference Books

There are more valuable books on fishing than we can list here. The following titles are mostly recent works by contemporary authors that are basically "how-to" oriented. These are available in many bookstores or obtainable direct from the publisher or from the various outdoor book clubs.

BERGMAN, RAY. *Trout.* Alfred A. Knopf, N.Y.

BROOKS, JOE. *Trout Fishing.* Harper & Row, N.Y.

DUNAWAY, VIC. *Modern Saltwater Fishing.* Winchester Press, N.Y.

EVANOFF, VLAD. *Surf Fishing.* Harper & Row, N.Y.

FLICK, ART. *Master Fly-Tying Guide.* Crown, N.Y.

GINGRICH, ARNOLD. *The Well-Tempered Angler.* Alfred A. Knopf, N.Y.

———. *The Joys of Trout.* Crown, N.Y.

HENKIN, HARMON. *Fly Tackle.* J.B. Lippincott, N.Y

JORGENSEN, PAUL. *Dressing Flies for Fresh- and Saltwater.* Freshet Press, N.Y.

KREH, LEFTY. *Fly Fishing in Salt Water.* Crown, N.Y.

———. *Fly Casting with Lefty Kreh.* Crown, N.Y.

KREH, LEFTY AND SOSIN, MARK. *Practical Fishing Knots.* Crown, N.Y.

LIVINGSTON, A. D. *Advanced Bass Tackle and Boats.* J.B. Lippincott, N.Y

LYMAN, HAL, AND WOOLNER, FRANK. *The Complete Book of Striped Bass Fishing.* A.S. Barnes, N.Y.

MARINO, VINCENT. *In the Ring of the Rise.* Crown, N.Y.

McCLANE, A. J. *McClane's New Standard Fishing Encyclopedia.* Holt, Rinehart and Winston, N.Y.

McNALLY, TOM. *Fisherman's Knots.* J. Philip O'Hara, Chicago.

———. *Fly Fishing.* Harper and Row, N.Y.

MIGEL, MICHAEL, AND WRIGHT, LEONARD, JR. *The Masters on the Dry Fly.* Lippincott, N.Y.

———. *The Masters on the Nymph.* Lippincott, N.Y.

NETHERBY, STEVE. *The Expert's Book of Freshwater Fishing.* Simon and Schuster, N.Y.

REIGER, GEORGE. *Profiles in Saltwater Angling.* Prentice-Hall, Englewood Cliffs, N.J.

————. *Fishing with McClane.* Prentice-Hall, Englewood Cliffs, N.J.

SCHWEIBERT, ERNEST. *Trout.* E. P. Dutton, N.Y.

SHAW, HELEN. *Fly Tying.* Ronald Press, N.Y.

SLAYMAKER, SAMUEL R. *Simplified Fly Fishing.* Harper & Row, N.Y.

SOSIN, MARK, AND DANCE, BILL. *Practical Black-Bass Fishing.* Crown, N.Y.

SOSIN, MARK, AND CLARK, JOHN. *Through the Fish's Eye.* Harper & Row, N.Y.

STRUNG, NORMAN, AND ROSKO, MILT. *Spin-Fishing.* Macmillan, N.Y.

SWISHER, DOUG, AND RICHARDS, CARL. *Fly-Fishing Strategy.* Crown, N.Y.

WALKER, ALF. *Fly-Fishing Techniques.* Pagurian Press, Toronto.

WATERMAN, CHARLES. *Fishing in America.* Holt, Rinehart and Winston, N.Y.

————. *Modern Fresh- and Saltwater Fly Fishing.* Winchester Press, N.Y.

WEISS, JOHN. *Advanced Bass Fishing.* E. P. Dutton, N.Y.

WHITLOCK, DAVE, AND BOYLE, ROBERT. *Fly Tier's Almanac.* Lippincott, N.Y.

WISNER, BILL. *The Complete Guide to Salt- and Freshwater Fishing Equipment.* Winchester Press, N.Y.

WOOLNER, FRANK. *Modern Saltwater Sport Fishing.* Crown, N.Y.

WULFF, LEE. *The Atlantic Salmon.* A. S. Barnes, N.Y.

Index

Page numbers in **boldface** indicate illustrations.